About the Author

Lily is a mindset and life coach, stress management consultant, speaker, journalist, columnist and podcaster. Using her signature, neuroscience-informed approach, *The Priorities Method®*, Lily cuts through wellness clichés to empower people to navigate the chaos of modern life with more clarity, resilience and ease.

Praise for Prioritise This

'Sign me up immediately. This beautiful, joyous and life-affirming book will change the lives of its readers, and the more the better, frankly. It is a magisterial manifesto for our times, and a science-backed, practical Bible for how to thrive in a world that seems designed to overwhelm us. I have lived according to Lily's philosophy for years, so it is invaluable to have it collected in one exquisite, unputdownable volume'

Amol Rajan, broadcaster and journalist

'This book cuts through the noise of hustle culture with calm, sensible advice that helps you focus on what truly deserves your energy'

Ashley James, broadcaster, campaigner and author of Bimbo

'In a world full of self-help gurus offering quick fixes, Lily Silverton is a breath of fresh air – bringing thoughtful, evidence-based advice that delivers real results'

Melissa Hemsley, bestselling author of Real Healthy

'I felt seen – this book helped me bring order to the chaos in my life'

Angela Scanlon, broadcaster and author of Joyrider

'Great advice for balancing the demands of modern life – a book I'll give to all of my busy friends'

Adrienne Adhami, wellness coach and author of Decisions That Matter

'The book for our overwhelmed age'

Zoe Blaskey, bestselling author of Motherland

'So relatable and empowering. A roadmap to a purposeful and satisfying life'

Suzy Reading, psychologist and author of How To Be Selfish

Prioritise This

Prioritise This

A Practical Guide for Thriving in a World
That Won't Slow Down

Lily Silverton

First published in Great Britain by John Murray One in 2026
An imprint of John Murray Group

1

Copyright © Lily Silverton-Parker 2026

The right of Lily Silverton to be identified as the Author of the Work has been asserted by her in accordance with the Copyright, Designs and Patents Act 1988.

Author photograph © Sarah Cresswell

All rights reserved. No part of this publication may be reproduced, stored in a retrieval system, or transmitted, in any form or by any means without the prior written permission of the publisher, nor be otherwise circulated in any form of binding or cover other than that in which it is published and without a similar condition being imposed on the subsequent purchaser.

A CIP catalogue record for this title is available from the British Library

Hardback ISBN 978 1 399 82863 5
Trade Paperback ISBN 978 1 399 82994 6
ebook ISBN 978 1 399 82870 3

Typeset by KnowledgeWorks Global Ltd.

Printed and bound in Great Britain by Clays Ltd, Elcograf S.p.A.

John Murray Group policy is to use papers that are natural, renewable and recyclable products and made from wood grown in sustainable forests. The logging and manufacturing processes are expected to conform to the environmental regulations of the country of origin.

John Murray Group
Carmelite House
50 Victoria Embankment
London EC4Y 0DZ

John Murray One
Hachette Book Group
123 South Broad Street
Ste 2750
Philadelphia, PA 19109, USA

www.johnmurraypress.co.uk

John Murray Group, part of Hodder & Stoughton Limited
An Hachette UK company

The authorised representative in the EEA is Hachette Ireland, 8 Castlecourt Centre, Dublin 15, D15 XTP3, Ireland (email: info@hbgi.ie)

For Dolly, Zev and Dan. You are *my* priority.

Contents

A Note	xi
Introduction	xiii
1 Stress	1
2 Habits	39
3 Saying No	67
4 Overwhelm	85
5 Procrastination	113
6 Failure	135
7 Rejection	153
8 Comparison	171
9 Moving Forward	189
Final Thoughts	209
Resources	213
List of Practices	217
References	219
Acknowledgements	229

A Note

This book wouldn't have been possible without the openness of my clients and the companies I've worked with, as well as the guests from my podcast and experts I've interviewed for magazines and papers over the years. I'm also indebted to my teachers, both past and present. This book is an amalgamation of everything I've learned and discovered combined with my own experiences as a coach and writer – the resulting approach is what works for me and my clients, and I sincerely hope it will resonate and connect with you too.

> **A note about confidentiality**
>
> All 'clients' referred to in this book have either given written express permission to be included, or their stories and personal details have been extensively modified to make them unrecognisable.

Introduction

priority *noun (priorities)*
1 *the right to be or go first; precedence or preference.*
2 *something that must be attended to before anything else.*
3 *the fact or condition of being earlier.*
Chambers 21st Century Dictionary online, 2025

It's June 2016 and I'm in a stark and impressive office in Paris's Left Bank. Sitting next to me is my boss – the editor in chief of a leading UK magazine – beside him, two other members of our team. We arrived from London on the Eurostar last night and leave tomorrow evening, and in this time we won't see much of the city. It's mostly the inside of boardrooms, interspersed with the inside of the sleek black town car that's ferrying us between back-to-back meetings with the advertising clients that fund our publication. These guys are *important*; without them we would have no magazine at all. They pay our way.

This is our last meeting of the day, and it's with one of the biggest luxury fashion brands in the world. The women and men sitting across from us are doing it justice – it seems 'must appear intimidatingly expensive' is the first prerequisite on any job application to work here. I feel scruffy in comparison and am a bit jittery from too much coffee but the meeting seems to be going well – they've agreed to advertise with us, which is great news. After all, if we lost advertisers, I'd probably lose my job. Not because my boss is horrible (he's actually great), but because budgets are tight and my position as features director – the one I'd been working towards for the best part of a decade – would be the first to go if cuts were required. So, in theory, I should feel happy.

And yet, I don't. Not about the fact that they are advertising – I'm thrilled for the magazine. I just don't seem to care so much about my *own* place in all this anymore. For my entire career I'd worked towards becoming 'editor' or 'editor in chief' of a magazine. That had been my *ultimate* goal. But now, as that ambition began to look attainable, it no

PRIORITISE THIS

longer felt like what I wanted. I loved my colleagues, my boss, the work itself and the creativity of the industry, but – much like the too-tight, *towering* heels I'd watched the French PR hobble down her winding office stairs in – my job didn't fit me. It did once, but not anymore . . .

A painful break-up had brought life into sharp focus; what mattered to me now, at 32, was so different from when I'd started out at 23. I'd had enough of the perpetual stress, total exhaustion, competitive busyness and constant comparison (though, I must note, much of it self-inflicted). I was done with the travel, late nights, freebies, shows, openings, parties and the like (even though most of them *were* as much fun as they sound). I adored culture, fashion and art (still do!) but I didn't want to peddle it anymore. And, while I'd recovered from the eating disorders and depression that had plagued my life for 15 years, I could increasingly see that a job in the fashion world, which prizes thinness, was not the best place for me. My priorities had changed; *I'd* changed – it was time for a change.

So, I did what any normal person would do – I bored my closest friends to death about wanting to leave for 18 months before actually doing it! But in that time I did prepare my exit . . . I'd practised yoga since my early teens, and an experience at an ashram in India in 2012 had helped me finally overcome my mental health struggles,[*] so I'd known for some time that I wanted to go back there to train as a yoga teacher myself. In late 2016 my boss graciously gave me time off to do so, which set me on the path towards what I do today. After that first training I doubled down on the thought-repatterning and mindset aspects of yoga that had supported my recovery, seeking out courses that offered more of the same. I became increasingly interested (read: obsessed) with answering the question: how can I better navigate the unbridled *chaos* that is modern life? And through setting out to do just that, I discovered coaching – immediately connecting with its forward-thinking, science-backed approach, as well as how it aligned with and built upon the mindfulness and mindset trainings I'd already done. Then, fairly on, and through launching my podcast, *Priorities*, I realised that what fascinated me most about this work was the concept of priorities itself. I'd watched my own shift and change through my career in the arts, ultimately leading to that realisation in Paris. I'd observed the negative thought patterns I'd held for so long lose their

---

[*]To be clear – I don't believe this is the *only* thing that helped; many things led to my recovery, medication and therapy among them.

INTRODUCTION

strength through learning to prioritise new thoughts and habits – ones that helped rather than harmed me. And I'd seen the positive change in clients when we focused on priorities over, for example, simply setting goals or discussing habits. In 2022 I formalised my own coaching approach – *The Priorities Method*® – that puts priorities at the forefront of self-development and personal change, and in 2023 I released *The Priorities Method Journal*, a tool to help put that idea into practice. And that (in a wildly reductive nutshell) is how I find myself here, writing a book on priorities and modern life.

WHY PRIORITIES? WHY MODERN LIFE?

Let's be honest, I work in this field because *I* need help. I am (and always will be) my first student, which means I'm very much on the boat or plane, or any other transportation analogy you might prefer, with you. I've built a career around the fact that *I* find modern life challenging, and if you've picked up this book, I imagine you do too . . .

In 1971 the Nobel Prize-winning economist Herbert A. Simon coined the term 'attention economy' to describe our capacity to engage with the many competing demands on our mental focus. Simon explained the term by saying: '[I]n an information-rich world, the wealth of information means a dearth of something else: a scarcity of whatever it is that information consumes. What information consumes is the attention of its recipients. Hence a wealth of information creates a poverty of attention.'[1]

This statement could not be truer today. While 'modern life moves too fast for us to adapt' isn't a new thought (indeed the Romans were saying it millennia ago), over the past 25 years, Western society has changed and progressed at near unparalleled speed. When Simon coined the term 'attention economy', I doubt he had any inkling of the 'wealth of information' that would flood and transform our world. (He especially couldn't have predicted Reed Hastings, Netflix's CEO, describing his biggest competitor not as Amazon or Apple TV, but as 'sleep'. Yikes.[2])

Technology has transformed how we eat, sleep, move, interact, communicate and express ourselves – it's even changed how we *think*. Much of this change has been for the good. Medicine and healthcare have made huge leaps, communication is effortless, infrastructure and industry are more efficient, the sum of human knowledge is at our fingertips and sharable with a swipe – demanding more accountability from both individuals and organisations alike.

However, while it's clear that a good deal of today's world is a vast improvement on how humans have lived in the past, there's a flip side to all this progress. Evolutionarily speaking, we are a success story – with more than 8 billion of us wandering around, we're evidently equipped to survive the environment we have built. Yet, while our world is an extension of us, it can often feel that the conditions we've created, with every part of our lives transformed, don't seem to be the ones we're designed to even keep up with, let alone thrive in.

Technology may be phenomenal, but, as Hastings proves, it wants *all* your time. And although, like with anything viewed individually, the demands – a social media notification here, a Zoom meeting that could have been an email there – may seem inconsequential, or even banal, taken together they are leading us towards a 'poverty of attention'. Humans were never designed to process so many things at once, to have this much bidding for our attention.* The multifaceted strains of modern society are numerous and exhausting. We're overloaded, both individually and collectively – inundated by a daily torrent of information, distractions, options and data. All of it seemingly important and urgent, all of it desperately vying for our energy, attention and time. There's that email you have to reply to NOW, those shoes you must buy IMMEDIATELY, the success that is ALREADY OVERDUE, and all the rest . . . We're tethered to our smartphones – carrying the whole world's (highly curated) thoughts and experiences in our pocket, always right *there*, available to compare our own life to via a quick glance at a screen. We're encouraged to chase meaningless goals, to think busy equals successful, and to define our self-worth by how productive our days may appear. We are expected to be constantly available and 'on'. We expect ourselves to be able to 'do it all' . . .

In sum, it's *a lot*.† And, once you combine this fast-paced world with an ancient nervous system, ill-equipped as it is to face these distinctly modern challenges (not to mention the difficult circumstances or traumatic events that everyone experiences to a varying degree over

---

*Remarkably, in 2023 it was noted on a Leftronic blog that an overwhelming 90 percent of the world's data was produced in the previous two years alone (https://leftronic.com/blog/how-fast-is-technology-growing-statistics). I would assume that changes with AI in the years since have increased this statistic even more dramatically.

†Dare I say it, even self-development/productivity books can just add to the burden! Not this one, of course.

INTRODUCTION

their lifetime), it becomes easy to find yourself prioritising mindsets, behaviours and relationships that don't serve you, floating directionless through a life that feels at once both too empty and too full.

But it doesn't have to be that way.

We may live in a world we're not designed to thrive in, and we may be evolving more slowly than our technology is advancing, but luckily, as humans, we *are* extremely adaptable – good at learning to live in new situations with new conditions, quick to acquire different behaviour patterns and ways of living. Your brain is constantly creating new neural pathways while pruning away old ones.[*] Your brain is constantly changing.

Prioritise This will help to change your brain for the better so that it can cut through the noise, overwhelm and relentless pace of modern life. It'll help you update your system to adapt to the world you live in, to stop fighting against the chaos (a losing battle) and start carving a path across it instead. Using a system of principles and practices drawn from the fields of coaching, neuroscience, mindfulness, positive psychology and stress management, you'll uncover the daily steps and big-picture thinking that'll help you declutter your world, change your mindset and build a life that feels empty and full in all the *right* places instead. If that sounds like what you want, what you need, what you *deserve* . . . then read on.

Factors that affect how you respond to life

- Experiences
- Knowledge
- Memories
- Beliefs
- Mindset
- Perception
- Social circle
- Family
- Health
- Genes
- Age
- Sex

ABOUT *THE PRIORITIES METHOD*®

As I mentioned earlier, *The Priorities Method*® (*TPM*) is an approach to self-development that empowers you to focus on what truly matters –

---

[*] Also known as *neuroplasticity*.

whether that's a person, habit, thought, idea or goal. Over the years, I've developed ten principles to support this. On the surface, they're straightforward lessons for living – ideas on how best to show up for yourself and the people you care for – but simple doesn't mean easy. There's often a wide gap between reading something and actually living it, and none of us are immune to life's chaos or the pull of distraction. I wrote these principles because I need them too, and I still return to them as reminders.

As you read through them, use the reflection questions at the end of each one as your first step towards prioritising what matters to you in life. The chapters that follow will help you embody the principles by putting them into action; the more you do this, the more instinctive they'll become.

1. YOUR PRIORITIES = THE SUM OF YOUR LIFE

In a world of endless distractions, the first principle is the most important. If you forget everything else in the book, remember this . . .* *What you prioritise day-to-day becomes the sum of your life.* The minutes, hours, thoughts, people and behaviours you give your attention to all add up. That's why half an hour scrolling socials or constantly checking emails isn't just a small habit – it's your life being spent. Our time here is short and precious, and whether we fill it with harmful thoughts, draining people and mindless habits, or with what uplifts and sustains us, is down to what we prioritise. Ask yourself: what am I really prioritising, in my thoughts and behaviours, and what is that adding up to in my life?

2. THE MYTH OF BALANCE

We're sold the idea that balance is attainable, but, in reality, life is *messy*. It's a continuous juggle of competing priorities, stresses, changes and curveballs, and perfect equilibrium simply doesn't exist. True balance is less about rigidly dividing our time and more about how we *feel* about the way we spend it. That means embracing 'seasonal unbalance': leaning into the natural tilts of life, letting priorities shift, and accepting that sometimes we'll be disciplined and grounded, and at other times we'll be up late with children's needs, work deadlines or drinking martinis with friends. Real balance is flexible, forgiving,

---

*Also, please don't forget everything else.

INTRODUCTION

sometimes messy, even. Ask yourself: what might seasonal unbalance look like in my own life?

3. WE CAN'T DO IT ALL, BUT WE CAN DO A LOT
We grow up being told we can 'do it all', but no one can keep every plate spinning at once without smashing something along the way. Life's demands, distractions and inevitable clashes between our wants and needs mean we will always drop a few – and that's okay. The point isn't to lower your ambition but to let go of the notion of perfection, to accept that while you can't do everything all the time, you can do a lot really well when you choose wisely. Ultimately: if everything is a priority, nothing is. Free yourself from unrealistic expectations, *prioritise*, and find yourself on far steadier ground. Ask yourself: how do I try to 'do it all', and what might it look like to do less but better, instead?

4. UNDO THE TO-DO
To-do lists are brilliant. They're simple, accessible tools that bring order to the chaos, and even reward us with a little dopamine hit when we tick something off. But it's worth remembering their *sole purpose* is to help us manage our tasks and focus on what's important. They're not there to make us feel like a failure when we don't complete them. Especially since we never *will* complete them – life isn't a neat list, it's a game of whack-a-mole and the moment you finish one task, another pops up. Don't ditch your lists, just make sure to release the pressure they hold over you and use them as the support they're meant to be, not as proof of your productivity or worth. Ask yourself: how do I use my to-do list, and how does it make me feel?

5. BUT, FIRST, DE-PRIORITISE
Prioritising isn't just about deciding what matters most; it's also about deciding what *doesn't*. We have finite personal reserves, and to make room for the people, habits and goals that align with the life you want, you have to de-prioritise. Saying no to tasks, habits and even people can feel uncomfortable, but without it, your energy, time and focus will always be overdrawn. Still, it's worth it, because nature abhors a vacuum and, if done mindfully, that space you've created will be filled with what you truly value. This is all we can hope for in our short, precious life. (And also, I assume, why you are reading this book.) Ask yourself: what do I need to de-prioritise?

6. LIVE IT, DON'T FIX IT

Life is complex. It's beautiful and ugly, quiet and loud, simple and overwhelming. You won't feel joyful and purposeful all the time, because 1) you'd be intolerable and 2) that's not how life works. Despite what social media might suggest, the aim isn't to mould yourself or your days into a 'perfect' version, but to live them as they are. You are not broken, and you don't need fixing. Growth, change and challenges are all part of being human – steer through life with a 'live it' mindset and it's much easier to see yourself and your circumstances through a compassionate, constructive lens. Ask yourself: where in my life am I trying to fix things, rather than simply live them?

7. REAL SELF-CARE, WITHOUT THE SELFISH

True self-care isn't about matcha lattes, sheet masks or perfect bathroom cupboards; it's about the habits and practices that support your inner and outer world. It's being kind in your thoughts, words and actions, listening to your body and showing up for yourself, while at the same time remembering that the goal isn't to retreat into yourself at the expense of others. Real-life wellbeing means caring deeply for ourselves, but also remaining mindful of the impact we have on those around us. Ask yourself: what does real self-care, without the selfish, look like in my own life?

8. BE THE KIND-FLEX

I'm not sure how I feel about made-up words, but here we are – I'll let you be the judge! Kindness and flexibility are the foundations that make all the other *TPM* principles possible. Without kindness, we beat ourselves up when life doesn't go our way, and without flexibility, we break against its constant changes. Together, they allow us to be compassionate, forgiving, adaptable and resilient, with ourselves and others. Don't be a pushover – boundaries and self-respect remain essential – but practise the 'kind-flex', and you will move through life with more grace, ease and steadiness. Ask yourself: how do kindness and flexibility show up in my life, and where could I bring in more?

9. PRIORITISE JOY

I use the word 'joy' over its synonym 'happiness', because I think happiness can feel like a destination, always out of reach, whereas joy has more room to exist alongside everything else in life, including sadness. Research shows it's often not the big 'impressive' life events that sustain us, such as getting married or a promotion at work, but rather the tiny, overlooked moments – think: a good cup of coffee, a walk on a crisp morning, a message from a friend. These small pockets of joy add up to help us feel more connected and alive, and, when we notice and appreciate them, our brains actually begin to look for more. Ask yourself: what small things bring me joy, and how can I notice and seek them more often?

10. USE YOUR WHY
Finally, there's your 'why'. Your 'why' is the deeper reason behind your choices, the force that keeps you going when life gets hard. It could be 'because I want to teach my children kindness', or 'because my health matters more than late-night scrolling' or 'because I'm worth it'. Your whys connect you to the bigger picture and ground you in what matters most, helping you focus on the process rather than obsessing over outcomes. The clearer you are on your whys, the easier it is to live a life aligned with your true priorities. Ask yourself: what are my big whys, the reasons that drive me and keep me moving forward?

HOW TO GET THE MOST OUT OF THIS BOOK

With those in place, let's move on to the book that they've shaped . . . *Prioritise This* is divided into nine chapters, exploring nine aspects of contemporary living that I believe to be the best intervention points for a more content mind and life. The topics set out here are not unique to 21st-century life – it's human nature to experience stress, to struggle with rejection and failure, and so on. However, our modern world uniquely exacerbates both the volume and intensity of these experiences and our emotional responses to them. And, while the challenges of modern living can be viewed through environmental, cultural and social lenses, this book delves into the everyday struggles we all encounter as individuals. These are:

1. Stress
2. Habits
3. Saying no
4. Overwhelm
5. Procrastination
6. Failure
7. Rejection
8. Comparison
9. Moving forward

PRIORITISE THIS

Apologies, it's not the most light-hearted list . . .* Yet, across these chapters I'll share with you the learnings, prompts, systems, practices and processes that'll enable your brain to finally carve a path through the chaos that is modern life.

Most books of this kind are written so that you start the beginning and end at the end. Not this one. I would recommend reading Chapter 1: Stress first, as it lays a bit of the groundwork, but, ultimately, each chapter is an island unto itself, so flip to wherever feels right for you. If you've recently experienced a break-up (I'm sorry, if that's the case), it could be Chapter 7: Rejection. If you're spending too much time on social media and not enough on an important work, school or personal project, then perhaps Chapter 2: Habits or Chapter 5: Procrastination. If you feel like everything is too much, then Chapter 4: Overwhelm is your best launch point. Conversely, if you're feeling motivated to make inspiring plans for the months and years ahead, then dive straight into Chapter 9: Moving Forward. If you have absolutely no idea where you want to start, then begin at the beginning and work your way through – although the book can be read in any order, I have organised the chapters in the one that I think works best. And, of course, all the chapters are interconnected, every single topic affecting the others in some way, shape or form.

When it comes to the practices found throughout the book or online,† know that *their purpose is to help*. They are here because I've learned from years of experience that they shift theory and words ('transform your life, blah blah blah') into tangible, real-world change. They are not here to stress you out, and I do not, in any universe, expect you to do them all. I've included a wide variety to ensure there's something for every type of mind, learning style and general mood. Do the ones that work for you, skip the rest. Also, honestly, if you read the book without doing a single one, your brain's capacity to weather modern life will still be better than before you picked it up.

Hmmm, what else?

Well, this book is not a first-edition Tolstoy that needs handling with kid gloves, so *use it*. Fold down pages, highlight passages, take pictures of quotes or exercises, spill coffee on the cover and scribble your own notes and doodles along the way. The more you do this, the

---

*As Gloria Steinem once wrote: 'The truth will set you free, but first it'll piss you off.'
†Go to https://www.prioritisethis.com/.

INTRODUCTION

more *The Priorities Method*® approach will become part of your life. It's yours – don't hold it at a distance, *get involved.*

Speaking of which, if a quote or learning really resonates, I recommend jotting it down somewhere – use the notes app on your phone, text it to a friend or scribble it on a Post-it note to stick by your desk or on the fridge. We absorb and remember information more effectively after writing it down, and I know that the various Post-it notes on my office wall help me to stay on track when life gets in the way. The practices and learnings in *Prioritise This* are cumulative – reading or trying them once is unlikely to shift entrenched thought or behavioural patterns, but with repetition you'll begin to see real change. Remember your brain is a muscle like any other – you wouldn't expect to have huge biceps after one session at the gym and nor should you expect to have completely transformed your life after reading a few pages. Consistency may sometimes feel boring, but it's also *key.* (You may also notice that many of the topics in this book overlap and reinforce one another and that for this reason there is some degree of repetition. I am aware of this and I am aware that we learn through repetition.[*])

Having said that, if you try an exercise or prompt and find it unhelpful or anxiety-inducing, stop immediately and do not try it again until you feel safe to do so. Don't worry about getting anything 'right'; follow your intuition and listen to what you need. There is no right or wrong way to read this book; there is only *your* way.

Please know that the suggestions in this book are by no means exhaustive. I do not, for a second, think that my way is the only way,[†] or that I know it all. In fact, the more I learned and discovered about the topics in this book through writing the book, the more I changed my mind (and then sometimes changed it again). While this book is informed by my neuroscience trainings and readings, I am not a neuroscientist. I am a writer and coach, and though I've tried to be rigorous in my research, it's possible I've got some things wrong. Moreover, neuroscience, coaching and wellbeing[‡] are all fast-moving fields, so it's equally possible that, by the time this book comes out, some of what

---

[*] We learn through repetition. We learn through repetition. We learn through repetition . . .
[†] I'd actually suggest running as far away as possible from anyone who says theirs is the *only* way to create change – there are many good ideas and books out there, and different methods work for different minds and stages in life.
[‡] If you bristle at the sound of that word, as I know many do, go with 'your state of relative mental and physical ease' instead. Not so snappy, but it means the same thing.

I've written will be obsolete. I do not have all the answers; I simply have some that, in my experience, work well. All I can really say is that this book is not a prescription, but an *invitation* for you to take what you need, and leave the rest.

Finally, before we start, I think it can be useful before you read a book like this to consider what you hope to get out of it. You picked it up for a reason (P.S. Thank you for doing that!) and the more you can keep that at the forefront of your mind, the more this book and *TPM* will work for you. So, what's your priority for the book? It could be to reduce stress and overwhelm, declutter your life, better navigate failure, stop procrastinating, slow the f*ck down, or some combination of all of the above. What do you need to *prioritise*? What's your *aim*? This will help maintain your focus, so keep your answers in mind, jot them down or share them. (Also, be prepared for them to shift gradually, or in an instant – change is normal, natural and to be expected, so revise them anytime you need to.)

Finally, *finally*, I'd like to add an important caveat . . . This book has been written to offer support with better managing the *generalised* challenges of modern life. It cannot do much about the systemic change that is ultimately needed in our societies, nor does it offer any kind of formal support for anyone with undiagnosed or severe psychological or physical health problems, or anyone suffering from extreme levels of stress or anxiety or dangerously low self-esteem. If you are struggling right now, I see you – please don't suffer in silence. A book is absolutely no substitute for in-person support – *seek help as soon as possible*. Reach out to your family and friends and/or an appropriately trained professional, such as your GP, a councillor, psychologist or therapist (I've included a list of useful support organisations at the end of the book).

IN SUM

Just before we dive in, I want to make it very clear that nothing you do, including, sadly, reading this book, will change the fundamental nature of modern life. Short of going to live in a remote cave somewhere,* the demands on your attention will, in all likelihood, just keep

---

*The Himalayas will forever appeal to me!

INTRODUCTION

growing. *Prioritise This* will not offer you a life free of the challenges of twenty-first-century living, so if you picked it up hoping your daily myriad of worries and distractions would disappear, I'm sorry, you will be disappointed.

I cannot do that for you, and I don't believe any other coach, book or system (no matter how shiny, expensive or well packaged) can either. If that's what you're looking for, this is not the book for you. It will not solve all your problems; life will continue to be challenging and fast-moving, because, well, that's what life *is*.

However, if you're looking for the best possible *guide* through the challenges, a system to *support* you through life's inevitable ups and downs, a framework to help *bolster* you from the difficulties you face, then you're in the right place. We all have automatic responses, conditioning, life experiences and genes that we know play a huge part in how we interact with and experience the world – this book is designed to help us move from that place of knowing what we need to do, to actually doing it.

Prioritise This won't build you a 'perfect' life. But it will build you one that feels less overwhelming, more purposeful and focused . . . and, ultimately, inimitably *yours*.

CHAPTER 1

Stress

● ● ●

'*The impediment to action advances action. What stands in the way becomes the way.*'

Marcus Aurelius, Meditations, Book 5[1]

Whenever I meet someone for the first time and explain what I do for a living, the number one question they ask is: 'Does that mean you never get stressed!?'

Reader, as I (and my entire family) can attest to, I get stressed.

My job doesn't make me invulnerable to the daily stressors we all face. I still find life overwhelming, exhausting, frustrating, anger-inducing, wearisome, annoying and the rest. In fact, I think the reason I do my job well (or at least hope I do) is because I'm not the equivalent of some army general sitting comfortably at a desk far from the war, giving orders over a warm cup of tea. I'm in the trenches with you.

However, while I'm with you, it's also not my first tour. So, I have an entire toolkit, filled with stress management techniques, approaches and exercises that it's possible you may not (*yet*) have yourself.

I've built this toolkit up over the past ten years and it helps me to 1) prevent negative feelings of stress from creeping up too often in the first place and 2) manage them well when they do get through. If we stretch this army analogy (perhaps to its limits?), you could think of me as a medic, with a bag full of lifesaving equipment, but it's not for your body, it's for your mind. And rather than treating you, I'll be teaching you – you'll be treating yourself.

This chapter is dedicated to sharing those learnings and tools. You'll discover the updated neuroscience around stress, determine how to spot and prevent approaching burnout, discover how to harness stress in a positive way, and uncover a wide range of practical strategies using your body, mind and environment to put theory into action. My aim is for you too to feel equipped to better navigate yourself through this hectic world.* The potential for stress won't disappear – in stressful situations it's natural to experience negative emotions; feeling nothing would be unrealistic, deeply concerning even. Stress will still be there; it's *you* that will change.

There's a lot to say about stress, and it's essentially my mastermind subject, so this is the longest chapter in the book. Make yourself a drink (of any kind) and settle in . . .

WHAT EVEN IS STRESS?

While the word 'stress' gets thrown around a lot (including by me), and we all know what it *feels* like to be stressed, have you ever considered what it actually is, or why we experience it in the first place?

The World Health Organization (WHO) – which tends to be reliable on such things – defines it as 'a state of worry or mental tension caused by a difficult situation'.[1] One useful way to break this down is to think of stress in two parts: first, as a stimulus i.e. the difficult situation,† and second, as a response i.e. the resulting state of worry or mental tension. The response of stress is thought to occur when *the perceived demands on your life outweigh your perceived capacity to handle them.* (Note the use of the word 'perceived' here; it'll be important later.)

Though stress often gets a bad rep – and yes, this chapter *is* dedicated to minimising its more harmful effects – it's important to recognise that stress isn't bad for you. As humans, we *need* stress. As early twentieth-century researchers Robert M. Yerkes and John Dillingham Dodson showed,‡ we rely on its stimulus to help us grow,

---

*Or at the very least find your inbox less overwhelming . . .

†'Stimulus' can also be further broken down into *external* (e.g. from the environment or social happenstances such as divorce or a car crash) or *internal* (e.g. illness or emotional trauma).

‡This is known as the Yerkes–Dodson law, which describes the relation between stress and performance. Simply put, it shows that our performance improves with stress, but only up to a point. When stress levels rise too high, performance starts to decline.

adapt and thrive, and the stress response – both psychological and physiological – has played a crucial role in keeping us alive as a species.

This 'worry or mental tension' is part of our evolutionary biology: our nervous system developed the stress response hundreds of thousands of years ago as a way to trigger action – to help us respond to opportunities, overcome challenges or escape threats. Yet while the sources of those stressors have changed over time, our bodies continue to respond in much the same way today.

> ### Worry
>
> Worry is a common experience and deeply connected to stress. Those persistent, repetitive thoughts that pull us away from the present moment and lead us to fixate on 'what if?' scenarios are often the ones that tip us from *'I'm actually okay!'* to *'Actually, I'm really not!'* The studies on worry examine its causes from multiple angles, including neurobiology, sociocultural influences and individual cognition.
>
> Central to this is the *default mode network* (DMN), a brain system active when we are not engaged in a specific task. During periods of worry and rumination, this network becomes overactive and hyperconnected, resembling a crowded room where everyone is speaking at once. This heightened activity keeps the mind trapped in unhelpful, repetitive thinking rather than focused on the present. At the same time, there's a decrease in activity in brain networks responsible for higher-order cognitive control and reasoning, such as the prefrontal cortex. And this reduction makes it difficult to regulate thoughts and escape the cycle of worry.

We'll come on to those shifting parameters, and the neurobiology of the stress response, in a moment. But first, if you're someone who sees stress as something to be avoided at all costs, let me share with you a story about a CEO I once worked with who thought the same . . .

PRIORITISE THIS

A MINDSET SHIFT*

A few years ago, I was brought in to deliver a stress management programme for a small, female-founded advertising agency in London. They were growing rapidly – every day presented new challenges and the founder/CEO was struggling to manage the impact this was having both on her own wellbeing and that of her team.

We got on well in our discovery call,† but midway through our first session we reached a slight impasse. It became clear that we had different ideas about what a 'stress management programme' involved. Essentially, she wanted me to show her how to eliminate the stress that comes with growing a company.

Now, obviously, I couldn't do that. I'm not a magician. While I could see certain pain points in the organisation that were likely contributing to feelings of overwhelm (and flagged these), my role was never to take away her stress. I was there to help her *manage* stress, and a key part of that was supporting her to recognise and accept that growing a company is inherently stressful (as well as that the alternative – *not* growing it – would arguably be more so).

By the end of that first session, her mindset had shifted – from 'This stress is *killing* us' to 'This stress is *building* us'. Over time, she let go of the idea of stress as something to be avoided, which allowed us to more easily implement the interventions you'll read about in this chapter and throughout the book. This led fairly quickly to a positive shift in both how she and the company operated (and, ultimately, flourished).

Culturally, the general messaging tends to be that stress is *bad*, to be avoided like the plague. And I'll hold my hand up to say that, in the past, I've been guilty of perpetuating that message myself. But over the past eight years I've come to view that approach as unhelpful, because, as we all know: *we can't avoid stress in life*. While it's important to acknowledge and understand the potential negative impacts of stress (some of which are proven and serious), we've also developed

---

*The first of hopefully many in this book!
†The initial Zoom call I'll have with clients or a company that's interested in working with me. It's like a first date – where you decide whether you get on and would be a good fit.

as a society a collective *fear* of stress itself. And this makes us stressed *about* stress.*

Yet research shows that not all stress is harmful. One landmark study in 2012 found that it's not necessarily stress itself that is damaging but our *belief* that stress is bad for us that causes the harm. A negative perception of stress can generate damaging physiological responses which then *trigger* the stress reaction. And, perhaps most fascinatingly of all, the people in that study who reported high levels of stress but *didn't* view it as harmful had the *lowest* mortality rates in the sample. In short: view stress as a challenge rather than a threat, and it seems you may even live longer.[2]

Just so you know, this is not a call for toxic positivity – I believe that approach is *the most* unhelpful response to the reality of being human. I'm not suggesting you ignore life's struggles or pretend everything's fine when it's not. I'm suggesting the opposite. Don't push away your feelings; acknowledge and lean into your difficulties. It's terribly clichéd, but we don't grow despite challenge, adversity and stress; we grow *because* of those things.

Let me share with you a small personal example of my own... Writing this chapter has honestly been the most stressful part of this book. The subject matter is vast, the science is complex, and the stakes feel high. When I focus on how stressful it is to write about stress and start worrying about feeling stressed, I freeze up. I get stressed. But when I reframe my feelings of stress as an indication of how much I *care* about this chapter (and book), then they can be used to spur me on instead. *Welcoming* them makes me feel calmer, clearer and more able to sit and type.

And this is why any stress management intervention begins with the crucial mindset shift that *stress is not bad for you*. Reframe it as natural and normal – perhaps even beneficial† – and you'll be in a far better position to thrive in this fast-moving modern world.‡ With that in mind, let's look at how your nervous system has evolved (or, more accurately, *hasn't*) to help you do just that.

---

*In coaching we refer to this as a version of a 'secondary emotional disturbance', whereby we have an emotional response or reaction to an emotional experience – another example could be feeling ashamed about feeling anxious. Where possible we, unsurprisingly, want to try to minimise them.
†Even though, yes, I know, sometimes it f*cking sucks.
‡FYI: there's a great TED Talk by Kelly McGonigal called 'How to make stress your friend' if you're interested in exploring this idea further: https://www.youtube.com/watch?v=RcGyVTAoXEU

OLD HARDWARE

Stress is clearly not unique to twenty-first-century life. In fact, I imagine there are far fewer truly stressful stimuli for most people in, say, the UK today, compared to those who lived during the Victorian era.

However, what modern life does exceptionally well is create conditions that amplify our emotional reactions and introduce challenges and situations that feel novel and demanding to our brain. Our nervous system evolved over millions of years to handle certain conditions, only to be faced by a dramatically changed world in the last hundred years, and even more so in the last 30 since the arrival of the internet (and *even* more so over the past few years, with advances in AI).

While humans are incredibly adaptable, we have now altered our environment so rapidly through agriculture, industrialisation and technology that we haven't yet had time to fully adjust. Our 'stress response' developed to help us to (among other things) react quickly to concrete, immediate, physical threats – such as being chased by a hungry tiger or encountering an unfriendly tribe. It was biologically designed to reallocate your energy in times of 'stress'; it was not designed to manage intangible, psychological challenges, such as constant email notifications, a 24-hour news cycle or emotionally taxing social media apps.

So, although many physical threats of the past have been reduced or ruled out, they've been replaced by increasingly abstract ones. The very same, era-defining technological advances that are meant to make life easier often do the opposite.* And, in simple terms, your nervous system is like an *old computer*, one that lacks some of the updated hardware modern life requires. It doesn't work optimally with its environment. My work is about helping us develop that hardware, so we can better manage the growing pains of being mismatched with our environment and keep our systems running as smoothly as we can.

---

*James Gleick's book *Faster* brilliantly explores the concept of 'hurry sickness', and this idea that the more time-saving strategies and devices we have, the more rushed we feel.

MADE TO ORDER

The stress response itself is incredible – it influences how you think, feel, behave and even how the body functions.* At its core, it prepares you for action – your brain interprets a threat, challenge or opportunity as something needing a response and then triggers your body to react. This happens *involuntarily*, meaning your body reacts before you're consciously aware.

However, despite popular opinion, this response isn't confined to a single region or system in your brain, nor is it a simple on/off switch. Also, it's not hardwired – it is dynamically *constructed*.

Think of your brain like a high-end restaurant, crafting your feeling of stress to order. There's no precooked 'meal' sitting in the fridge, waiting to be heated up and served. Instead, it's using fresh ingredients every time, coordinating a response between your cognitive, emotional and physiological networks based on the stimuli it encounters – your experiences, the events, sensory input, memory and more.†

This bespoke response works through two distinct systems in the brain. First, the autonomic nervous system (ANS) rapidly releases adrenaline and noradrenaline from your adrenal glands. These hormones activate the sympathetic nervous system (SNS), which increases your heart rate, breathing and other bodily functions.‡ This response is quick and acute – it doesn't last long.

The second system, the hypothalamic pituitary adrenal (HPA) axis, responds more slowly (if still incredibly fast). It triggers the release of cortisol, also from adrenal glands, into your bloodstream. Unlike the fleeting ANS response, the effects of HPA activation can linger. And, while cortisol serves an important function in your body (having too little is deeply dangerous), chronic elevated cortisol is linked to negative effects including high blood pressure, weakened immune function and osteoporosis.[3] Stress may sometimes be good for you, but lingering cortisol stores are categorically not.

---

*There is not one system untouched by its effects – from the musculoskeletal, respiratory, cardiovascular, endocrine, gastrointestinal and reproductive.

†Yes, it might use the same (unhelpful!) ingredients over and over again, and how to encourage it to find new, more helpful, ingredients is something we look at later in the chapter.

‡I imagine you're all too familiar with the fight–flight–freeze (FFF) response, which is an extreme version of this.

Any stress intervention programme therefore needs to work *with* these systems, to help you turn up the volume on your 'resting' system – the parasympathetic nervous system (PNS)* – and turn down the volume on your SNS when it's not required. Much of this chapter will help you to improve your ability to modulate your PNS and SNS, as well as bolster the networks between different areas of your brain. It'll also show you how multiple factors, including the *type* of stressor, affect your stress response, with each response triggering different levels of hormones in different configurations.† And through all this you'll learn to better regulate your stress responses so that you can cook up a response that's not just a 'best guess' but *the* best guess for you.

YOUR KALEIDOSCOPE

With that brief lesson on the brain complete, the most important takeaway is this: stress is *highly subjective*.

Now, before you throw your arms up in despair, no, not all stressful stimuli are created equal – the death of a partner and a delayed Amazon delivery are clearly incomparable.‡ But, generally speaking, a 'situation' is fairly fixed – a broken toe is a broken toe, a divorce is a divorce. What isn't fixed, what is *subjective*, is our experience, perception and interpretation.

For every situation we encounter, we bring with us a lifetime of accumulated context – our current mood, past experiences, personal biases, assumptions, cultural background and understandings of the world. We each arrive from a different starting point, which is why two people can face the exact same scenario and respond in different ways. In essence, we look at life through a unique kaleidoscope – one shaped by everything we've experienced, learned and felt so far.

Think of two people (Bob I and Bob II) stuck in a traffic jam.

Bob I is late for an important meeting and, moreover, firmly holds the belief that being late is akin to a mortal sin. For him, this traffic jam is *terrible* – he's frazzled, frustrated, simmering with stress. Bob II, on the other hand, is not only more relaxed about punctuality but also

---

*Also part of the ANS: think of it like the yin to the yang of your SNS.
†For example, you may be surprised to hear that when you respond to a stressful situation with anger (the *Fight* response) you have higher levels of noradrenaline than adrenaline and cortisol in your body.
‡I did just compare them, but only to show how incomparable they are.

doesn't have anywhere he urgently needs to be. In fact, with three loud teenagers at home, Bob II is relishing the peace of listening to a podcast in his car. He doesn't feel stressed at all.

Same situation, completely different experience.

Of course, certain situations in life are inherently stressful, painful, difficult or deeply unfair. But, when it comes to the everyday stressors that make up the background hum (or foreground drilling) of life, mindset and context play an enormous role. As the Stoic philosopher Epictetus famously said, 'We do not see things as they are, we see them as we are.' Stress is a combination of what brings us stress, *and* what we believe and think about that stress.

A TALE OF TWO BRIDGES

I'd like you to imagine two bridges.

The first is the iconic Golden Gate Bridge in San Francisco – striking, solid, seemingly never-ending. It spans a vast expanse of water and holds strong under the weight of almost anything, including enormous (and I mean *enormous* – this is the United States, after all) HGVs, lorries and the like.

The second bridge couldn't be more different. It's a tiny, wobbly, wooden structure crossing a quiet stream somewhere in the British countryside. Several planks are missing, the remaining ones are rotting – the whole thing looks it might collapse under the weight of a large rabbit, let along anything with four wheels.

Human beings are like bridges – each of us can carry different loads and we each have a unique breaking point. Your wellbeing (or how strong *your* bridge is) depends on a balance between the resources you have[*] and the challenges you face – that is, what life throws at you.

But, unlike actual bridges, we aren't fixed.

We evolve, change and adapt as we move through life. And how we respond to our experiences (whether tough or joyful) plays a role in shaping who we become. Personally, I felt like the Golden Gate Bridge after my first child was born; by the time my second arrived my affinity lay more with the rickety wooden one. And right now (and I mean *right now* at the time of writing since I might feel *completely* different in an hour) I'm somewhere closer to the Golden Gate again.

---

[*]Both internal (thoughts, beliefs, health, etc.) and external (support system, finances, environment, hobbies, etc.).

What about you? What kind of a bridge do you feel like today?

The reality is, we can't control much of what happens to us in life (see the 'Control the controllable' box below). We can't avoid pain or heartbreak. We can't magic away our commitments, problems or responsibilities – and we certainly can't do that for anyone else either. Life is going to life. *That's what it does.*

However, the more we can develop our bridge – by building resources and resilience – the better able we'll feel to manage stress (and life) when it comes our way. And it *will* come.

That's why stress requires a 360-degree approach, one that addresses how we support ourselves through our bodies, minds and the world around us. There are many coaching frameworks that can help us do this, but my go-to is my tutor Dr Sarah McKay's neuroscience-informed model: *Bottom-Up, Outside-In, Top-Down*.[4] It offers a clear, practical way of understanding how different brain–body pathways influence our thoughts, feelings and behaviours, and how we can tap into these to navigate stress more effectively. I've adapted the model below, with Dr McKay's kind permission. Small caveat: McKay's framework can be used in any order – I've chosen to lead with Bottom-Up, followed by Top-Down, ending with Outside-In as I've found this sequence to be most effective.

Control the controllable

One of the most liberating lessons I've learned is this: some things are within your control, some things you can influence, and some things are out of your hands. That might sound painfully obvious, but grasping and accepting this framework has changed my entire relationship with stress.

The Zone of Control captures this idea:

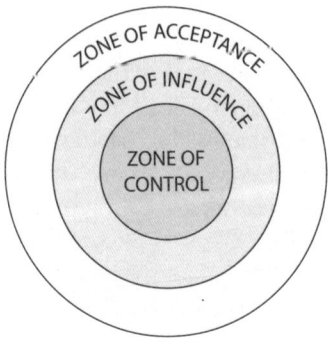

- At the centre is your **Zone of Control** – these are the things you have direct power over: how you speak, the boundaries you set, the decisions you make, how you react to things.
- Surrounding that is your **Zone of Influence** – the things you don't directly control, but where your actions or input can make a difference. For example: how your team at work operates, your child's bedtime routine, a friend's mood, a project outcome.
- Outside both of these lies your **Zone of Acceptance** – things that affect you but are ultimately beyond your control or influence. The weather, the economy, other people's beliefs, behaviour or opinions, political decisions, global crises, your past.

Most of us spend a *lot* of time and energy in the outer circle – worrying, ruminating, overthinking, trying to control what people think of us or fix problems that aren't ours to solve. And, the more we operate in this area, the more powerless and overwhelmed we feel. So much of our stress can come from trying (read: failing) to exert control over the uncontrollable.

What you want to do is draw your focus back inward, and *control the controllable* instead.

Stop micro-managing everyone around you, redirect your attention towards your own actions and mindset – towards your Zone of Control.

This doesn't mean being perpetually calm and nonplussed by others. I'm certainly not! We all waste energy on things we can't change from time to time. It's more about being aware of *how* you can look at things differently. Of seeing what you can't change and instead focus on where you *can* make a difference instead.

So: what's stressing you right now? And, more importantly, which zone does it fall into? Ask yourself: what are the stressors I can control and what are those I can't?

PRIORITISE THIS: BOTTOM-UP

We'll begin with *Bottom-Up*, which refers to any signals from the body and lower brain areas that influence your brain state – including sensory input, instinctive reactions and physiological experiences. Think of this as how your body impacts your brain, with bottom-up strategies using physical and sensory practices to help regulate your nervous system.

Through this lens, let me be the millionth person to remind you to do these four simple things that you absolutely already know you need to do to improve your ability to navigate stress:

1. Aim for seven-plus hours of sleep a night.
2. Eat a balanced diet that leaves you feeling energetic and well.
3. Drink water. A lot of it. More than you think.
4. Move your body – not just with planned exercise, but generally throughout the day.

These basic building blocks of health might seem painfully obvious, but also they are proven to work![5,6] And let's be honest – when you are stressed, these basics are the first to go. You might reach for the wine bottle more often or skip your morning workout because you stayed up late doom-scrolling. You *can* address stress without focusing on these areas, but in my experience this is a good place to start.

And perhaps the very best place of all is with sleep. I know firsthand – from periods of insomnia and from having small children – that not sleeping makes *everything* harder. It impairs our ability to regulate emotions, manage overwhelm and survive stressful times.[7] Yet, in the UK alone, 37 million people are estimated to be chronically sleep-deprived.[8] Tellingly, studies show that even an extra 30 minutes of sleep each night can make a substantial difference to your cognitive and physical health.[9]

Now, I know that, if you have insomnia, having a non-sleep-expert suggest you just 'improve your sleep!' is insulting. I'm not writing this part for you (though I *feel* you and hope things improve). If, however, your sleep could be better, and you haven't yet tried these consistently for at least three months, give them a go.

> ### Painfully boring notes on sleep hygiene (so boring they may help you fall asleep!)
>
> - Go to bed and wake up at roughly the same time every day, even on weekends.
> - Make your sleeping area as quiet, dark, relaxing and cool (temperature, not décor) as possible.
> - Limit your use of electronic devices – TVs, computers, smartphones – for 30 minutes to 1 hour before bed and after waking.
> - Turn your smartphone off and put it in another room, or use *Do Not Disturb* so you're only alerted to emergencies.
> - Avoid large meals, caffeine or alcohol immediately before bedtime.
> - Include carbohydrates in your evening meal – studies suggest they increase brain uptake of tryptophan, which converts to serotonin and melatonin, improving sleep.[10]
> - Move your body during the day – physical activity helps you fall asleep more easily (avoid high-intensity exercise close to bedtime; gentle stretching is better).
> - And, on a general note, it's worth considering whether stressing about your sleep is making your sleep worse as well as whether any sleep-tracking device is *actually* helping you – don't just rely on the data: if your device says you didn't sleep well, but you feel good, stick with that instead.

TEN MORE (SCIENCE-BACKED) BOTTOM-UP STRESS INTERVENTIONS*

1. **Mindfulness and meditation:**[11] as a meditation *and mindfulness* teacher, these are two practices I consistently recommend. They give the mind a break, bring you into the present (i.e. away from spiralling thoughts about the past or future) and help bolster the

---

*You don't have to do them all – remember these are just suggestions! If you hate meditation or don't cope well with cold water, that's fine, ignore them. (Or, you know, try them anyway and see how you get on . . .)

PNS. They may not be for everyone, but studies do repeatedly show them to be effective for managing and preventing stress. There are meditations both in the book and online, but if you'd like to try a specific mindfulness-based one, you can find it on the Prioritise This website.

2. **Cold water:**[12] the science goes that cold water puts your body under positive stress and stimulates the vagus nerve – the largest cranial nerve in the body, crucial for nervous system regulation – which in turn helps slow your heart rate and regulate cortisol. I love cold-water swimming, and go weekly all year round,* but for the days I don't, I dunk my face in a bowl of ice water until just before brain-freeze kicks in (FYI: also brilliant for reducing puffiness after a bad night's sleep or big night out). Cold showers are another great option.

3. **Fermented foods:**[13] our understanding of the gut–brain axis is still growing, but studies suggest that healthy gut bacteria can reduce stress. If you're a fan of fermented foods like kimchi, then it's worth upping your daily dose of them; if you're not, don't force yourself – I imagine that'd just make you more stressed.

4. **Standing on one leg:**[14] standing on one leg clearly improves physical balance, but it also requires focus, which can bolster brain health and reduce stress overall. I do this sometimes while brushing my teeth – balancing for one minute on each leg (also known as habit stacking, as you'll discover in Chapter 2: Habits).

5. **Massage:**[15] massage also stimulates the vagus nerve and can even lower blood pressure. Whether it's professional or self-massage, gentle touch anywhere on the body helps (reflexology, in particular, comes up frequently in studies). Avoid deep tissue or sports massages as they may trigger the SNS instead.

6. **Deep belly breathing:**[16] I'm a broken record on recommending breathing deeply into your belly (diaphragmatic breathing). It helps reconnect you with your body, balances your nervous system and can even help ease back pain. It activates the vagus nerve (that guy again!) and has been shown to lower physiological and psychological stress. You might also explore other breathwork styles such as box breathing or the 'physiological sigh' (see the end of the chapter).

---

*How do you know if someone is a cold-water swimmer? Don't worry, they will tell you! (Same joke as vegans, I know.)

7. **Step outside barefoot:**[17] grounding – making direct physical contact with the earth – has been shown in research to reduce stress and promote healing. It's a little harder to do during winter, but worth trying whenever possible.
8. **Mindful distraction:**[18] this technique has been shown to dampen the SNS response in your brain and increase the networks that can help with reasoning and thinking. To try it for yourself, set a timer for three minutes and during that time focus on what you can see, hear or smell. Label it: *there is a chair, it is brown, there is a computer, it has a keyboard* and so on . . . If you become emotionally involved in an object and start feeling stressed, draw your attention back to labelling instead. In sum, give yourself a mental break.
9. **Yoga or somatic movement:**[19] I mean, this clearly won't be the first or last time someone has mentioned stress and yoga in the same sentence . . . But the reason yoga comes up so often is because it has been repeatedly shown to be effective at calming the nervous system. There seems to be something in the combination of mindful movement with breath awareness in yoga (and other somatic practices). Even a few minutes can make a difference.
10. **Rhythmic activities:**[20] rhythmic movement has a calming effect on the nervous system, with the repetition creating a meditative state that can settle the body and mind. Activities like walking, running, dancing or drumming have been shown to help regulate breathing and heart rate, promote mindfulness, and encourage the release of endorphins, all contributing to stress reduction. Extra points (i.e. benefits) when practised with others.

PRIORITISE THIS: TOP-DOWN

Now that we've covered some of the physiological foundations, we can turn to the *top-down* approach, which explores how your thoughts, beliefs and experiences – *your mind* – both contribute to stress and can be used to manage it. (FYI: I *love* this stuff.)

Let me begin by sharing with you an analogy I heard during my first trip to the ashram in 2012. It changed the way I see my brain and my ability to navigate this world, for the better, for ever, and to this day remains one of the most impactful things I've ever learned . . .

Imagine a towering rockface, with water cascading steadily over its surface.

At first, the water flows uniformly, washing over every inch of the rock. But over thousands of years it begins to wear into the stone, carving out grooves. Once those form, the water no longer spreads evenly across the rock; instead, it flows into these paths instead because *they offer the least resistance.* They've become the most efficient way for the water to travel from top to bottom.

Your brain works in much the same way.

Think a thought once, and not much happens.* Yet think it over and over, for months and years, and it carves out a groove of its own. You won't see it *physically* in the brain, but that thought strengthens the neural networks and internal conversations around it. It becomes part of your mental landscape.

And once that thought groove exists, your brain defaults to it. It chooses familiar thoughts *automatically*, not because they're true or useful, but because (like the water flowing down grooves in the rock) they provide the path of least resistance. Well-trodden neural pathways use less energy, and your brain is wired to conserve energy whenever it can. Familiar thoughts are effortless, whereas new ones are demanding. So, like water down a rockface, your mind flows towards what it already knows.

This is why you might find yourself thinking, 'This is just how I am,' or accepting your thoughts as unquestionable truths. But familiarity doesn't equal fact, and just because a thought is well worn doesn't mean it's helpful or true.

There is another path, however. Your brain has the capacity for *neuroplasticity* – meaning it can change, adapt and form new networks. You have the power to rework your thoughts. You can gradually weaken some of those old, automatic grooves and start to build and strengthen new ones.

It's not easy, or quick. But it *is* possible.

I know – because I've done it.

When I was unwell it felt as though 90 percent of my thoughts were self-critical. Inside my head I was constantly berating myself in a wide range of creative ways, from the size of my wrists (insane, I know) to how I spoke to others. Everything was ammunition for self-criticism. My eating disorder started in my early teens, hit its peak around 17, and held me in its vicelike grip until my mid- to late twenties. My

---

*There are, as always, exceptions – some thoughts like those from a traumatic event can be laid down in your neural networks instantly.

depression came a little later but it had been percolating beneath the surface for some time. And, once it took hold, it still managed a full decade inside in my head. It wasn't a few months – or even years – of harmful thought patterns that I had to undo and relearn. I was trying to untangle *decades* of mental conditioning.

It sounds wildly reductive to say that I decided to change my thought patterns and be happy and well and then I became those things, especially as I also spent years in various therapies and on antidepressants all of which (mostly) helped in their own way. That's not what happened.

But, when I came across the metaphor of the water and the rock, something clicked. I guess I was finally ready to hear that *I* might play some part too. Until then, I'd mostly believed that I was 'broken' (*this is just how I am*) and placed any hope I did have of recovery on external sources – *this* therapist might work or *that* medication will make a difference. To be clear, I'm not suggesting the responsibility for recovering from a mental illness should rest solely on the individual. But I do know that, *for me*, when I started to take personal responsibility for my thoughts and gain some 'power' over them, everything began to change.

This isn't a book aimed at addressing serious mental health conditions like those that I lived with.* However, I wanted to share my story here because the lessons I learned – about rewiring my brain and reshaping my thought habits – are the very ones I use with my work today. And I know from experience that they can be usefully applied in *any* stressful or challenging situation, including those covered in the rest of the book. What I've seen, time and time again, is that an active cognitive view has a huge impact, that prioritising the thought 'This is what I'm telling myself about this situation' versus 'This is happening to me and I have zero part to play' can bring about real change.

The more you actively challenge your unhelpful thoughts, the more your brain will begin to doubt them – and, eventually, start to question them automatically. The less you'll feel hijacked by your thoughts, your stress, or whatever else that's unsettling your mind.

But it does take energy, time and consistency.

Annoyingly, you can't confront a thought once and expect it to disappear. Just like building physical strength, mental strength requires

---

*There is, however, a list of Resources offering this kind of support at the back.

regular effort. Muscles grows with consistent training, and while they might need less attention once they're strong, if you stop working them, they atrophy. The same goes for your mind.

I think of my mental health and my thoughts as part of a lifelong exercise programme. These days, I may not need to train as hard as I used to, but I'm never going to stop doing it entirely.

And, if I were recommending this programme to someone just starting out – something like the lightest weights in the gym – I'd suggest beginning right here, with these four questions . . .

FOUR (LIFE-CHANGING) QUESTIONS

I ask myself these four 'Socratic' questions in almost every challenging situation – whether I'm frazzled by a big, last-minute corporate project or worn thin by the relentless (sometimes monotonous) demands of parenting. I think they are the most helpful questions I know . . .

The four Socratic questions are:

1. Is this situation or problem I'm thinking about *real* or *hypothetical*? (I.e. is something actually happening right now, or am I spiralling about something that might happen in the future?)
2. Are my thoughts *logical*? (I.e. would a scientist agree with my logic? Where is the evidence for my thoughts? Do they follow reason?)
3. Are my thoughts *rational*? (I.e. do they make sense in proportion to the situation, or are they exaggerated, distorted or emotionally driven?)
4. Are they *helpful*? (I.e. where are they actually getting me?)

And this last one, for me, is the most important of all. Because if my thoughts aren't helping me move through a situation with more clarity, compassion or perspective, if they're not nudging me closer towards my goals or nurturing a healthier, more grounded mindset, then what *are* they doing?

The thoughts you prioritise directly shape how you experience stress.* When you learn to prioritise more helpful thoughts, you don't just manage stress better, you change the way you experience it.

---

*When I say this, some people can (understandably) start to feel defensive – that is, it's not my fault that I think these thoughts, I can't help it! While I agree wholeheartedly that it's not your fault, I would also suggest that, if you believe you can't help, that could be a thought you need to work on changing!

Try this: bring to mind a stressful situation and walk yourself through the four Socratic questions. Jot down the answers or say them out loud – sometimes, simply seeing or hearing your thoughts is enough to reveal how senseless, unhelpful or even self-sabotaging they truly are.

And if they *are* harming you or holding you back, the next question becomes: *what can I do about it?*

SITs AND SATs

This is what you can do about it!

Once you're comfortable challenging your thoughts using the four questions, you're ready to move on to the next topic: learning how to identify different types of unhelpful thoughts and discovering more constructive ones to replace them with. Psychologists have long studied what are commonly known as *thinking errors* – patterns of thought that tend to increase stress, undermine effective problem-solving and generally make life tougher.

These errors are categorised in various ways depending on the context,* but for the purposes of this chapter we'll refer to them as *stress-inducing thoughts* (SITs) and *stress-alleviating thoughts* (SATs).

As the names suggest, SITs are thoughts that trigger or intensify stress while SATs are cognitive strategies that help us challenge and reframe unhelpful or inaccurate perceptions of events and stress itself.[21] By actively disputing stress-inducing thoughts, we can begin to form more balanced beliefs and adopt healthier approaches to coping and problem-solving. This marks a shift from being passive recipients of stress to taking an *active* role that includes accepting *some* responsibility for our thoughts.

You'll find a full list of SITs and SATs as well as *stress-alleviating behaviours* (SABs) *and stress-alleviating feelings* (SAFs) on the next page. For now, let's take a closer look at a few examples to understand why these kinds of thoughts make life more difficult, and what we can do to change that:

---

*You may have heard them phrased as 'self-restraining thoughts' and 'self-propelling thoughts', 'health-inhibiting thoughts' and 'health-promoting thoughts', or even 'task-interfering cognitions' and 'task-orientated cognitions'. The acronyms are as follows – SRT/SPT; HIT/HPT; and TIC/TOC – and some of them will be mentioned in the chapters ahead. All you need to know is that they are all simply different ways of describing variations on the 15 thinking errors that SITs and SATs are based on.

SIT 1: All-or-nothing thinking. Seeing things in black-and-white terms, without recognising any middle ground. This type of thinking frames an experience as either a complete success or total failure.

For example: *I am always stressed.*

SIT 2: Catastrophising (or Awfulising). Exaggerating the importance or impact of an event, blowing it out of proportion and often imagining the worst-case scenario.

For example: *If I lose my job, it will be the end of the world.*

SIT 3: Mind reading. Assuming you know what others are thinking – usually something negative – without any real evidence. Sometimes you might infer this from vague cues, or even without seeing any behaviour at all!

For example: *I'm sure I'm going to get fired because I was late on that project.*

Sound familiar so far . . . ? I know it does to me.

So now let's look at how we can use SATs to challenge and replace SITs, in order to give our minds less cognitive kindling for the emotional fire.

SAT 1: Relative thinking. When you notice yourself falling into extreme, all-or-nothing thinking, practise introducing nuance by looking for the grey areas and keeping things in perspective.

For example: *Yes, there are stressful things happening in my life right now, but there are also moments – even if brief – when I feel calm and relaxed.*

SAT 2: De-magnify or de-awfulise. Whatever the situation, there's no benefit to blowing it out of proportion. Remember the last of the four Socratic questions: *Is this thought helpful?* A situation or event may be painful and difficult, but seldom is it 'the end of the world'. Create some distance; see the wood from the trees.

For example: *If I lose my job, it may be awful for a little while. But I am good at what I do, and I will find another job (perhaps an even better one!).*

SAT 3: Seek evidence. Challenge mind reading or assumptions by searching for real evidence that supports (or contradicts) your stress-inducing thoughts. This might mean asking someone directly or testing your assumptions through action.

For example: *This is the only project I've been late on. No one has mentioned anything about being fired. I can schedule a meeting with my boss to explain and discuss next steps.*

As you practise challenging your thoughts, you'll start to notice which SITs show up most often for you. From there, you can identify the SATs that best help you rebalance your thinking and reduce negative stress.

Ultimately, what I want you to do is *talk back to your brain*.

Don't automatically accept every thought that arises as fact or truth. Instead, learn to consistently – but *compassionately* – question your thoughts.

Bear in mind, however, that challenging your brain can be tiring and difficult, especially when you're just starting out. It's essential to do so with compassion,* to remind yourself that you're not being critical of your thoughts and beliefs to tear yourself down, but to support yourself more fully. It might feel sometimes as if you're constantly criticising yourself, or as if your mind is broken. I've felt that way too. Keep going. Keep challenging those SITs and replacing them with SATs – over time, you'll shift into a place where your brain is more often working *with* you, rather than against you.†

And always remember: your brain is trying to keep you safe – it just sometimes does this with 'unhelpful' and negative thoughts. I go into this 'negativity bias' in Chapter 3: Saying No, but for now know that your brain highlights negative thoughts to protect you. It believes it's doing the right thing. And sometimes it is! But, also, often it's not. In those times, let it know it's off track and offer up a new thought or belief (one that helps rather than harms) to hold on to instead.

When I catch my own brain slipping into a SIT, I take a deep breath and say: 'Please, brain. No. Be quiet. You're not helping me right now.'‡

You can find your own way of saying it, but the idea remains the same: let your brain know that although it thinks it's helping, it isn't. View it like a well-meaning child who's just drawn all over the wall with a marker. They don't understand the difference between a wall and a

---

*Self-compassion is an important *top-down* strategy.

†I like to lean on the legal concept of 'beyond a reasonable doubt' (which states that the evidence for a case in a criminal court must be so strong that there is no reasonable possibility that a defendant is innocent) applying it to my thoughts and asking myself: Is this true beyond reasonable doubt? Often, the answer is a resounding *no*.

‡The language I actually use is less PG, but I'd only suggest telling your own brain to f*ck off if you can maintain compassion while doing so. Otherwise, it may feel aggressive and overly self-critical.

piece of paper, *yet*. So, you'd explain it to them, calmly and kindly. Your brain is similar. With certain thoughts, you'll need to patiently retrain it – again and again and again.

Speaking from experience, I still have to challenge my brain around certain thoughts, beliefs and insecurities, especially if I'm tired or stretched too thin. My brain tends to revert to old, unhelpful patterns – I'll feel more negative about my body, or more uncertain and insecure – and will know that I need to work a little harder to counter those thoughts and take care of myself.

One more important topic connected to *top-down* strategies is to be mindful of not *identifying* too much with your stress. First, constantly telling yourself you are stressed is like repeating a mantra to yourself – it's a self-fulfilling prophecy: believe you are always stressed and you will always feel stressed. Secondly, when you've spent a lot of time feeling stressed or worrying, it's a natural step to assume that it's part of your personality – 'I am a worrier!' and so on. But adopting an emotional experience into your identity makes it harder to separate from. I had this with my eating disorder: it became so much a part of who I thought I was – *of my identity* – that recovering from it became much harder. Try saying to yourself: 'I currently suffer from stress', rather than 'I am always stressed'. You don't have to have a relentlessly optimistic mindset at all times but know that studies repeatedly show the health-protective effects of a positive outlook.[22] Where possible, cognitively reframe stressful situations, recognise the difficulty and challenge of a given moment, but also catch yourself when you're falling into overly negative, stress-inducing patterns of thinking. Always ask yourself: *how is this helping?* And: *is there the slightest possibility I'm looking for a way to make life hard?* See where the answers take you. As the late artist Andy Warhol said: 'Sometimes, people let the same problem make them miserable for years when they could just say, So what. That's one of my favourite things to say. So what.'

SITs checklist

Are you . . . ?

- jumping to conclusions
- mind reading
- assuming your view is the only possible one
- paying attention only to the negative side of things

- overestimating the chances of disaster
- exaggerating the importance of events
- assuming you cannot do anything to alter the situation
- expecting yourself or others to be perfect
- condemning yourself (or someone else) on the basis of a single event
- using a double standard
- fretting about how things should be instead of accepting and dealing with them as they are
- blaming yourself for something that is not your fault
- thinking in all-or-nothing terms
- using ultimatum words (must/should/have to/got to) in your thinking
- taking things personally that have little or nothing to do with you
- predicting the outcome instead of experimenting with it
- concentrating on your weaknesses and neglecting your strengths
- posing questions that have no answers.

ALTERNATIVE STRESS-ALLEVIATING THOUGHTS, FEELINGS AND BEHAVIOURS

THOUGHTS

1. What are other ways of looking at this situation?
2. Am I looking at the whole picture?
3. What might be a more helpful way of thinking right now?
4. What SITs am I employing? How could I replace them with SATs?
5. What is the probability my thoughts will happen?
6. Have I had experiences in the past that suggest that this thought might not be completely true *all* the time?
7. Can I really predict the future? Is it helpful to try? What is more helpful?
8. Am I exaggerating how bad the results might be?
9. If a friend or loved one were in this situation and had this thought, what would I tell them?

PRIORITISE THIS

BEHAVIOURS

1. What could I do in the moment that would be more helpful?
2. What's the best thing to do (for me, others, or the situation)?
3. If my feared situation happens, how will I handle it? What coping skills can I use? What have I done in the past that was successful?
4. Am I needing to work on acceptance, letting go of control, being okay with less than perfect, or having faith in the future and myself?
5. Do I need to take five deep breaths into my belly or go for a walk? (The answer is always yes.)

FEELINGS

1. What might it feel like if I acted/thought differently?
2. When I'm not feeling this way, do I think about the situation differently?
3. Are there any strengths or positives in me or the situation that I may be ignoring?
4. What else might this anxiety/stress/worry be related to? Is it really about feeling X instead?
5. Tell yourself: this feeling will pass.

Orange visualisation

To help you understand the power of our thoughts, try this quick visualisation. (Don't worry if you're not a 'visual' person – I can't picture things clearly,* and it still works on me.)

Close your eyes and imagine I've just placed a fresh orange in your hand. Feel the weight of it. Run your fingers over the skin. If you can, picture its vibrant colour.

Now bring it up to your nose. Smell the sharp, citrusy tang of its peel.

Next, imagine it's been sliced open. See the beads of juice glistening between the segments. Bring one of those segments to your mouth and bite into it. Taste the burst of sweet, tangy juice filling your mouth, trickling down your throat.

---

*I actually have aphantasia, which is an inability to visualise.

Now pause. Is your mouth watering slightly? Do your taste buds feel activated? Can you almost taste the orange?

That physical response – the salivation, the slight jaw tension, the anticipation – has been triggered *entirely by your thoughts*. And if simply imagining something as banal as an orange can provoke a noticeable bodily reaction, just think what the constant stream of anxious or stressful thoughts might be doing to your system on a daily basis. (FYI: you can also do this experiment the other way round – try to feel an emotion such as stress, anger, guilt or shame *without* any thoughts, images or pictures in your head. As you'll discover, it's basically impossible to feel an emotion unless you have a thought or picture in your head). Thoughts aren't just in your head – they shape your body, your chemistry and your experience of the world. Learning to manage them can help you learn to manage your stress.

PRIORITISE THIS: OUTSIDE-IN

The final part of Dr McKay's model that we'll explore looks outward at the role the external world plays in shaping how your brain experiences life. Think: context, environment and other *outside-in* influences on stress. The good news is that there are *many* possible intervention points we can use.

Too often, these kinds of strategies are dismissed as 'obvious', but, as you will surely get tired of me repeating: *obvious works*. These aren't ground-breaking suggestions, but they are proven, effective and often surprisingly easy to implement.

Let's start with environmental optimisation, which simply means adjusting your physical surroundings to better support your mental and physical health. This could look like removing your phone from the bedroom, reorganising your furniture, changing your lighting or decluttering your space. The priority here is small changes that can create subtle shifts in your stress baseline.

Here are two simple, science-backed suggestions to start with today:

1. **Maintain a daily routine.**[23] Having some form of regular schedule is consistently shown to improve mental health and reduce stress. It helps you use your time more effectively and gives your brain a

reassuring sense of structure and predictability. Create a routine that works for *you* and do your best to stick to it, even loosely.
2. **Make your bed.**[24] Yes, really. Achieving this small goal early in the day creates a micro-win, giving your brain a hit of dopamine and lowering cortisol. No matter what happens next, you've done something; you've *started*.

From there, we can move into your digital environment, which has quickly become one of the biggest sources of background stress and mental noise. I go into digital decluttering and smartphone interventions in detail in Chapter 4: Overwhelm, but for now ask yourself two quick questions:

1. Roughly how much time do you spend on social media sites each week?
2. Roughly how much news do you consume?

I'm not here to demonise the internet or tell you to log off for good. I just want to stress that none of us are designed to absorb the scale of suffering broadcast in a 24-hour news cycle, especially not via social media, where news is often sensationalised, repeated, sometimes even false. The terrible things that happen in the world are real, and it's valid and human to be concerned. However, the term *headline stress* is also real, and if you feel constantly anxious, overwhelmed or helpless after scrolling, this could be part of the reason.

A 'media diet' might help, and here's what that could look like:

- Write down a stressful headline on paper – this slows your processing and can help you absorb it with more perspective.
- Turn off news notifications on your phone.
- Set a 15-minute timer when checking social media.
- Avoid news/socials for the first hour of your day.
- Avoid screens at mealtimes.
- Add in regular tech-free time where possible.

If the news is making you feel powerless (as it does me sometimes), try moving from passive consumption to active engagement. For example, if climate change headlines are weighing on you, look into joining a local group, donate or volunteer. Meaningful action, however small, can counter helplessness. Doing something – *anything* – is good for the psyche.

And that brings us on to an often overlooked but remarkably effective stress intervention: *acts of kindness and service.*

Research unfailingly shows that helping others – whether through volunteering, offering support or simply being kind – reduces stress levels and improves emotional wellbeing.[25] It seems that by redirecting your attention outward, you give your brain a break from its own worries. It also affords you a sense of agency and purpose, both of which are neuro-protective in times of negative stress.

Small acts count – check in on a friend, offer to help a neighbour, write a positive review for a local business. These gestures can increase levels of oxytocin (the 'connection' hormone), lower blood pressure, and activate the brain regions associated with reward and bonding. It also reminds you that, even in difficult times, you can still make a difference. In sum: being kind doesn't just help others, it helps *you*.

Now, shift your attention to another underrated intervention for stress: *nature*. Studies show that time outdoors, whether forest bathing, gazing at wide landscapes, seeking a sense of awe[26] or simply walking in a park, can increase heart-rate variability (a marker of wellbeing), reduce pain, improve sleep and boost mood. Nature is good at reminding us we're part of something bigger, so put down your phone, get outside, look at the sky. Feel small, in a good way.

And finally, *connection*.

Human connection is *the most* powerful *outside-in* support there is.

The people around you – how much you see them, how deeply you feel seen by them – can dramatically affect your stress resilience. Think of connection as an emotional buffer: it may not remove stress, but it does give you more strength to carry it. Social support improves brain function, reduces illness and even extends life expectancy.[27]

So please, don't isolate. Share how you're feeling with someone you trust. Prioritise closeness, even if it's just a phone call. (Not a text or a DM. A *real* phone call.)

In fact, maybe put this book down right now and make that call?

THE TRIAD

The most effective, sustainable behaviour and mindset change happens when all three levels of Dr McKay's model work together, and finding what truly works for you is a *personal*, ongoing experiment. What helps in one moment might look different from what helps your best friend, or even from what worked for you that morning. The main goal of this chapter, of any stress intervention programme, is to discover what supports *you* best in each moment.

To help with this, I've included a downloadable, PDF table on the Prioritise This website outlining possible interventions across the three categories: *bottom-up, outside-in* and *top-down*. Take some time to explore it and identify the ones that feel useful or interesting to you.

Use this as a starting point to create your own personalised stress-intervention plan. One where you are prioritising the thoughts, behaviours and support structures that feel helpful, the ones that work for you.

BURNOUT

I can't very well write a chapter on stress without talking about its more aggressive, insidious cousin: burnout. Like stress, the word is overused, tossed around to describe being tired or needing a break. But, as anyone who has experienced it will tell you, burnout is much more than that.

WHAT IS BURNOUT?
Psychologist Herbert Freudenberger first coined the term 'burnout' in the 1970s to describe a state of chronic physical, emotional and mental exhaustion. Today, it's widely recognised (although not formally classed as a psychiatric disorder) as a condition most commonly linked to pressures at work, but it's also increasingly connected to the pressures of home life – particularly caregiving and emotional labour – as well as digital demands and the increased blurring of personal and professional boundaries. There isn't an approved list of symptoms for diagnosing burnout, however it is generally defined by three core elements: *exhaustion* – persistent fatigue that doesn't improve with rest; *depersonalisation* – a loss of empathy or emotional withdrawal from others; and *reduced performance* – a sense of ineffectiveness, where even simple tasks feel unmanageable.[28]

In essence, burnout is the result of unmanaged, prolonged stress. It's what happens when the stress response, which is meant to be temporary and helpful, becomes chronic. Your brain and body stay in a constant state of activation, eventually wearing down the systems that keep you thinking, feeling and functioning. And let's call a spade a spade – the relentlessness of modern life is often what drives us there.

While mild burnout can still look 'functional' from the outside, severe burnout leaves the brain struggling to access the cognitive resources it requires. You may be there, but really, you're not.

WHAT CAUSES BURNOUT?

Burnout doesn't happen overnight. It creeps in, as the saying goes, gradually then suddenly. Stress becomes burnout when the demands placed on you consistently exceed your internal and external resources (aka, your bridge).

The most common causes include:

- **Chronic work stress:** heavy workloads, too many deadlines, unclear expectations, lack of autonomy or recognition
- **Home overload:** juggling caregiving, managing childcare, household demands, emotional labour
- **Personality style:** perfectionism, Type A tendencies,* high neuroticism, low self-efficacy
- **Lifestyle habits:** always being 'on', poor boundaries, lack of downtime, constant digital engagement
- **Cultural messaging:** productivity equals worth, success is linked to self-sacrifice, busyness is a badge of honour.

Women are particularly vulnerable to burnout, as they are more likely to manage a 'second shift' of unpaid domestic work, even alongside full-time jobs. However, anyone who feels overworked and undervalued, or has pressures on them that they can't handle, is at risk.

HOW IS BURNOUT DIFFERENT FROM STRESS?

While burnout is caused by stress, it's not the same thing. Stress feels like *too much* – too many tasks, too many decisions, not enough time. But with stress, there's often hope that, if you can just get it under control, things will improve. Burnout, on the other hand, feels like *not enough* – not enough energy, motivation or care left to give. You're basically empty.

And while stress is often associated with high cortisol levels, burnout is more commonly linked to a depletion of those same stress

---

*Type A personalities are ambitious and competitive; they can often be workaholics.

hormones, leaving you mentally and physically flat. If stress feels like drowning in responsibilities and commitments, burnout feels like sinking to the bottom.

THE (SURPRISING) SIGNS OF BURNOUT
Though we tend to know when we're stressed, burnout can sneak in, unnoticed until it's taken hold. And, while the classic signs – exhaustion, low motivation, dread – are well known, burnout can show up in more subtle ways. Here are ten less-expected symptoms to watch for:

1. **Constant irritability**: little things feel disproportionately annoying and your tolerance for everyday life is thin.
2. **Overwhelm at minor tasks**: even small requests feel like too much – decision fatigue is the norm.
3. **Slipping self-care**: routines you once relied on (exercise, sleep or even brushing your hair) quietly fall by the wayside.
4. **Procrastination**: you're not getting anything done and you can't pinpoint why. (FYI: it may be because your brain is overloaded and protecting itself by avoiding any more input.)
5. **Memory blips**: you find yourself forgetting words, appointments or conversations more than usual.
6. **Escapist daydreaming**: you can't stop imagining quitting, escaping or hitting reset on your entire life.
7. **A cynical or pessimistic outlook**: you've lost the ability to see the positive, even in things you used to enjoy.
8. **Physical symptoms**: headaches, gut issues, frequent colds – our bodies are good at telling us something isn't right with our minds.
9. **Emotional numbness**: you feel increasingly removed from your emotions; you may even feel . . . *nothing*.
10. **Disconnection**: even surrounded by people, you feel alone or unseen, and this leads you to withdraw, including from those closest to you.

We all have bad days (or weeks). However, if this is your normal, I'd suggest paying attention. Burnout is reversible, but this is easiest to do when it's caught early and treated seriously.

THE THREE RS APPROACH

This is the coaching framework I use for *mild* burnout. If, however, you suspect you may be experiencing *severe* burnout, I do recommend seeking professional support. Either way, and above all, please know that you are *not* broken; you simply have limits. And just as we care for a pulled muscle or painful back, we need to care for mental burnout.

Step 1: Recognise. Ask: what is it about my job, home life or circumstances that's driving this feeling? At the same time, think about how your burnout warning signs show up – physically, emotionally, mentally. Awareness is, as always, the crucial first step.

Step 2: Reverse. Where possible, change the source of stress: ask for help, reduce your load, set clearer boundaries and so on. If none of that is immediately possible, support your recovery: sleep, screen breaks, nature, quiet, human connection – all the interventions mentioned above.

Here are two things you can try:

1. **Start and finish your workday.** Set boundaries; don't check emails the moment you wake up or long into the evening. Create structure and stick to it.
2. **Shift your mentality from input to output.** If you're able to control your working day then stop counting the hours you work and focus on the results you produce instead. This approach is both more efficient and less draining.

Step 3: Resilience. What you want to think of here is building *mental immunity*, of building your 'bridge' so that you're more robust the next time life piles up.

Ways to do this could include any of the *bottom-up, outside-in, top-down* strategies we've looked at in this chapter as well as many of the learnings from other chapters such as Chapter 6: Failure. (We also go into resilience itself in detail in Chapter 9: Moving Forward.)

Yes, these are individual strategies – and I know that system-level, organisational changes are urgently required. But if you're waiting for those to happen before you help yourself, you may end up waiting a while. So make sure you start somewhere. *Anywhere.*

Burnout doesn't mean you've failed or that you can't keep up. It just means you've been carrying too much for too long without enough support. I've seen many people thrive after recovering from burnout, so, if you're in it right now, please know that this doesn't spell the end.

DO NOT LEAVE IT AT THAT

Reaching the end of this chapter doesn't mean the end of your stress. (I'm sorry, I wish it did too!)

Stress is complex – there is no tidy arc with a beginning, middle and end. How you experience it is shaped by so many factors, from what's going on in your life, to your history, biology, wiring, how well you slept last night, and even how much water you've drunk that day. *Everything* plays a part. Two people in the same situation (think Bob I and Bob II) can experience it entirely differently, and that difference doesn't mean anything except that we all have limits, that we are all human.

I know that on bad days – those all-consuming, black-hole kind of days – it's hard to imagine ever feeling differently. When you're in it, stress can feel like your *entire* reality. It's easy to think *this is just how I am*, or *this is how life is* . . . and leave it at that.

Please do not leave it at that.

You can change the way you respond to stress. Your stress response is shaped not just by instinct, but by perception, context and learning, and you can train your brain to reinterpret and regulate these responses, to improve your emotional regulation and resilience. You have the ability to shift how you think, behave and support yourself in difficult moments.

With patience and consistency, you can learn to prioritise more helpful thoughts and habits over unhelpful ones. And the more you challenge those automatic responses, the more your brain will begin to do it for you, until helpful thoughts become more habitual and accessible. Until *they* become the ones you prioritise.

Your experience of stress will ebb and flow. Sometimes it'll feel motivating; at others, debilitating. Sometimes the strategies in this chapter will feel powerful; at others, impossible. That's the nature of living. The aim isn't to eliminate stress entirely – remember, *stress is not a bad thing* – it's to build up your internal strength, so you can meet your life with more capacity and care.

There are a couple of well-known quotes often shared in stress coaching:

'It's not the stress that breaks you down, it's the way you carry it.' (Lou Holtz)

'The greatest weapon against stress is our ability to choose one thought over another.' (William James)

And while I believe both hold truth – in that stress shapes how we see the world but how we see the world can also shape stress – I also think they can feel reductive, especially when you're facing real, painful challenges. They can make it sound as though managing stress is just about thinking differently, and that if you're struggling, it's somehow your fault.

It's not.

Some stressors – caring responsibilities, financial pressure, illness, trauma, complex family dynamics – are not things you can simply put down. Your thoughts are not responsible for what happens to you, and you can't 'mindset' your way out of those.

That's really why I'm writing this book – to create a space that recognises the full reality of life, one that counters the painfully simplistic, overly positive messages I've read elsewhere. I want to embrace the full picture, the social, emotional, physical and cognitive layers of stress. To acknowledge that, yes, your thoughts play a part, but so does your body, environment and circumstances. I want to encourage a narrative where cognitive strategies are offered but alternative forms of support, such as social connection, time in nature and acts of service are deemed equally important.

Because sometimes, the difference between a stressful situation and a situation in which you feel stressed *is* your ability to prioritise one thought over another. But also, sometimes changing your mind with your mind is the hardest thing of all. When you can't prioritise that better thought (and believe me, sometimes I can't either, *and I do this for a living*), then choose the next best one. The thought that lets you be kind to yourself for not choosing the other one, that allows you compassion for struggling in the first place.

And if that fails, look elsewhere: nature, connection, breathwork, friends, music, movement, meaning. There's no one right tool. The aim is to find what your brain will accept, adopt and use to support you.*
Prioritise whatever works, whatever makes you feel more like you.

---

*And if you haven't found anything that works in this chapter, then look at the others, too, particularly Chapter 4: Overwhelm and Chapter 5: Procrastination.

The suggestions put forward in this chapter are not ways to 'fix' your life, but ways to reinforce yourself from within. Think of them as internal scaffolding for your bridge; they will better equip you to hold everything else up. So, ask yourself: *what do I need right now? What would help me feel supported? What can I actually do today (as in right now) to meet myself with care? What might make me feel even 1 percent better?*

Ask yourself again and again . . . and again.

Because, sometimes, the answers really are life changing.

PRIORITISE THIS

- Stress is complex and multifaceted.
- Stress can be treated as an ally, not an enemy.
- Don't fight your difficult emotions; learn to be with them and support yourself through them (but don't wallow in them).
- Stop trying to control the uncontrollable.
- Approach any stress intervention holistically using your body, mind and environment.
- Familiarise yourself with the signs of burnout in order to be able to intervene in time.
- Take the time to discover which interventions work for *you* and then prioritise them in your life.

PRACTICES TO HELP WITH STRESS

THE PHYSIOLOGICAL SIGH

Breathwork has been shown to help prevent and manage stress, so if you haven't tried it, I suggest giving it a go. One of the simplest techniques is the 'physiological sigh' – first identified in the 1930s as something we naturally slip into during deep sleep or in claustrophobic environments. It's essentially a built-in reset for the body. The science goes that when we're stressed, our breathing becomes shallow and carbon dioxide (CO_2) builds up in the bloodstream, which can leave us feeling agitated. A physiological sigh fully expands the alveoli (the tiny air sacs in the lungs) and clears out that excess CO_2, creating a rapid calming effect. More recently, neuroscientist and podcaster (and sometimes divisive character) Dr Andrew Huberman has popularised the practice, highlighting research that shows its impact on stress reduction, mood and even sleep.[29] It only takes seconds and can be done anywhere – at your desk, on the bus, even from bed.

How it works:

1. First relax your shoulders and unclench your jaw.
2. Inhale deeply through your nose until your lungs are nearly full.
3. Inhale again – a short, sharp top-up breath – to completely fill (even overfill) your lungs.
4. Exhale slowly through your mouth.
5. Repeat two or three times.

THE ABCDE MODEL

The ABCDE model is a stress management technique developed by Albert Ellis,* which provides a framework to help show how thoughts and beliefs may impact our responses to situations (stressful or otherwise). It can enable you to identify negative, unhelpful SITs and learn how to replace them with more helpful SATs, improving emotional regulation and your capacity to navigate

---

*a pioneer of Rational Emotive Behaviour Therapy – I'm trained in Rational Emotive Behaviour Coaching.

challenging situations with greater ease. As you can see below, the model has five stages to go through, unsurprisingly, in order from A to E . . . I've included a fictional example to help explain the process; read through that then try it with a real-life example of your own. Experiment with different situations and examples as this will provide an idea of your general thought/behaviour pattern, and so where you need to focus on change. And, FYI, this model can be used with many topics from the book – for example if you have a habit you want to change, a break-up you're trying to get over or an unhelpful pattern of comparison on social media. It's applicable in so many circumstances, as you'll soon discover for yourself.

> **A – Activating event.** What is the situation or event that's causing you to feel stressed?
>
> **B – Beliefs.** What are your thoughts and beliefs around the situation?
>
> **C – Consequences.** What are your emotional and behavioural responses to the situation?
>
> **D – Disputation.** How can you challenge your thoughts and beliefs around the situation? Use your top-down strategies here.
>
> **E – Effective new belief/strategy.** What would be a different, more helpful way of thinking about and approaching the situation?

Go to the Prioritise This website to find an extra Mindfulness meditation practice.

STRESS

A Activating event	B Beliefs and thoughts (SITs)	C Consequences (emotional + behavioural responses)	D Disputation of column B	E Effective new belief/strategy to move forward
Anticipation of failing my driving test. Goal: Remain calm during the test.	I will definitely fail. If I fail, it's the end of the world. Failure is terrible. The instructor will think I look too nervous and anxious. They won't like me.	Angry at self. Depressed, anxious, worried, overwhelmed and nervous. Palms sweating, heart racing. Not able to fully concentrate during driving lessons and studying sessions.	It's also possible I won't fail, I don't know that I will! Not true it's the end of the world – it might be embarrassing but I can always re-take. Many people fail their first time. it's okay to fail sometimes. The instructor probably won't notice, and if they do they are very used to people feeling nervous and anxious – this won't affect what they think of me.	Meditate for five minutes before driving lessons and study sessions. Study a tiny bit every day to help with feelings of overwhelm. Leave house early the day of the test so don't need to rush at all. Practice 'Coping visualisation' (see Chapter 6: Failure). Remind myself many people take the test and don't pass first time. If possible, explain to instructor how nervous I feel.

A blank copy of this table is available on the Prioritise This website.

CHAPTER 2

Habits

● ● ●

'The chains of habit are too weak to be felt until they are too strong to be broken.'

Samuel Johnson

My morning routine reads like a self-righteous social media post.

Every weekday I get up at around 6 a.m. after at least seven to eight hours of sleep (aided by various supplements and sometimes mouth tape). I hydrate with an electrolyte-infused glass of water and caffeine-free tea, followed by meditation (while wearing a red-light face mask) then yoga, Pilates or strength training. Breakfast (full-fat Greek yoghurt, nuts, seeds, fruit) is non-negotiable, and my accompanying oat latte is decaf (with collagen, because I am easily influenced). A few times a week I take a sauna and/or a cold swim.

I know, nauseating.

However, 20 years ago, at university, my mornings looked quite different. I'd wake around 9 or 10 a.m. after four to five hours of sleep, often due to either hunger-induced insomnia or partying. I'd start the day with strong coffee and a rollie, skipping breakfast and dragging myself to my first lecture with an empty stomach and a pounding headache. While partying is hardly rare among students, my partying – as well as my lack of self-care – was excessive, routine and self-destructive.

Same person, two radically different sets of habits.

As I explored in the Introduction, what we do repeatedly – *what we prioritise* – shapes the sum of our existence. Life is formed by habits, rituals and routines. My life was once formed (and informed) by habits that weren't just unhelpful but unsafe. I relied on them for valid reasons, including most notably that they helped me manage the emotions I tried hard not to feel. But I also couldn't be happy in my life without changing them – my habits, so deeply embedded, *had* to stop for me to have any hope.

Habit change and formation can get a bit chicken and egg. Is it the thoughts, cognitive processes and emotional regulation techniques that help us to alter our actions? Or does altering our actions rewire how we think? Both can be true (such a dull answer), and, as with every chapter in this book, the key to change lies with what works for *you* in any given situation.

While I'd been actively trying to recover from my mental health struggles since I was 18, my recovery only truly happened ten years later, after (as I wrote in Chapter 1: Stress) that thought-seed of change was planted in my mind at the ashram in India. However, at the same time, I instinctively knew that nothing could *really* change internally until I changed my habits externally. Two weeks later, on New Year's Eve 2012, I stood in one of the most beautiful places I've ever been, a stretch of the Karnataka coastline only accessible by foot, stared out at the picture-perfect sunset with leaping dolphins (really!) and made an internal promise to never intentionally harm myself again.

And I never have.

Habits shape both our own little world and how we perceive the world at large; they *define* our lives. As such, a good understanding of them is crucial to putting into practice much of the advice and guidance in this book. If you want to change your SITs into SATs (Chapter 1: Stress), comprehending how a *thought habit* can be created in your brain will help you do that. If you want to minimise your overwhelm (Chapter 4: Overwhelm), then changing your digital habits is an impactful first step.

And, if we zoom out to *The Priorities Method*® itself, any enquiry around habits really becomes the question: *what am I prioritising in my life?*

If you don't like the answer, this chapter is for you.

At the core of any behaviour change is the desire to start, stop or do something differently. Over the next few pages, we'll look at evidence-based strategies that'll help you do just that. You'll discover the neurobiology at play with habits, explore some of the common barriers to change (including why human nature can interfere with the best of intentions), and create a blueprint for sticking with your habits, even when life turns upside down. The subject of habits lies at the core of my work, and I've repeatedly seen how changing or creating them can be game-changing for not only achieving long-term goals but, more importantly, living a life in line with what's important to you.

So, let's explore how we can do all that.

WHAT IS A HABIT?

Broadly speaking, a habit is a settled tendency or practice – 'something that you do often and regularly, sometimes without knowing that you are doing it'.[1] It can also be characterised (less charitably) as something that is *hard to give up*. Habits can be helpful or harmful, physical or mental, conscious or unconscious. They can be the morning walk you never miss, or the mindless scroll every night before bed. They can be brushing your teeth, or telling yourself you're not good enough. In essence, a habit is anything you do repeatedly, including how you *think*.

There's an important distinction to be made, however, between *conscious* habits and *unconscious* ones. Your brain operates with two internal systems – your *reflective* system and your *impulsive* system. Conscious habits (like cooking a healthy breakfast or going for a walk after work) live in the reflective system. They require effort, attention and decision-making. Unconscious habits (like biting your nails when you're anxious or how you react to a perceived rejection) operate from the impulsive system. They happen automatically, often without you even realising.[2]

And according to researchers at Duke University, more than 40 percent of your daily life is run by unconscious habits.[3] From how you drive a car to how you speak to a colleague, many of your responses are part of what author Gina Cleo calls the 'invisible blueprint' of everyday life.[4] And while this blueprint can be frustrating at times, it also protects your brain from overload. We make an estimated, staggering, 35,000 decisions every day[5] – if you had to consciously consider even a fraction of those, you'd find yourself face down on the floor before breakfast.

Your brain does this to conserve energy, delegating the mundane so it can focus on the complex. For example, think of cleaning your teeth – the act itself is a conscious habit, but the *way* you brush is unconscious.* Ultimately, your brain can't redecide *every* detail in life, so it sets a pattern and follows it. Yet as psychologist Wendy Wood notes, 'Much of what we do is repeated not because it's rewarding, but because it's easy and we've done it before.'[6] This is why even habits you *don't* like can feel so hard to change – they are deeply embedded in your context and routines.

And while you may have heard or read that it takes just 21 days to form a new habit, this is sadly a myth. As always, the truth is more complex and less convenient. A 2009 study found that, on average, it takes roughly 66 days to establish a habit.[7] But those findings also depended on the person, context and behaviour. In reality, it can take from as little as 18 days to as long as 254 days to establish a habit. And, for some people (sorry!), certain habits never become fully automatic. Don't view it as a personal failure; it's just a reflection of how your brain responds to a particular pattern. And it's also why consistency and commitment are so vital.

(One quick, important point: habit and severe addiction are not the same. While severe addiction shares some neural pathways with habit, it also involves dependency, compulsion and often withdrawal. Habits can be overridden, whereas severe addiction typically needs a different level of intervention. I don't go into addiction in this chapter: if you or someone you know requires support, please do refer to the Resources at the back of the book.)

YOUR BRAIN ON HABITS

Let's take a look at what happens in your brain when a habit forms.

Your habits are stored in a part of the brain called the basal ganglia. Once a behavioural pattern becomes familiar, the brain creates a kind of 'chunk' that can be triggered automatically by a cue that it encounters. At the core of this is a principle from neuroscience called Hebbian learning, summed up in the catchy phrase: 'Neurons that fire

---

*Mine is: top right side first, never enough time on the back left molar (much to the annoyance of my dentist). Test it for yourself next time you clean your teeth – what's your unconscious way of brushing?

together wire together.' Every time you repeat an action or thought, you strengthen the neural pathway associated with it. As we covered in Chapter 1: Stress, over time it then becomes the *default* – the well-worn groove that your brain automatically takes. Each time you repeatedly think or do something, you literally reshape your brain to make that thought or action easier for the next time.

This is the transition from *declarative* memory (effortful, conscious learning) to *procedural* memory (automatic, unconscious behaviour). It's why a professional pianist plays without looking at the keys while I stare intently at my fingers when learning a new piece. With practice and repetition, actions become embedded.

Then there's dopamine – the reward chemical, which as I'm sure you know, makes you feel pretty good. A neurotransmitter, it plays an essential role in regulating pleasure, motivation and (yes) reward systems in the brain. Dopamine gets released either before or while you do something your brain perceives as gratifying – eating, exercising, connecting with someone, ticking a task off your to-do list. It's your brain's way of saying: *do that again*!

This reward system can be incredibly helpful, especially when it reinforces habits that positively impact your wellbeing (both in the moment and long term), but it can also be hijacked.

Dopamine is just as happy (often happier in fact) to reinforce habits that feel good in the moment but don't serve you in the long term – like bingeing Netflix, doom-scrolling, or reaching for sugar, caffeine or alcohol as a panacea to life. These fast-acting 'sources' provide a brilliant pick-me-up in the moment, but they can also lead to a change in the dopaminergic pathways in your brain (such as excessive dopamine release), which can negatively impact your focus, mood and wellbeing overall. They also train you to favour *instant gratification* over more meaningful, slower forms of fulfilment – for example, a spontaneous online shop gives a faster dopamine hit than taking a long walk with a friend. The former feels more gratifying to your brain, even if the latter leaves you feeling more satisfied (with none of the regret of a late-night, drunken online shopping haul).

And this is why new habits, particularly those that take longer to 'pay off', can feel difficult at first – your brain hasn't yet linked them with reward, so any desire to do them is weak. But the more you repeat the behaviour (or thought), the more your brain begins to connect it to dopamine, and the easier it becomes to do it.

And if you've ever wondered why it seems that all your good habits fall apart when you're under pressure or overwhelmed, know that you're not imagining it. A 2009 study proved what we all know experientially – under stress, we default to habits rather than conscious decision-making.[8] Behaviour doesn't exist in a vacuum, and challenging times make us more likely to fall back on any familiar action or thought pattern, including unconstructive ones. The stress hormones cortisol, adrenaline and noradrenaline shift your brain from goal-focused behaviours to automated habitual behaviours, which is why at the end of a difficult day you reach for your phone instead of a book. Your brain is trying to help, just not in a hugely helpful way.

Ultimately, your brain is doing what it's designed to do – conserve energy and reduce effort in order to keep you alive. But if you want to live in alignment with your priorities and values, *rather than your wiring*, and have habits that reflect that, it's important to find a way to make your brain work for you.

WHY IS CHANGE HARD?

Okay, we're almost on to the good stuff!

But before we look at how to change or create a habit, let's understand why it is that change often doesn't happen, even when we *really* want it to.

First, y*our brain craves familiarity*. It prefers to stick with what it knows as that requires less energy and is less dangerous. Big changes threaten your brain, so it often steers you away from them.

Second, *information does not change behaviour*. If it did, there'd be no need for this chapter (or this book, or my job); I could simply tell you why a habit is good for you and then . . . off you'd go! The NHS would be saved, we'd all be hydrated, no one would smoke, I'd never forget to floss . . .

Clearly, that's not how it works.

Health knowledge alone doesn't reliably lead to behavioural change.[9] We all *know* we're supposed to drink water, stretch, sleep more, move, be self-compassionate and all the rest . . . It's just that knowing isn't enough.

Third, *motivation is wildly unreliable*. Motivation refers to the drives (i.e. wants and needs) that propel us in a direction or towards a goal. We will go into this topic in more detail later in the chapter (as well as in Chapters 5: Procrastination and 9: Moving Forward) but for now let's note that, while it's great, it can't be trusted. Motivation comes in spikes and dips, and is hugely affected by stress, sleep, hormones, blood sugar and more. Basically, I wouldn't count on it.

Fourth, *we all have psychological barriers to change*. Thoughts, feelings, ideas, fears, beliefs, images . . . everything that goes on in our heads on a daily basis can create a mental environment that is unreceptive to the new.

WHAT MAKES CHANGE EASIER?

The astronaut Chris Hadfield once explained that when you're in space and something goes wrong, 'You don't rise to the challenge, you fall back on your systems.'[10] The same is true of behaviour and mindset change. You don't rely on your ability to think on your feet; you create systems and processes and then lean heavily on them to help you achieve whatever it is you're hoping to achieve.

And luckily there's a whole host of systems to choose from, from health psychology models to self-monitoring exercises.[*] Here are two behaviour change systems that I find effective, especially when used together:

1. COM-B[11]

This model looks at how, in order to perform or change any behaviour, three things are required:

1. **Capability** – your physical and psychological abilities in relation to a behaviour – that is, *Can I do this?*
2. **Opportunity** – the aspects of your environment (social and physical) that make a behaviour easier – that is, *Is my outer world making it possible?*
3. **Motivation** – what makes you want to perform a behaviour – that is, *Do I want to do this above all else?*

---

*A good example of the latter is the ABCDE model in Chapter 1: Stress.

In essence, if you don't have the abilities/skill (capability), the conditions (opportunity) or the drive (motivation), you won't do the thing. You need to have some degree of all of them in order to enact change.

2. THE TRANSTHEORETICAL MODEL (CYCLE OF CHANGE)[12]

This is one of the most commonly applied theoretical and clinical frameworks in the UK, used across a broad spectrum of behaviour and mindset change, including smoking, daily application of sun cream, addressing school bullies and weight control. It breaks habit change into six stages:

1. **Precontemplation** – you are not yet considering a change.
2. **Contemplation** – you are thinking about changing (let's say in the next six months).
3. **Preparation** – you are planning for change (let's say in the next month).
4. **Action** – you are actively making the change.
5. **Maintenance** – you are working to sustain or maintain the change.
6. **Relapse** – you've fallen back into the behaviour, but hopefully will loop back to action very soon.

Finally, as we covered in Chapter 1: Stress, never underestimate the power of your *social support systems* for habits. It may not be a recognised behaviour change model, but the people we surround ourselves with, the lessons we learn from them, the norms we absorb, the access they have, the emotional scaffolding they provide and how much they encourage or support us can mark the difference between successful and unsuccessful change.

Now you're ready to change or create a habit, and you've got your systems to help you do so. Where do you start?

CHOOSING A HABIT

Not all habits are created equal. Some are harder to adopt or shift, while others are catalysts that can create ripples of change. Choosing the *right* habit at the *right* time can vastly increase your chances of success.

K came to me in 2022 with the simple goal of 'I want to feel healthier.' It's a worthy aim but also a vague one – 'healthier' will mean different things to different people, and there are dozens of ways to get ourselves there. To help K narrow his focus, we used a simple coaching model called Impact–Likelihood–Spillover (ILS) to clarify the best starting point for him.

First, I asked K to jot down a few habit changes that might move him closer to feeling healthier. Together, we landed on three options:

1. Quit drinking wine during the week.
2. Go for a brisk walk most days.
3. Eat smaller portions at dinner.

Then, I asked him to score each habit from 1 to 10 in response to the following questions:

1. **Impact:** if I change this habit, how big of a positive impact will it have on my life?
2. **Likelihood:** how likely am I to follow through with this habit right now?
3. **Spillover:** if I change this habit, will it naturally improve other behaviours too?

To his and my surprise, *walking* came out on top. It felt realistic and motivating – and he also noted it would likely help him sleep better, reduce stress and boost his mood. Still, he admitted: 'I wouldn't have picked it on my own. It doesn't feel very *serious*.'

Let me be clear: *the best habit is the one you will prioritise.*

Not the one that seems most impressive, or looks best on paper, or your best friend swears by. It's the one that's achievable *and* meaningful for you, *right now at this moment in time*. The one that will create momentum, the one you can build on.*

I love the ILS model because it encourages you to meet yourself where you are, rather than where your inner perfectionist *thinks* you should be. It brings a bit of clarity to the unavoidable uncertainty of change.

This model also works great when you *have a very specific outcome in mind* but are unsure which habits will best get you there. For example, with quitting smoking, possible interventions could include chewing nicotine gum, journaling every time a craving hits, calling a friend or using a craving timer app.

---

*Charles Duhigg calls this a 'keystone habit'.

Try it yourself:

1. Think of a habit you'd like to start or stop, or a goal you want to reach.
2. Brainstorm three to five small habits or actions that could help you do this.
3. Score each one from 1–10 using:
   - **Impact:** how much of a difference would this make?
   - **Likelihood:** how likely am I to stick with this right now?
   - **Spillover:** will it positively influence other behaviours or areas of my life?

The one with the strongest combined score is your best place to start.

HOW TO CREATE A NEW HABIT

There are many brilliant pop-psych books that focus solely on this subject and are worth a read if you want to go into depth,* but for now here are the most essential, science-backed ideas that actually work.

First, at its core, every habit should serve a *goal*. What is it you want to create or change in your life? What's your bigger aim? What's your *why*?

Every habit (good or bad) runs on a *loop*, and once you're clear on a direction, you can use the *habit loop* below to build your desired habit:

CUE → CRAVING → RESPONSE → REWARD

- The **cue** is what triggers the behaviour (a time, place, emotion or action).†
- The **craving** is the desire it sparks (I want to relax / feel good / check out).
- The **response** is the habit itself (scrolling, stretching, smoking, snacking).
- The **reward** is the pay-out (dopamine hit, distraction, relief, familiarity).

---

*I like B. J. Fogg's *Tiny Habits* and James Clear's *Atomic Habits* – both are in the Resources section at the end of the book.
†A cue helps create less need for cognitive energy, memory, willpower, motivation and so on – when you have a defined cue, encountering that trigger will lead your brain to fire off neural pathways to do that action without you even needing to think about it.

To make a new habit stick, you want to make each part of this loop work for you. James Clear's *Atomic Habits*[*] simplifies this into four key rules:

1. Make the cue obvious.
2. Make the craving attractive.
3. Make the response easy.
4. Make the reward satisfying.

Let's go back to my client, K and his habit of a daily brisk walk – this is how he applied these four steps:

1. **Cue:** he left his trainers and socks ready by the door (obvious).
2. **Craving:** he chose a gripping podcast he only listened to on walks (attractive).
3. **Response:** he committed to just 20 minutes (easy).
4. **Reward:** he scheduled a warm shower or bath straight after (satisfying).

As a result, the habit *stuck*.
Try it for yourself . . .

1. Pick an action that supports your goal – this is your *response*.
2. Pair that action with a simple, easy cue – remember, this can be internal or external. For example: *when I make my morning tea (cue), I will take my supplements (action)*.
3. Make the cue more *attractive* by, for example, buying or making a nice pill box.
4. To reinforce it, think of a *reward* – a walk, a treat, a gold star sticker – whatever works for you.

HOW TO CHANGE OR BREAK AN EXISTING HABIT

Habits are ingrained pathways (and often less about what we want than what we repeat), so know that changing or breaking a habit isn't

---

[*]While this is Clear's formulation, it's heavily influenced by Charles Duhigg, behavioural psychology (Skinner, Pavlov) and B. J. Fogg.

really about willpower, but rather about *reworking* the systems that are in place. Here's the two-step plan I'd recommend you begin with to shift a habit that no longer serves you:

1. START WITH AWARENESS

Clearly, before you can change a habit, you have to notice it. But this means more than just knowing what it is you want to change, you also have to pay close attention to:

- your cues (what triggers it)
- your emotional state (how you're feeling before it happens, i.e. is an emotion actually the trigger?)
- your environment (where you are, who you're with, what's happening around you)
- the reward (what you're getting from it, even if short-lived).

Make a note of these things. Often, we quickly beat ourselves up for repeating a behaviour or habit, but rarely do we pause to examine *why* or *when* we do it. Once you know more about what the loop looks like for you, the more easily you'll be able to disrupt it.

2. REPLACE OR RESTRUCTURE

Since habits are ingrained pathways in the brain, there are two main approaches we can take to breaking them:

1. You can *replace* a habit with a new, desired behaviour.
2. You can *restructure* your environment, so the cue disappears. (This disrupts the pathway by taking away the trigger.)

For example, if your habit is scrolling in bed at night:

- Replacing might look like keeping a book next to your bed to read instead.
- Restructuring might look like charging your phone outside the bedroom.

With the former, you are taking the ingrained pathway and rerouting it, using it to layer on a 'better' habit. This is perfect for when the advice of eliminating the cue is impossible (an approach sometimes known as Charles Duhigg's 'Golden Rule of Habit Change'[13]). In essence, you replace the routine, but keep the cue and reward the same. For example, many of my clients want to change their digital habits – such as not scrolling through emails and socials *the moment* they wake up, before even drinking a glass of water or brushing their teeth. For them, *waking up* is the cue. We clearly can't change that, so we replace the habit – pop a glass of water by the bed and drink that first thing instead.

However, with the latter option of restructuring so that you remove or change the cue entirely, you effectively weaken the whole habit loop.* This is the principle behind the less catchy but equally effective anti-Hebbian model – *If neurons no longer fire together, they stop wiring together.* Focus on eliminating or changing the trigger and your neural pathways simply aren't engaged in the same way.

With either approach, it's worth knowing that the first few days or weeks of breaking a habit feel hard because your brain is still firing along old neural pathways. The less you engage with a habit, the weaker those become. Bear in mind that the reward of an unwanted habit is often short yet the regret of giving into it can be very long. With each skipped loop, it takes less energy to resist or change the habit. Over time, unused pathways get pruned. In real terms: the less you do the habit, the less your brain defaults to it. And then, the reward starts to come from *not* doing it instead.

WHAT WILL HELP ME DO ALL THIS?

Now comes the boring but essential part: *consistency*. Habit change doesn't require intensity, it requires repetition, so here are a number of strategies that when prioritised will help you actually stick with it . . .

KEEP IT MICRO
The smaller and easier the habit, the more likely it is to stick. Don't lower your standards, but focus on building confidence over perfection – one push-up is better than no push-ups; one non-alcoholic beer is enough to interrupt a loop. Something small that you can stick with is preferable to some grand gesture you only do once – remember, your brain resists big shifts, so micro-habits feel safer and more doable. And, with consistency, they *grow*.

---

*This is also referred to as 'Shrink the cue, starve the loop'.

USE IMPLEMENTATION INTENTIONS

This is a fancy name for a simple but powerful idea:* 'When/If X happens, I will do Y.'

For example:

- When I brush my teeth, I will stand on one leg for a minute each side.
- When I turn on the kettle, I will do five squats.
- If it's 7 a.m. on a weekday, I will do five minutes of meditation.

This works because it links your new habit to an existing action or cue, which means you don't need to remember to do it or rely on motivation – the trigger's already part of your day, making it easier to prioritise. Think of it like *mental programming*.

HABIT STACKING

Closely related to this idea is habit stacking – where you take a habit you already do reliably and 'stack' a new one on top. The formula looks like: 'After [insert current habit], I will [insert new habit].' For example:

- After I make my morning coffee, I will write one sentence in my journal.
- After I take off my shoes, I will do 30 seconds of stretching.

The brilliance of habit stacking is that it builds on existing routines. You're not reinventing your day, but instead anchoring a new action onto something you *already* do. In an ideal world, in time the stacked habit becomes second nature too.

TEMPTATION BUNDLING

Again, related to the idea of habit stacking (we're stacking ideas themselves!) you can take it one step further by pairing your habit with an activity that feels appealing. This links what you *want* to do with what you *should* or *need* to do, making the habit more attractive to your brain. For example:

---

*Implementation intentions have actually been shown to improve success of desired behaviour by up to a staggering 50 percent (https://pmc.ncbi.nlm.nih.gov/articles/PMC5730820)

- I'll only listen to my favourite podcast when I'm folding laundry/cleaning the house.
- I'll get a pedicure while I trawl through this email inbox from hell.

COMMITMENT DEVICES

These are techniques and systems that help by making it unappealing (possibly even costly) to not stick to your habit. For example:

- pre-paying for a gym membership
- scheduling a work-from-home day for a big project with a friend that you wouldn't want to let down.

TIE IT TO YOUR IDENTITY

One of the most powerful ways I've personally found to make a habit stick is by attaching it to the person I want to be. For example, I hate flossing but know it's important for health. So, instead of saying to myself 'I want to floss more', I'll say 'I am the kind of person who cares about their dental health'. And who can argue with that? This subtle mindset shift aligns action with *identity*, so that every time you repeat a habit you reinforce that identity. And I think that when you shift your language from *what you do* to *who you are*, your brain listens differently. Ask yourself: *who do I want to be?* Then create habits that match:

- Don't 'run' – *be a runner.*
- Don't 'try to write a book' – *be a writer.*
- Don't 'exercise more' – *be someone who moves their body with care.*

This is called *noun–verb manipulation*. It ties your habit to your sense of self – and self-image – and is an excellent driver for change. Ultimately, think lifestyle change, rather than habit change.

USE THE 'HABIT DISCONTINUITY EFFECT'

Behaviour change experts have shown that habit change is more effective during big life transitions, like moving house, changing jobs or becoming a parent.[14] Known as the 'habit discontinuity effect' or 'fresh start effect',* these moments disrupt your usual patterns and create a

---

*The 'fresh start effect' was discovered and coined by behavioural change expert Katy Milkman. Her excellent book *How to Change* is included in the Resources section at the end of this book.

window for rewiring. You can take advantage of this by intentionally pairing a new habit with a new context. For example:

- Starting a new job? Use that first week to establish a morning walk.
- Moving home? Rework your digital habits alongside your new space.
- Feeling uplifted by the back-to-school energy of September? Channel it to start working on a big goal.

In essence, new context equal new cues which equal new habits. And while these are all examples of big moments, you can also create smaller transition moments for yourself (think: a haircut or a brand-new journal/notebook*).

REMOVE PINCH POINTS
When you're trying to build a new habit, you want to be eliminating as much friction (aka pinch points) as possible. If your goal is to drink more water, don't wait until you're frantically rushing to a meeting to realise you're thirsty – fill up a large bottle and place it on your desk. If you want to go to the gym, lay out your workout clothes the night before. If you want to eat better, chop up veg ahead of time, or keep go-to healthy snacks in your bag. The more straightforward it is, the more likely you are to do it. In other words: make life easy for Future You.†

TRACK IT, STAY ACCOUNTABLE
This is not about perfection (it never is), but rather *visibility*. By tracking your progress – tick a box, cross off a day on your calendar, send a 'Done it!' text to a friend, use a habit tracker (you'll find one on the *Prioritise This* website) – you send tiny signals that create a dopamine hit in your brain and reinforce the loop. A streak builds momentum and keeps you accountable. (And leans into the idea of *gamifying* your habits, to make them more appealing to your brain.) Research has shown that we are 65 percent more likely to meet a goal if we

---
*Never underestimate the motivating allure of new stationery.
†I cover this idea of Future You (versus Present You) in detail in Chapter 9: Moving Forward.

commit to someone, and this increases to 95 percent if we have a specific accountability appointment with that person.*[15] So, yes, track your habits, with someone else if you can but for yourself if not.

CELEBRATE SMALL WINS, *UNPREDICTABLY*

Your brain loves rewards, so lean heavily on that reward segment of the habit loop and celebrate your small victories. But, and this is weirdly crucial, don't give yourself *predictable* rewards – you'll find out exactly why (and how to do this) in the motivation section later in this chapter. For now, think about how you can reward and celebrate your wins, and know that predictability is not your friend.

FOCUS ON THE PROCESS, NOT THE OUTCOME

I know it's never easy, *for anyone*, but please don't obsess over results. Instead, immerse yourself in the systems that get you there. Rather than 'I want to run a 10k', try 'I want to move my body outside three times a week.' Focus on the here and now – the process is the reality of what you prioritise day to day; the process is what will *stick*.†

BELIEVE YOU CAN

Self-efficacy – your belief in your own ability – is one of the strongest predictors of long-term success.[16] As the saying (generally attributed to industrialist Henry Ford) goes: 'Whether you think you can or think you can't, you're probably right.' And when (not *if*) you slip, don't catastrophise or give up. Just get back on track whenever you can.

DR SARAH'S MCKAY'S BOTTOM-UP, OUTSIDE-IN, TOP-DOWN MODEL

Dr McKay's bio-psycho-social model, which I explored in detail in Chapter 1: Stress, can be usefully applied with habits too. For example, if you know you're the kind of person who leads with your thoughts (*top-down*), then mind-focused habit interventions could be the best starting point. If you have a thought-based habit you want to change (e.g. negative thinking), then getting out of your mind and into your

---

*Hence that's why people hire coaches!
†We go deeper into this topic in Chapter 9: Moving Forward.

body (*bottom-up*) with somatic practices and environmental changes (*outside-in*) may be better instead. In sum: play to your strengths.

REMEMBER YOUR PRIORITIES
You know by now that *what you prioritise becomes your life*. Reminding yourself of what's important and of value to you, and asking yourself whether your current habits align with that, can be very impactful for instigating change. It's also much easier to change or build a habit when it aligns with your priorities. Ask: *why is it important to me to change? How is it more important that the familiarity of my current life?*

FOCUS ON WHAT'S WORKING
When we think about changing a habit, we often zoom straight in on what's *not* working, on what we're doing *wrong*. But this kind of deficit mindset can easily de-motivate us. Instead, ask yourself: *what's already working well in this area of my life?* It could be that you're already doing part of the habit without even realising, that you've succeeded with similar habits in the past, or even that you know there's a time of day or environment that makes you naturally feel more focused. Identify what *is* going well (even if it feels small), and you'll show your brain that progress is possible. And by reinforcing competence rather than just effort, you begin to build the kind of self-belief (and neural pathways) that support lasting change.

KNOW THAT SELF-CONTROL IS FINITE
The act of change is *hard*. Sorry but it just is. Change demands effort, energy and commitment. It's hard to maintain self-control, and life's demands make it even harder. If your self-control is depleted (from, say, managing a stressful workday or not snapping at your children), you'll have less of it to use for your habits. Simply put: the more demands you have on your life, the less resources you have for other things. Stress, fatigue and decisions all impact your cognitive energy[*] – they all make you more likely to have that third glass of wine or eat the whole box of chocolates even after they've stopped tasting good. To help manage this, you want to be replenishing your self-control when and where you can with things like rest, breaks in your workday, time

---
[*]This is also known as 'ego depletion'.

with loved ones and reducing the potential for decision fatigue. Ask: *what depletes my self-control?* and *what replenishes it?*

WHAT WON'T HELP ME DO ALL THIS?

Even when we know what habit we want to change, *and how to do it*, we can still find ourselves completely stuck. This is where *barriers* come in – the internal and external blocks that stand in the way of you following through. A barrier could be practical (not enough time), emotional (fear of failure), psychological (limiting beliefs) or environmental (surrounded by cues that reinforce the old behaviour). We also don't always recognise them; they can be invisible or unconscious and we can internalise them as laziness, weakness or lack of willpower – which is not only untrue, but *unhelpful*. Here are a few barriers to change for you to look out for:

SELF-RESTRAINING THOUGHTS (SRTs)

One huge hurdle for us all is our thoughts, that internal voice that gets a bit loud when we're trying to make a change or life gets tough. Can you identify any SRTs or HITs (both similar to the SITs we covered in Chapter 1: Stress) that pop into your head when you try to make a change? These often sound like:

- 'I'm too tired.'
- 'What's the point?'
- 'I always mess this up.'
- 'This won't work for me.'

These thoughts and mindsets aren't facts,* and once you identify them, you can start to challenge them – lean on the Socratic questions and stress-alleviating thoughts and behaviours from Chapter 1: Stress. *Talk back to your brain.*

ENVIRONMENTAL FRICTION

Barriers aren't just in your head; they're in your space too. If your environment is full of triggers for the habit you're trying to break, if it's hard to access the tools you need for the habit you're building or if you

---
*Remember: don't believe everything you think!

have friends and family who don't support your change, this all adds friction. Ask: *what can I do to reduce friction?* For example:

- Prep gym clothes the night before.
- Keep your journal visible.
- Delete apps that lead to distraction.
- Add cues in your space that support a new habit.
- Create boundaries with unsupportive friends/family.

EMOTIONAL LOAD

Change requires cognitive and emotional energy, which, as we all know, some days we just don't have. That's normal and okay, but bear in mind that stress and overwhelm are proven to get in the way of habit change. Ask yourself:

- Am I drained, overwhelmed or exhausted?
- Has (as above) my self-control been depleted?
- Am I asking too much of myself right now?

If the answer is yes, don't give up your habit altogether but rather *scale it down*. A habit you can stick to twice a week is much better than one you go all in on then abandon after three days. (Also refer to Chapters 1: Stress and 4: Overwhelm for help with stress and overwhelm.)

READINESS TO CHANGE

How ready you feel for change can mark the difference between a successful habit and an unsuccessful one. Without a feeling of readiness, it's much harder to impact change. Ask yourself:

- On a scale of 1–10, how ready am I to change this habit?
- If I'm not at a 9 or 10, what would help me move one point higher?

Change isn't all-or-nothing; it's a *process*. You're allowed to be scared and unsure and to move slowly, just don't let that stop you from taking that first step. Consider how you can make yourself feel *more ready* instead.

YOUR BEST PARTY FRIEND

As I mentioned earlier in this chapter – and more than once in the book – I think motivation is fickle. Or, as my tutor Dr Mary Collins once said: 'Motivation is like your best party friend: fun to have around, but you wouldn't trust them to get you to the airport on time.'

That said, recent research at the intersection of neuroscience and psychology has deepened our understanding of what drives goal-directed behaviour – and how we can use that knowledge to boost motivation in sustainable ways. While your 'party friend' might not show up every day, you *can* learn how to give them a nudge.

Motivation is largely driven by the neurotransmitter *dopamine*. This isn't the 'pleasure' chemical, as it's often described, but rather, it fuels desire, attention and *movement* towards a goal. (Some call it the 'molecule of more'.) Other chemicals, like serotonin and oxytocin, are more about *being okay with what you already have*. Dopamine, on the other hand, is about anticipation; it pulls you into the future. It makes goal pursuit feel exciting, and can also make you feel perpetually restless.

Your dopamine neurons are always firing at a steady rate, but when a reward is better than expected they surge, or when worse than expected they dip. This is known as a *reward prediction error*.[17] And, once a reward becomes *predictable*, your dopamine response *fades*. This is why novelty and surprise are so appealing to us as humans and can actually help boost motivation.

There are two main types of motivation:

- **Extrinsic**, which is when you're driven by external rewards or consequences – things like money, grades, praise, approval or fear of punishment. For example: studying medicine because your parents expect it.
- **Intrinsic**, which is when the drive comes from within, because the task feels enjoyable, meaningful or interesting. It's tied to your sense of satisfaction, growth or identity. For example: playing tennis because you genuinely love it.

While we all use a mix of both, intrinsic motivation – the kind that comes from within – has been shown to fuel greater persistence, creativity and satisfaction over the long term.[18] And, according to *self-determination theory*, we can increase intrinsic motivation by fostering three key ingredients: autonomy (having choice), mastery (feeling competent) and connection (feeling supported or purposeful).

On one very simple level, if you want to sustain motivation for a behaviour, you have two options – you can reduce the amount of motivation the behaviour requires (i.e. make the action more automatic by turning it into an unconscious habit) or you can look at how to boost motivation itself. Let's look at the latter.

FIVE SCIENCE-BACKED WAYS TO BOOST MOTIVATION

Here's how to apply the research in ways that my experience has shown will help you to actually stick to your habits:

1. **Use variable rewards.** This is why slot machines, video games and social media are so addictive – the unpredictable, novel nature of the reward keeps dopamine levels high. While it's not always easy to replicate for yourself in real life, adding a small element of *surprise* or *variety* can keep things feeling fresh. Randomly choose your post-run treat or don't give yourself a reward every time you stick to a habit but make it *unpredictable instead*.* Mix it up to keep your brain (and your dopamine) guessing.

2. **Offer choice and control.** Research shows that having a sense of control over how and when we pursue a goal makes the outcome feel more meaningful and makes us more likely to stick with it.[19] Try it with a habit, letting yourself choose the how, when or where. For example, 'I'll take my vitamins either before breakfast or after dinner' – same outcome but this phrasing gives flexibility and choice.

3. **Game your own brain.** Create small, joyful incentives that reinforce the habit. For example: pair a habit with something pleasurable (e.g. listen to a podcast *only* while walking), make it social (e.g. send a 'done it' text to a friend) or give yourself a small reward after completion (favourite snack, star on a chart, guilt-free scroll).

4. **Focus on the reason.** Motivation is stronger and more consistent when it's anchored to your 'why' – your underlying reason – rather than relying on moment-to-moment emotions. You might not *feel* like doing something, but remembering what it's in service of can

---

*Using dice or an online random number generator for this.

help you act anyway. Instead of 'I don't want to run', try 'I may not feel like it, but I run because I want to feel strong.' Your reason doesn't need to be profound, it just has to matter to you.

5. **If it's not intrinsically motivating . . . make it extrinsically rewarding.** Not every habit starts off fun, enjoyable or meaningful, and that is more than okay (it's also life). In these cases, external motivators can be effective at giving you a boost. Start with something small – like music or a treat – to get you going. Over time, those external rewards can lay the groundwork for more intrinsic drives to take over. For example, fold laundry while watching your favourite show, until that becomes an established habit for you.

(As with so much in this book, these four strategies are framed as personal tools – but they can absolutely be used to support others who might need a boost.* I see this in action whenever I go into companies like Meta to run workshops. Their workspaces are full of built-in motivators such as ever-changing gourmet snack options (novelty + choice + external reward), and initiatives that encourage passion projects within and outside the company (autonomy + purpose). These perks are clever ways of boosting motivation by tapping into how our brains work (and also, let's be honest, excellent ways to get employees to remain loyal . . .)

Motivation is not a magic bullet. It's fleeting and inconsistent, and I don't recommend relying on it above your systems. However, when you understand how it works – and how to work *with* it – you can create an environment where motivation is both more likely to show up and stick around. Basically, don't wait for the 'party friend' to get you to the airport on time – set an alarm, book a cab, and then maybe – *just maybe* – they'll manage to meet you at the gate.

ONE DROP EVERY DAY

Habits and behaviours sit on a spectrum. There are good ones – meditating, brushing your teeth – and bad ones – unhappily scrolling, smoking. And then there's everything in-between. Ultimately, a habit either moves you closer towards or further away from what's important to you.

---

*There have been several studies over the years that have actually suggested bribing your kids and teens to improve their habits is not a bad idea . . .[20]

And while it's not easy to undo habits or create new ones, it's absolutely possible.

I've seen it over and over again with clients; I've lived it myself. And everything in this chapter is designed to make it easier. Don't wait for the perfect moment or the ideal conditions to start – think small, simple changes. The brain is capable of incredible plasticity, but it also has limited capacity for change at any one time, so look for low-hanging fruit – changes that require less willpower, energy and time. Ones that are quick, low-effort, easy to implement and not too disruptive to your regular routine. Think: manageable tweaks rather than massive interventions. Link your habits to how you see yourself. Stack new behaviours onto existing loops in your brain. Challenge your thoughts. Reward yourself. Do what you can to increase your motivation and take advantage of motivation waves to keep you going. Ask yourself motivational questions such as: *what would my life be like if (INSERT HABIT) did/didn't exist? What's the easiest win I could make this week? What would feel meaningful but doable? What change might unlock momentum elsewhere?*

All this will make you more likely to stick with your habits, which will make you more likely to see good results. And the more you see good results, the more you'll stick with them – you'll create a positive habit loop. And the more you do them, the less motivation, willpower and cognition you'll require. Eventually, they may even become automatic, freeing up your mental energy for bigger, more demanding tasks.*

And remember, habits and behaviours *accumulate*. We tend to expect too much progress in a week while underestimating what we can achieve in three or six months. Imagine a glass filling slowly with water – one drop every day. At first, you may not see much change, but after a while (even with evaporation, aka setbacks) that glass will suddenly be full. This is how small, consistent changes become real-life transformation. Drop by drop.

Moreover, know that the real difference between those who succeed and those who don't is getting back up after the fall. Life isn't a straight line – it twists and dips and sometimes hits you really f*cking hard in the face. I had many moments of this on my recovery from my mental health struggles, and I continue to have them with my general

---

*I always like to think of Steve Jobs wearing the same thing every day to reduce the daily decisions he needed to make. (Elizabeth Holmes of Theranos fame did the same, but she's not one to emulate.)

life today. Nothing ever stays the same, so expect lapses; what truly matters is that you keep moving in the right-ish direction.

Other chapters will support you greatly here too:

- Chapter 5: Procrastination will help you tackle self-sabotage.
- Chapter 6: Failure will help you reframe setbacks so they don't derail or destroy you.
- Chapter 8: Comparison will support you in building the internal foundation needed to sustain change.
- Chapter 9: Moving Forward will support you in setting and achieving goals in your life.

Self-efficacy really is key. The more you believe you can change, the more likely you are to change.[21] And often, the best way to build that belief is to make change easier. Start where it's simple, then let success snowball and build from there. *You can do hard things*, and you're not aiming for perfect; you're aiming for progress . . .

Just one drop. Every day.

PRIORITISE THIS

- What you do repeatedly becomes your life.
- Your brain prefers a shortcut and a short-term win, but you can use this to your advantage.
- Don't rely on motivation, rely on systems that you've built for yourself.
- There are many ways to make habits easier to start and stick to – find the ones that work for you and lean on them.
- Consider your own barriers to change, such as your thoughts or the emotional load you have on in life.
- Rely on the proven ways to increase your motivation and willpower.
- Progress doesn't come from intensity or perfection; it comes from consistency.
- Self-efficacy is crucial – believe in your ability to change.

PRACTICES TO HELP WITH HABITS

WHAT I DO IN A WEEK

As we all know too well, the demands of modern living make it easy to find yourself existing on autopilot, absorbed in the details of day-to-day life. This exercise invites you to evaluate your days, and, in doing so, consider whether you're prioritising the habits and people that are truly important to you, or getting bogged down by distractions and unhelpful tasks.

How it works:

- Grab a piece of paper and write down everything you do in your week (either in a list format, or a spider diagram). Think of your month as well, for example, you may go to yoga only once a month – include it.
- Once you've written everything down, evaluate each activity and habit using the following criteria:
  - Does this NOURISH you?
  - Does this DRAIN you?
  - Does this fulfil a sense of PURPOSE?
  - Does this fill you with JOY?
  - Is this NEUTRAL?

The answers will help you figure out what you need to be doing more of and what you need to be doing less of – i.e. which habits, people and actions to prioritise and which to de-prioritise. (FYI: some may fall into more than one category – for example, an activity can be purposeful, but also draining at times too.)

PLAYING THE TAPE

This technique is one to use if you're facing a strong urge to engage in a behaviour you want to change – whether it's reaching for another drink, skipping the gym, bingeing, doomscrolling or reacting in anger. It helps you mentally *zoom out* of the moment and grounds you in the long-term consequences – both negative and positive. It's widely used in recovery circles and supported by research on mindfulness and visualisation – one study even found that vividly imagining the consequences of giving in to a craving (like chocolate) significantly reduced the craving itself.[22]

How it works:

- Take a deep inhale and exhale. Ground yourself in the here and now.
- First play side A – *what happens if you give in?* Visualise or imagine yourself going ahead with the urge – ask: what does this feel like in the moment? What are the consequences (physical, emotional, mental, social, spiritual)? Imagine the immediate relief or reward you will feel, but also consider how you'll feel in a few hours, or tomorrow or any time in the future.
- Now play side B – *what happens if you don't?* Visualise or imagine resisting the urge – ask: how does that feel? What are the long-term gains you are making? What would your future self thank you for? Would you feel pride, clarity, calm or a sense of agency?
- Remind yourself, many urges pass within 20 minutes if you don't feed them. Know that resisting and not giving in is an investment in your future self.

BEST POSSIBLE SELF

This exercise invites you to imagine a time in the future when you are living your life as your 'Best Possible Self'. This will help you see the impact of possible habit changes in your life by embodying them. So, spend a few minutes thinking about that time and that version of you and then write down a detailed description of your life, including answers to these five questions:

1. How have your habits have changed?
2. What has happened?
3. Who is around you?
4. How do you feel?
5. How have *you* changed?

Go to the Prioritise This website to find an extra Habit tracker practice.

CHAPTER 3

Saying No

● ● ●

'The difference between successful people and very successful people is that very successful people say no to almost everything.'
Warren Buffett

If you've ever tried to put shoes on a toddler, you'll know how easily they say, 'NO!' As the parent of a three-year-old, I feel like I hear it a million times a day, and it drives me mad – many of his 'nos' are disproportionate, unconstructive, even dangerous. His constant refusal to play ball for what appears to be no apparent reason can be testing.

But I also respect him for it. For while it's clear to me that some of them are misplaced, they evidently make sense to his growing and developing brain. And I want my son to lay down those crucial neural networks – to learn how to assert his needs, preferences and desires, to discover his boundaries and feel confident defending them. In essence, I very much want to *be* the parent of a child who knows when and how to say no. I just don't particularly want to have to *parent* them all the time . . .

Saying no is important. Very important.

It marks the difference between a life that feels mostly led by others or at the complete whim of your impulses, and a nourishing, uncluttered* life that feels like yours.

---

*Or at least *less* cluttered.

Saying no helps us create boundaries and stop ourselves from drowning in commitments or resentment. It strengthens our connection with our 'self', demonstrates respect (both inwardly and outwardly), protects our best interests and preserves our mental and physical health. It helps us stay on top of our priorities, feel productive, maintain a manageable schedule and ensure our time and energy is put towards the projects and people that matter. Ultimately, it imbues life with a greater sense of autonomy and purposeful direction.

And yet we stop doing it so much as adults.

In part this is a good thing. If I said no to you in response to the kinds of requests my son says no to – 'Could you please stop pulling every single one of our books off the shelf?' – I don't think you'd want to spend any time with me.* Testing boundaries is an essential part of being a child; it's how they begin to understand and make their way in the world. Then, ideally, as evidenced by my six-year-old, they do less of it as their comprehension and sense of identity develops.†

But as adults we often swing too far the other way. There are many reasons why, and I'll go into them in a bit, but the outcome is the same – we end up letting our impulses run wild and/or other people's desires and needs define the pace of our lives.

In any healthy relationship (including with ourselves) there's a balance to be struck between being selfish and selfless, between saying yes and saying no. I find the analogy of an ice cream swirl useful, where a mixture of one person's wants (vanilla) is blended with another's (let's go chocolate). Sure, it'll never be a perfect mix, but it should be an equal-ish blend. Too much or little of one and it's not a swirl anymore – it's one main taste, with an afterthought. It's *unbalanced.*

Your wants, needs and desires should never be an afterthought, and nor should those of your loved ones. My goal in this chapter is to reawaken your ability to say no and help you enable the people around you to feel they can say it to you too. We'll explore the reasons we struggle to say no, run through why it's so important, and then use all that to build a mental toolkit that'll enable you to create a balanced flavour to your relationships and your life.

---

*Nor, understandably, read this book.
†Obviously, this is not a straight line, and it all ramps up again tenfold when puberty hits . . .

SAYING NO

THE HARDEST WORD

We start off in life saying no to almost everything – it's one of an English-speaking baby's most frequent first words, firmly in the top ten, alongside 'mama' and 'banana'.[1] That primordial, powerful no that I hear so often is the original assertion of the self against the other – of my son differentiating himself from me.

However, as we grow older, the less interested we become in differentiation and the more we try to fit in. Consider being a teenager, when nothing matters more than the opinion of your peers – I'm sure you can remember a time when you felt, or made a friend feel, that yes was the only available option. (Of course, teenagers don't lose their capacity to say no to their primary caregivers; this remains robust.) Yet, even as adults, saying no to requests or invitations can still feel deeply challenging.

So, why do we struggle, as Nancy Reagan once implored in that now-infamous anti-drugs campaign, to 'Just Say No'? (Spoiler: it's a *bit* more complicated than she made it sound.)

Well, your brain has two main priorities – survival and conservation of energy – and, from its perspective, saying no threatens both. You have an in-built, evolutionary preference for *approval.*

Before we move on to explore the psychology behind our resistance to saying no, here are some of the key reasons why we find it so hard, and why we should do our utmost to do it anyway.

Nine (good) reasons you find it hard to say no

1. You don't want to hurt anyone's feelings.
2. You think others may not like you if you say it.
3. You genuinely want to help.
4. You want to be seen as a team player.
5. You're worried it could affect your prospects.
6. You want to preserve your relationship.
7. You believe it's not nice to say no.
8. You feel guilty afterwards.
9. You instinctively say yes to everything.

Nine (very good) reasons you still need to say it

1. It will improve your mental wellbeing, fitness and clarity.
2. Being assertive pays off, in work and in life.
3. It helps you stay on track with your priorities and goals.
4. It helps prevent burnout.
5. It creates strong, healthy boundaries to your relationships.
6. It helps you get to know your own needs better.
7. It's self-care.
8. You can do everything else better if you're not overloaded.
9. It shows you can stand up for yourself.

THE NEGATIVITY BIAS

In psychology there's a phenomenon known as the negativity bias. Described by psychologist Roy F. Baumeister and colleagues in their 2001 study 'Bad is Stronger Than Good',[2] it explains that the brain responds more fiercely to negative stimuli than positive ones. This feels unfair from an individual standpoint: none of us wants to vividly remember the worst bits of life while the good stuff fades away. But the brain has a valid reason – from a survival standpoint it's crucial that we remember painful or frightening encounters, so that we can better identify and avoid them in the future. It's *trying* to keep us safe.

And when it comes to saying or hearing a no, regardless of how it's dressed up (ballgown, tracksuit or anything in-between), it'll always be perceived as negative. Your brain *automatically* responds more strongly to a no than a yes,[3] which for two reasons affects your capacity to turn down a night in the pub with your friends* or tell your boss you can't take on that extra project right now . . .

First, and most straightforwardly, we are an empathetic, caring species and do not wish to intentionally cause another person pain. Yes, there are exceptions, but for the majority, as our own lived experience of hearing no develops, the more we understand how painful it may feel. We know that saying it risks insinuating something negative

---

*There's also an extra, third reason at play here – your brain prefers the short-term reward it receives from staying out with friends, rather than thinking through the long-term consequences of that action. (I will explore this reason in detail shortly.)

about the person who's asked and/or their request. We become aware that no can hurt, and begin to avoid using it.

Second, as children, we were all, to varying degrees, told off or punished for saying no – for being impolite or 'rebellious', for refusing to obey and comply. In some cases, this is thought to lead to an overdeveloped negativity response, where the subconscious belief becomes: 'Saying no is bad, I must not do it.' In this way, a person never quite develops the communication skills or confidence necessary to assert themselves later in life. Saying no disproportionately triggers their *own* negativity bias, leaving them scared to say it at all. (I've heard therapists say this can be particularly true in firstborns, who often feel more pressure to be the responsible 'good child'.)

THE FEAR OF REJECTION

As social creatures, we rely on the people around us for our wellbeing. We crave human connection, have an inbuilt desire to belong, and generally don't wish to rock the boat in our relationships, preferring to keep the waters calm. (Sometimes we may want to ride our boat straight into a storm of epic proportions, but that's another topic altogether . . .) Mostly, we want to fit in.

Evolutionary psychologists believe that this innate need is driven by a memory imprint, located deep in your brain. In modern society we use (some may even say *overuse*) the term 'tribe' to describe a group of people with similar interests and values who take joy in being together – 'my tribe' and all the other saccharine memes. Yet, during hunter/gatherer times, when humans *lived* in tribes[*] you didn't just find comfort in your community, you relied on it for your survival. A no was dangerous – if someone didn't like your refusal, it could spell rejection from the group, which effectively meant death. While that's no longer the case, the brain is still scared of the potential conflict. Plus, our lived experience confirms that sometimes people really *do* reject us when we say no. It can happen. It does happen. We've all been teenagers, after all . . .

This deep fear of rejection can, as adults, lead us to tie our identity around being someone who always says yes. You may think of yourself as a helpful friend, or good team player. The one everyone can rely on, who juggles all the balls and makes things happen, who takes

---

*Some, of course, still do.

on everyone else's sh*t but never complains. It's possible in fact that you take great pride in this, viewing it as a core part of who you are. Therefore, why would you ever say no?

Then there's the connection between rejection and imposter syndrome, the psychological phenomenon characterised by persistent feelings of inadequacy and self-doubt. Now, I'm aware the thinking around imposter syndrome is mixed;[4] however, it comes up *all the time* in my work, often in relation to a lack of good boundaries and the ability to . . . say no! Ultimately, if you doubt yourself and feel as if you're not good enough (at work or in your relationships), then you'll avoid saying no. You won't want to refuse anyone, because of an underlying fear that someone will think you can't do your job properly, or belief that you're not worthy of love or support.*

THE LOVE OF DOPAMINE

As much as the brain is hardwired to avoid rejection, it is equally incentivised[5] to seek out dopamine – the reward chemical that plays an essential role in regulating pleasure, motivation and reward systems in the brain.[6]

Whenever we do something enjoyable – eat a good meal, go for a run, have sex, play an instrument, experience a rewarding social interaction – we experience a dopamine 'hit', with a little of the chemical released in our brain. This *positively* impacts our wellbeing – both in the moment and the long run, in terms of life satisfaction and happiness levels overall.

But those aren't the only activities that lead to dopamine release. As Anna Lembke, MD, explores in her best-selling book *Dopamine Nation*, we also get them from things that provide instant gratification – ordering a takeaway, flicking through Instagram, a random Amazon purchase. And these hits, though good pick-me-ups in the moment, *negatively* impact our wellbeing in the long run. They also wire our brains to prioritise forms of instant gratification (Amazon) above sustained fulfilment (curling up with a novel).

When it comes to saying no to your own impulses, dopamine is not your friend. Given free rein, your brain will almost always prioritise immediate, instant gratification[7] over something that requires energy

---

*FYI: you can and you are. And we explore this topic more in Chapter 8: Comparison.

and effort (remember, it wants to *conserve* energy, not expend it). The brain loves the hit it gets from quick, short-term rewards, and this makes it hard to resist doom-scrolling on Instagram or not hitting the snooze button. It takes more energy and gives you zero dopamine to say no to a night out – whereas saying yes gives you a nice little hit, even if the next day greets you with a splitting hangover and the haunting memory of a few things you absolutely shouldn't have said or done.*

Saying no to your impulses is in fact such a critical part of human behaviour that two Nobel Prizes have been awarded for research into it – first to Daniel Kahneman in 2002 and later to Richard Thaler in 2017. Their work showed how much of modern life is stacked against impulse control – we live in an 'impulse society', and where instant gratification is easier than ever, self-regulation becomes an increasingly radical (and vital) act.

THE CONSERVATION FACTOR

Finally, the brain's second priority – conserving energy – means that if a conversation or experience requires effort or will generate discomfort, its response is to shy away. Saying no involves both – we experience discomfort (from mild to extreme) at knowing we may disappoint someone, and we use effort to validate our reasons for saying no. The brain wants to conserve as much energy as possible and saying no challenges this. Whether it's to other people, or ourselves . . .

In my column in *ES Magazine*, I was once asked to give advice on saying no. The reader was a party animal who was becoming concerned that, despite creeping into their late thirties, they could never call it a night at a reasonable hour. Having once been in that position myself, I could empathise – and much of the advice I gave will be found in the next few pages.

In this instance you can almost *see* the neurobiology at play. He didn't want to leave his friends (fear of rejection plus negativity bias), he gets a dopamine hit from not leaving, and he conserves energy by giving in to his impulses. All of it leads smoothly towards: 'Yes! We *do* need tequila shots.'

---

*FYI: this isn't me saying you should always say no to a big night out if that's what you enjoy – I personally believe they have a solid place in life!

PRIORITISE THIS

THE CONSEQUENCES

In essence, the brain will always respond faster and more powerfully to a no than a yes. By creating a disproportionate emotional reaction, it stops us from saying no regularly in our lives. So, we take on burdens, spread ourselves too thin and believe that, in doing so, we're not 'hurting' anyone with a no.

Our brain *thinks* it's prioritising peace, that it's keeping us out of harm's way. But this approach isn't harmless – when we don't say no to others, we say no to our own priorities. An outward yes is often an inward no. We end up hurting ourselves.

If this all sounds familiar – like you yourself have said yes to 20 things this month that make you quietly resent everyone you know and maybe also yourself – know that you're not alone. I have definitely said yes to things I knew were a terrible idea mid-sentence (often while nodding enthusiastically).

This idea of an outward yes as an inward no was brought home to me when I interviewed journalist, author and LGBTQIA+ activist Amelia Abraham in Season 1, Episode 2 of my podcast, *Priorities*. 'Trying to do too much and being bad at saying no to things really affects your economy of time,' she explained. 'I easily spread myself too thin, so that I can't put my full attention on what I'm supposed to be doing. And then really simple things, that shouldn't even be considered self-care, become self-care.'

I think we all know how Amelia feels. How easy it is to find ourselves in a life that is so busy that we view going for a walk with a friend as self-care, rather than see it for what it is – a normal part of a healthy life.

PRIORITISE RESPECT

From this perspective, a kindly worded no communicates: 'My needs take priority here.' It defines the perimeters of the self; it says that while each of us loves, cares for and values the other people in our lives, we won't allow ourselves to be entirely led by them. It's an act of self-respect; by saying no you are choosing you.

My client S was confident setting boundaries at work and with friends, but, in her words, 'lost perspective in romantic situations'. After her divorce, she found herself struggling to balance her career and personal needs while sharing custody of her young daughter. She fell into old patterns – always saying yes, even when it felt wrong.

S's relationships became about her trying to please her partners – rather than 'What can they do for me?', it was always 'What can I do for them?' She found herself in relationships with women who would expect her to drop everything to be with them, but would also disappear for days on end. While I made it clear I'm not a relationship coach, she felt strongly that behavioural and mindset coaching could support her in breaking these patterns.

My approach to coaching is forward-thinking and action based – we never delved deeply into why S had developed this people-pleasing side of her (we left that for therapy) but instead explored how we could empower her to think and behave in ways that felt more helpful. We built up her sense of self-worth so that she could begin to appreciate the value of setting boundaries in relationships. We practised saying no to small things to strengthen the habit of saying no to the bigger stuff later on. Little by little, S began to understand her own boundaries, to assert herself, to say no.

When we consider S's story, it's easy to demonise her partners – to say that they didn't treat her with respect. However, while this may be true, S *also* didn't demonstrate respect. She never communicated her needs, she didn't set boundaries, she always said yes and, in doing so, played some part in building an unequal relationship. There are always valid reasons as to why we find ourselves in patterns like these; however, while we don't want to let other people define our needs, nor can we expect them to *always* anticipate them. In an ideal world we get to know ourselves to the point where we understand and appreciate our own needs and feel confident bringing clear boundaries and expectations into our relationships. (A tiny ask, I know.)

Ultimately, saying no doesn't just show self-respect; it demonstrates respect for those around you – it says: I'll meet you halfway.

YOUR CHOICE

The language we use – both in conversation and towards ourselves – is, clearly, very important. I often invite corporate clients to investigate the difference between saying: 'I *have* to reply to this email' and 'I *choose* to reply to this email.' Saying 'I have to' assumes you have no other available option, that it is a non-negotiable and a priority. 'I choose to', on the other hand, is a reminder that you have some agency – that the thousands of decisions we take every day are (within reason) choices. Someone else's urgent isn't necessarily the same as yours – no matter how many red exclamation marks they might add. Unless you're fairly certain you'll be fired or punished for it, know that sometimes you *can* say no to replying to that email in the moment. That it can wait until you've finished something *more important and urgent* to you (such as playing with your kids or enjoying your coffee).

Try putting it into practice this week by replacing an automatic 'I have to' with a more considered 'I choose to'. It may feel strange, uncomfortable, forced even, but it's also the best way to remind yourself that sometimes it is up to you whether to say yes or no, that, to varying extents, we choose what we prioritise. And, ultimately, we can all prioritise better choices – those that help us feel less stressed and overwhelmed and aligned with what's important.

Nine tips for saying no (and not feeling bad about it)

1. Remember your time and energy are limited. Look at your calendar if you need a reminder. Even if there is free time, rest is still a valid reason to say no.
2. Know your *why*. Being clear on your reasons makes it easier to say no *and* stick to it. It'll help you to respect your decision, even if someone else may not.
3. Pause before responding. Give yourself time to think not just short-term but also long-term. Don't let your people-pleasing, pleasure-seeking side take over. A moment of reflection beats a reflexive yes driven by pressure or habit.
4. Replace your automatic yes with 'I'll think about it.' This buys you time to make a thoughtful choice – not one based on someone else's urgency or wants.
5. Or, if you know it's a no, just say so. Clear is kind. Don't string someone along – it's better for everyone.
6. Keep it short and polite. Don't overexplain. A concise, respectful no builds clarity and conveys confidence, especially in professional settings.

7. Practise first. If you're feeling nervous, rehearse the conversation. Work through any potential conflict points. Knowing what you'll say will help defuse discomfort.
8. Flip the script. What would you say to a friend in the same situation? Probably to assert themselves and protect their wellbeing. Offer yourself the same advice.
9. Lead with compassion. A kind no still honours the relationship. Make it clear it isn't a reflection of their own worth, but rather about you needing to prioritise yourself. Use that cheesiest of all break-up lines: *it's not you, it's me.*

A MATTER OF HABIT

The best way to get better at saying no – whether it's to yourself when you want to stay out late, a demanding boss who has thrown another project onto your already overloaded plate, or an emotionally draining friend who takes more than they give – is by doing it. It's only by putting it into practice that you start to lay down the neural networks that'll make it easier the next time, and even easier the time after that.

However, if you're not used to saying no, it can feel challenging. Start small – resist the snooze button or don't reply to a non-urgent work email when it first comes in. With time and practice (and as you reap the benefits of saying no), your brain's negative reaction will lessen, and more positive associations will form.

Lean on the lessons in Chapter 2: Habits for help with this, while remembering that *what you prioritise becomes the sum of your life.* Making a *habit* of saying no – to distractions, temptations or other people's demands – when needed, allows for growth. That outward no is truly an inward yes – yes to prioritising your long-term objectives, yes to showing up for yourself, yes to your priorities.

But don't forget, too, that an inward no can *also* be an inward yes . . . Saying no to a late night in front of the TV or the voice telling you it's a good idea to look up your ex's new partner on socials (it never is) – every time you override urges such as these, you send yourself a message: *I can prioritise something better here.* Something that honours my continuing priorities, rather than my impulses.

And like any other habit in life, the more often you say no – whether to yourself or others – the easier it becomes.

EMBRACING A NO

Interestingly, as this habit develops, you'll find yourself more open to accepting a no when it's directed at you. In stress management coaching, we often look at how to strike a balance between *aggressive* and *passive* behaviour. Between being someone who stands up for themselves at the expense of others and someone who expenses themselves for the (perceived) benefit of others. This middle point is known as 'assertive behaviour' and is characterised by feeling able to ask for what you want, advocate for yourself, complain appropriately and give constructive feedback to others.

In the assertiveness training I run for corporate leaders, we focus not only on helping them develop confidence asserting their own rights,* but also on enabling their employees to feel they can do the same. Just as in relationships, a healthy business needs an environment where employees feel confident (within reason) saying no. This starts with improving the leaders' listening skills – not interrupting or overly anticipating what others might say is one of the most important tools *anyone* can develop to improve their relationships, whether at work or home. It may be obvious (clearly, I'm not the first person to suggest listening is useful) but in my experience it's a skill that can always be improved – I know I'm constantly working on it myself. Ultimately, as you'll know from personal experience, when we feel heard, understood and respected, we're far more likely to feel confident in speaking up and asserting our needs. *And* when we listen properly, we are more likely to understand and empathise, which, in turn, enables us to more easily take a no in our stride.

I'll give you a recent, personal example . . . A friend cancelled last minute on my birthday dinner. He messaged to say that his business partner was going to be in town and it was the only opportunity they had in the next six months to work together in person. He stated his reasons clearly, was very apologetic and offered to take me for dinner soon.

---

*As a leader, your ability to say no is a key part of your effectiveness. If you say yes to everything, you dilute your own impact and your team's. Strong leadership requires strong boundaries – the clearer you are about what matters, the easier it is for others to follow your lead.

Of course, my initial reaction was primal – I felt rejected, slighted and hurt. However, I then had a choice – I could dwell on that feeling, letting my brain compound it with every other rejection I've ever experienced until I ended up sad at the world *and* angry at him for 'making' me feel that way; or I could acknowledge and feel that emotional sting (which was there!), but then curb my runaway thoughts, listen to what he was saying and accept his reasoning. By saying no to me he was saying yes to himself and his new business. He was saying: *I love you, but this is so important to me that I'm still going to let you down. I'm choosing to prioritise myself and I hope you forgive me.*

I'm not saying be a pushover – if that friend made a habit of cancelling last minute, I'd start questioning the balance in our friendship. But the only thing I would have done by not forgiving him in this one-off situation is work myself up into an emotional frenzy in which I saw his no as a direct rejection. And that is a straight road to unhappiness and stress, especially if I reacted that way to every no. I'd be a mess! I chose to separate his decision from my relationship with him; I chose to *listen*.

(Oh, and if my friend was worried about how I'd react (or S was concerned about how her partners would respond), research shows they probably needn't . . . A 2023 study from the American Psychological Association found that we consistently overestimate the negative consequences of saying no – especially socially.[8] The inviter, it turns out, is more likely to focus on your reasoning than your rejection. In short: your no won't offend someone nearly as much as you think it will.)

ENABLING A NO

In the words of Mahatma Gandhi, 'A "no" uttered from the deepest conviction is better than a "yes" merely uttered to please, or worse, to avoid trouble.'[9] Studies have shown that people who feel forced or 'guilted' into saying yes can feel regret, resentment and frustration (I'm sure you can think of a few instances when you felt this way).[10] None of us want to feel as if we've cajoled someone into something – we want them to say yes because they *want* to, not because they feel there's no other choice.* With this in mind, the question becomes: how can we

---

*Like all things in life, there are exceptions – we may want a friend to say yes to something for their health, but know they'll need a bit of guilt-tripping first.

not only embrace a no but also help our loved ones say it? Surely, the answer is to tell them they can say no to us?

Apparently not. A 2024 study found that this can actually have the *opposite* effect, making it harder to say no.[11] Instead, it was shown that the best way to make someone feel comfortable is by telling them *how* to say it – give them a 'script' and that overrides the 'implicit scripts and norms of politeness' that make a no tough. The study used the phrase, 'If you'd like to refuse, please say the words, "I'd rather not" or "No, thank you"', though clearly that'd be an unsettling way to ask a friend for lunch. A less robotic version could be: 'I completely understand if you need to say no, if you do, please just say so. I won't be offended.' Or via email: 'I know you have a lot going on right now. If you reply saying you can't fit this in, I'll totally get it.' Clearly, it's not a huge leap from saying 'Feel free to say no!' but apparently the addition of some light 'script' makes a difference.

Ultimately, for all the reasons we don't like saying no and find it so hard to do, others feel the same. By taking a little pressure off the person you're asking, you create more room for their viewpoint, feelings and priorities: making a no easier and a yes feel more voluntary. I wouldn't recommend *always* making it easy for others to say no – stand your ground when it matters – but just remember that by creating more space for them to say no when they need to, they'll learn to do the same for you.

HOW'S NEVER?

My grandmother Dolly had a *New Yorker* poster on the wall in her kitchen that I like to remember when it comes to saying no. It was a cartoon of what appears to be a top-level executive standing in his high-rise office on the phone, with a speech bubble that read: 'No, sorry, Thursday's out. How's never? Does never work for you . . . ?'

Requests for your time will always be there – from family, friends, children, co-workers, social media, TV shows and more – but you can't achieve everything you want in life if you're always saying yes. To make time for your priorities, for the goals, dreams, people and activities you love, you need to say 'how's never?', both to others and yourself.

And while saying yes when we really want to say no can seem small in the moment, over time, those small compromises can stack up. Bronnie Ware, an Australian palliative care nurse, spent years listening to the stories of the dying and the number one regret she heard was that people wished they'd lived a life being true to themselves rather than trying to follow others' ideas of what makes for a good life. The number two regret was that they wished they hadn't worked so hard.* This chapter isn't just about boundaries; it's about building a life you won't have to apologise to yourself for. One that you won't look back on and regret you lived by someone else's priorities.

Saying no draws the line between *getting things done* and *getting done in*. It's your best defence against resentment, exhaustion and that heart-sinking feeling you get when someone asks, 'Just one more thing?' It stops us from becoming angry or resentful or spreading ourselves too thin. A no to one thing is a yes to something else, and it makes that yes even more impactful, because of the healthy boundaries you've drawn.

I had to say no many times to write this book. Both to myself and others. To learn to do this yourself there are a couple of uncomfortable truths to come to terms with . . . 1) sometimes people will think you're being selfish (perhaps you are); 2) you may disappoint and possibly offend them; 3) you will have to say no to things you really want to say yes to.

You can't be everything to everyone all the time. Let that guilt go; be okay with a bit of a fallout. Don't *always* choose you (you'd be an unbearable narcissist if you did) but prioritise yourself as much as you need to feel like your life is yours. Turn down energy-draining opportunities, people, activities and demands and you'll find that most people respect your boundaries. If they don't, that's their choice – remember, we can't control how other people will behave or feel. The only thing we can control is ourselves.

Boundaries are important for us all – they help us grow and develop as people. We need to knock against things, to have our sharp edges confronted and sanded off. To say no and to be told no.

So, what can you say no to today?

Safe in the knowledge that you can then say yes to something that really matters . . .

---

*Bronnie Ware's *The Top Five Regrets of the Dying* (Carlsbad: Hay House, 2011) makes for a moving read and its messages are hard to forget.

PRIORITISE THIS

- Saying no helps us avoid burnout and overwhelm.
- It's essential for helping us stay on top of our priorities.
- Yet our brains are hardwired to not say no.
- There are four factors involved in this – negativity bias, fear of rejection, love of dopamine and the conservation factor.
- It's possible to override this wiring by building and developing the habit of saying no.
- Saying no demonstrates self-respect and outward respect for others.
- It's important to also get comfortable with others saying no to you and you can help them feel more comfortable doing this.
- An outward no is an inward yes.

PRACTICES TO HELP WITH SAYING NO

QUESTIONS TO ASK YOURSELF BEFORE SAYING YES

Use these to check in with your priorities, needs and capacity:

- Do I have the time and energy for this right now?
- Am I saying yes just to avoid disappointing someone?
- What will saying yes cost me – emotionally, logistically or otherwise?
- Will this help or hinder my current goals and priorities?
- If I say yes to this, what am I saying no to?
- Am I scared of missing out – or of how they'll react?
- Is someone trying to gaslight, bully, coerce or use me?
- Is this truly aligned with the kind of life I want to create?
- Would I want someone I love to say yes in this situation?
- Do I need time in my diary to rest and recharge?
- Could my time/energy/attention be put to better use?

If your answers bring up hesitation, listen to that. Take a moment (or ten) so you decide how best to reply – not from fear or habit, but from clarity.

CREATE A TO-DON'T LIST

We're all familiar with to-do lists, and how they have the tendency to rule our lives . . . But one of the most effective productivity techniques is to flip that list on its head and instead write down the tasks or habits you *shouldn't* do.

Unlike a to-do list, which is generally used for short-term tasks that you can tick off, a *to-don't list* consists of tasks and habits that you want to avoid in the long term. These could be anything around you learning to say no such as . . .

- Don't reply to any work emails straight away.
- Don't use your phone in the first hour of the morning.
- Don't agree to invitations without looking at your diary.
- Don't smoke/vape on weekdays.
- Don't agree to see that draining friend this month.

Make a list of a few of your own. You may not necessarily be ticking them off in the same way you would with a to-do list, but it's helpful to see them written – so jot them down on a piece of paper, in a journal or on your phone.

Go to the Prioritise This website to find an extra practice: Alternative ways to say no.

CHAPTER 4

Overwhelm

* * *

'Start by doing what's necessary; then do what's possible; and suddenly you are doing the impossible.'

St Francis of Assisi

Here's a story I found on that most reliable of academic sources . . . *Reddit*.

A philosophy professor stood in front of his class at the beginning of their first semester. Silently, he picked up a very large, empty jar and filled it with golf balls. When no more could fit in, he turned to his students and asked: 'Is this jar full?'

'Yes,' they replied.

He then picked up a box of pebbles and poured them in, shaking the jar so that they filled the space between the golf balls. 'Is the jar full now?' he asked.

They agreed it was.

Next, the professor opened a bag of sand and poured that into the jar, where it packed the space between the golf balls and pebbles. Once more, he asked: 'Is this jar full?'

'Yes!' the students cried.

Finally, the professor pulled out two cups of hot coffee from under the table and poured them into the jar. The sand soaked up the coffee, filling any remaining empty space.

The students laughed.

'Now,' the professor said, as the noise settled, 'I want you to recognise that this jar represents your life. The golf balls are the truly important things – family, health, financial stability, close friends and much-loved passions. If everything else in your life were lost and only these remained, your life would still be full. The pebbles represent other important things that contribute to the fullness of your life – your job, house, car, bicycle, second-tier friends and so on. The sand is everything else – it represents the *small stuff*. If you put the sand in the jar first, there will be no room for the golf balls or pebbles. The same goes for life – if you spend all your time and energy on the small stuff, you will never have space for what's truly important to you. Take care of the golf balls first – the things that *really* matter. These are your priorities; the rest is just sand.'

A student raised his hand: 'What about the coffee?'

'I'm glad you asked,' the professor replied with a smile. 'It shows that no matter how full your life may seem, there's always room for a few cups of coffee with a good friend.'

THE SAND

In our fast-paced, demanding world, the sand is *everywhere*.

It's in your shoes, at the bottom of your bag, in between the cracks of your floorboards. Glance down and you'll realise you're standing in some sort of smartphone-related quicksand. We are drowning in the small stuff; we are *overwhelmed*.

And the reason you're overwhelmed is not because of anything that you are doing or not doing. *You* are not the problem. In the past hundred years our world has changed beyond recognition; while our grandparents and great-grandparents may not have been as busy as we are (indeed, they had none of our energy and time-saving technologies), nor were they faced with the endless deluge of information, data, visuals,[*] material possessions, distractions, competing demands and excessive choices that inundate us every day. Even just ten years ago,

---

[*]Past *Priorities* podcast guest Marine Tanguy writes brilliantly about the particular impact of visuals in her book *The Visual Detox*.

our lives, habits and routines (particularly around technology) looked wildly different from today . . .

The *Cambridge Dictionary* defines overwhelm as: BE TOO MUCH. Seriously, that's how it's written[1] – the capitalisation has nothing to do with me.

Now while this may be down to formatting, I'm also sure that, if I were to take creative liberty, I'd write it like that too – after all, overwhelm does feel as if you're living life in capital letters, your inner voice constantly screaming: *BE TOO MUCH.*

The feeling of overwhelm that we all know well – the sense that, no matter how much you try, you just can't keep up – can be short-term and short-lived or long-term and chronic. The cognitive and physiological impacts are wide-reaching, and while everyone experiences them differently, common signs and symptoms include: anxiety, irritability, forgetfulness, difficulty concentrating or sleeping, exhaustion, stomach problems, headaches, decreased concentration and joint pain. Studies have also even discovered a correlation between overwhelm and a reduction in the networks in the brain that encourage rational thinking and decision-making.[2] When your brain is tired, as in periods of overwhelm, it conserves energy for potential emergencies – complex, clear thinking not being one of them. We become more impulsive, lose our willpower and focus on short-term rewards over long-term gains, which in turn creates a torrent of unhelpful physical and mental responses, such as procrastination and negative self-talk. I imagine you can think of a personal example when overwhelm led you to experience some of or all the above; I certainly know I can . . .

There is no official diagnosis of overwhelm or reliable figures for the number of people living with it at any given time. Nor is there one recognised cause – it can be triggered by a variety of influences at work or home, or most likely some combination of the two; not only by recognisably stressful experiences (divorce, financial troubles, exams) but also by 'positive' ones (buying a home, getting a promotion, having a baby). Whatever the source, overwhelm occurs when the perceived demands on your life exceed your perceived capacity to handle them.*

---

*Keen readers may notice this is the same definition I used for stress in Chapter 1: Stress. Indeed, how stress and overwhelm occur is similar and they're often linked. Yet, as we also saw in Chapter 1, you can have stress in your life without feeling overwhelmed and you can feel overwhelmed without having any tangible stressor.

And boy, are our lives demanding! From the trivial – endless notifications from that annoying WhatsApp group – to the more serious – work stresses, caring responsibilities or financial worries – we are living through an era of demands. Try as we might to 'combat' this, our nervous system is ill-equipped to do so. Our (not insignificant) task, then, is to find our own way through. We may not be able to change the system itself, but we can teach *our* system to better cope; we may not be able to get rid of the sand, but we can place our golf balls and pebbles in the jar first.

Although periods of overwhelm are to be expected in a full and busy life, sustained overwhelm is no way to live. My aim for this chapter is for you to appreciate that any feelings of overwhelm are not your fault, and then begin to create for yourself a clearer path towards a life that feels less cluttered and frenetic.

We won't be trying to sweep the sand from the beach (an impossible undertaking if there ever was one); we'll be building a walkway over it instead.

THE EVOLUTION OF ATTENTION

Modern humans (i.e. you and I) have been around for about 300,000 years. For the majority of that time, our ancient ancestors lived predominantly simple lives – they hunted, foraged, built shelters, procreated, avoided predators and so on. Really, not much happened.

And because not much happened in their day-to-day lives, if your ancestor's attention *was* drawn – by a sudden movement or noise, for example – it was likely to be a predator or change in circumstance that required *immediate* attention and a readiness to react.

Their nervous system and brain (*your* nervous system and brain) thus developed to react aggressively to anything that seemed novel or out of the ordinary – a clever piece of evolutionary biology that's coming back to bite us . . . Your attention is a *limited* resource; you evolved to assign your brain power, physical energy and mental focus to one (*maybe* two) pieces of important information. You did not evolve to handle this many things vying for your attention at once – the numerous commitments, requests and distractions we're required to juggle fall beyond what our brain can reasonably handle.

And the thing with life is that it has a tendency to make us feel like *everything* is important. We are a product of our environment, and the combination of evolutionary biology with the do-it-all attitude of modern society leads us to take on more roles in our lives than ever before, and expect others to do the same.* We're supposed to have impressive and fulfilling careers, happy and nourishing relationships, strong and flexible bodies, fun and well-cared-for friendships, unique hobbies, stylish wardrobes, age-defying beauty routines, healthy gut-microbiomes, well-kept homes, a keen interest in politics/books/films/TV/music/the environment/AI and so on . . . And then, to further complicate things, in our world of opportunity and choice there's the omnipresent reminder of everything you're *not* doing – *I could be learning a new language right now with an app on my phone – why aren't I doing that!? Why am I so unproductive?*

It is, quite frankly, bloody exhausting.

The reality is that not everything can, or should, be a priority. When we're struggling to get those metaphorical golf balls in the jar, when life feels too crowded with sand, it's often because we're trying to prioritise too much.† The antidote then, is to see where and how we can prioritise better and for this I recommend a two-stage approach . . .

1. Minimise the amount of logistical and physical overwhelm – that is, change your external life.
2. Minimise the amount of *felt* overwhelm – that is, change your internal life.

We'll look at both, but before we do, have a think about some possible causes of *your* feelings of overwhelm. What's triggering you to feel like everything's too much? Is there anything (or anyone) in particular that's tipping you over the edge from 'regular level of expected busy' to 'drowning in my own life'? Write them down if you like (writing down a source of overwhelm has been proven to be helpful in combatting it), but even if you choose not to, hopefully even just thinking about them has given you a speck of clarity.

With that in mind, let's get into how to manage and minimise your triggers. First up, how to combat overwhelm in the physical and logistical realm, aka . . .

---

*Making us both a casualty and perpetrator of the overwhelm.
†Reminder: *You cannot do it all, but you can do a lot!*

PRIORITISE THIS

CHANGING YOUR EXTERNAL LIFE

In March 2022 I ran a workshop at a leadership retreat in London for one of my favourite corporate clients (I know, I shouldn't have favourites!) – the sales department of a global hospitality company. The US team had flown over, which took us to a group of 20 or so in total. To keep the retreat intimate, they held it at the home of one of the senior team members, rather than their office – it was a beautiful, unseasonably warm day, so we ended up in the garden.

As we sat in a circle on throws and pillows tossed on the lawn, I covered some of the topics in this book through a 'corporate' lens. Over the course of three hours (broken up with tea breaks) I ran through exercises and techniques to help with minimising the impact of stress, increasing openness and trust among the team, improving productivity using mindfulness and combatting cognitive overload and overwhelm in the workplace.

Attending this retreat was M, a woman in her late twenties who I'd worked with via the company for over three years. She's brilliant – open, receptive, smart. Everything you'd want from a member of your team. And yet, towards the end of the session, when we began discussing how to prevent burnout, M said something that made my jaw drop.

'I never switch off my phone . . . ever. I keep it on, next to my bed, all night.'

It wasn't the first time I'd heard this from someone, but still, it surprised me, and, by the looks on some the faces in the group, it surprised many of them too.

M's explanation was understandable: she's from Australia, her whole family lives on the other side of the world and she wanted to be available for them. I asked how often they called at night, and she replied 'never'. I then asked how often she was awoken or disturbed by random messages and notifications. 'Far more', she answered.

THE SMARTPHONE PROBLEM

I won't go into a full rant here on the importance of good sleep hygiene for managing stress and overwhelm (flip to Chapter 1: Stress if that's what you're after), I'll just repeat what I said to M, which is that your smartphone applies undue pressure to your nervous system that shouldn't be carried with you through the night. (It's bad enough having it all day.)

There are plenty of ways to silence the notifications on your phone while keeping yourself available for emergencies. If, like M, you don't know about them, please familiarise yourself – start with *Do Not Disturb* and go from there. I use notification blockers on my phone not just at night but also throughout the day – if I'm writing, for example, I'm only disturbed by calls from those on my 'favourites' list. (Yes, I *am* using one right now!)

Sleep hygiene aside, how *is* your relationship with your smartphone? The small device that's permanently in your hand, pocket or bag, and is, *by its very nature*, overwhelming. Remember, the apps on your phone or device are there for your time and attention – that's how tech companies make their money, and so they hire thousands of people whose job it is to ensure you engage with them as often as possible. It's *your* job not to. But, because smartphones are highly addictive, most people (me included) need to be reminded now and then.

FOUR QUESTIONS TO AUDIT YOUR PHONE USE

1. How and when do I engage with my phone?
2. Does it have free rein in my life?
3. Do I *always* carry it with me from room to room?
4. Is it adding to my sense of overwhelm?

If the answer to any of these is yes, I'd imagine you are a human person, and I'd also imagine you'd benefit from some digital boundaries . . . Stop checking your email and the apps every ten seconds. Turn off your social media and email notifications, unless you *really* need them for work – in which case switch them off on the weekends or whenever possible.* Try a brick phone, or use app blockers and the like to limit the time you spend scrolling. Put your phone on *Do Not Disturb* when working, sleeping or spending quality time with loved ones. Put your phone in another room whenever possible. Put your phone in a box and bury it in the garden . . .

---

*Oh, and don't worry too much about missing anything on socials. While you may forget your own parent's birthday, you're unlikely to forget to open a social media app if you already look at it frequently – we are so dependent on these apps, mindlessly opening them whether we're notified to do so or not.

Okay fine, maybe not the last one, but all the rest is incredibly obvious stuff that we all *know* we should do. The question is: *are you doing it?*

Overwhelm is complex but, on a simple level, smartphones make it worse. The sand the 'Reddit professor' speaks of – smartphones can easily become nothing but that. Minimising the amount of space your phone is permitted in your day and your life,* setting boundaries around your use, is the first step in getting those golf balls in the jar. Once you've done that, it's time to roll out those boundaries elsewhere . . .

The subject of boundaries is something clients often bring up in their initial session. Now I don't *think* this is because I attract clients who struggle with boundaries. I believe it's because we *all* struggle with boundaries, our brains and lives making them hard to set and adhere to, full stop. And yet they are *crucial* to feeling less stretched; it's only by protecting our time and energy, learning to assert our needs, saying no (see Chapter 3: Saying No) and drawing vital lines for ourselves that we can begin to feel more in control and less overwhelmed.

Following on from smartphones, social media and messaging apps are a good place to start . . . Here's a three-step checklist to help you regain some sovereignty over those spaces:

1. Set aside some time (10–30 minutes) to trawl through Instagram, LinkedIn, TikTok, Facebook, YouTube and any other social apps you use.
2. Remove, unfollow or mute people whom you don't remember meeting or who constantly post annoying/negative/unhelpful stuff.
3. Move on to WhatsApp – leave, mute or archive people or groups who are no longer relevant or who make you feel bad.

MULTITASKING AND THE SWITCH COST

I wouldn't be surprised if you're reading or listening to this chapter while doing something else. After all, technology has made it hard (strange even!) to focus on one thing at a time. Information comes at us from all directions, our phones ping incessantly, distraction is always one tap away. Everything vies for our focus and attention, and in a world of plenty, it's hard to choose. We juggle multiple devices, flick

---

*Refer to Chapter 2: Habits for some tips on breaking your habits around your phone.

between apps, keep endless tabs open. Even meetings and lectures – once immersive and in-person – are now on video, making it easy to be doing something else at the same time. Honestly, can you even remember the last time you watched TV without your phone somewhere nearby?

This ability to multitask, to seemingly 'effortlessly' swap from one thing to the next, is human nature. The fact that we can flexibly shift between what requires our attention has enabled us to thrive as a species, and we're pretty good at it as a result.* Our brains are built to be flexible. But that flexibility comes at a cost.

In fact, studies consistently show that the human brain is *incapable* of multitasking, that we cannot work on more than one cognitive task at a time.[3] What we think of as 'multitasking' is actually *task-switching*. And this incurs what psychology professor Anthony Sali calls a 'switch-cost' – the cognitive effort it takes to disengage from one task and reorientate to another. When you swap tasks, your brain has to store what you were just doing, refocus its attention and pick up the new thread. That transition burns through brainpower and drains attention, and the more these things are depleted, the more overwhelmed we begin to feel. We *think* we're saving time, but the research shows we almost always take *longer* and perform *worse* than if we'd done one thing at a time.[4]

How easily we switch is linked to something called *cognitive flexibility*, and it varies from person to person. In general, we're more flexible in young adulthood and less so with age – but this only applies to new situations (can't beat experience!). Our ability to switch increases in high-demand situations (like caring for a baby or navigating an unfamiliar airport), but declines when tasks require deep focus – like writing an article or having a meaningful conversation.

Importantly, *switch cost is highest when the tasks draw on the same mental resources* – for example, replying to emails while writing a report. Tasks that engage different brain networks tend to be less disruptive, which is why I can listen to piano music while writing but would struggle to watch TV instead.

So what's the takeaway? When it comes to cognitive flexibility, we're looking for a balance between too little and too much.† We don't

---

*Fun fact: 93 percent of people say they can multitask 'better than or as well as' the average person, which is, of course, statistically impossible . . .

†Attention-deficit/hyperactivity disorder (ADHD) can be thought of as persistent levels of high flexibility.

need to eliminate all switching – our brains are designed to flex – but *constant* switching will teach your brain to expect interruption, weakening your ability to focus and increasing feelings of depletion and overwhelm.*

To train your brain to multitask less and focus more, ask yourself:

- Do I *really* need to check my email or socials right now?
- What am I prioritising by switching my attention?
- Will this switch support or sabotage my goal?
- Can this wait ten minutes / one hour / until I finish what I'm doing?

Focus is a skill, and, like any other, it gets stronger the more you practise it. A few exercises or techniques in the book or online that can support this include Mindfulness meditation (Chapter 1: Stress, online – go to the Prioritise This website) and creating a to-don't list (Chapter 3: Saying No).

STUFF

I grew up surrounded by *things*. At my parents' home there were books, records and small knick-knacks everywhere. My maternal grandmother, whom I lived with intermittently over the years,† was a hoarder of genuinely epic proportions. It took us a year to clear out her house after she died. Either as a reaction or a predisposition, I naturally seek some degree of minimalism in my life. I'm not extreme: I don't have a 30-item capsule wardrobe, I keep most books I read, and have clung stubbornly to a few pairs of unfathomably high heels from when I worked in fashion that I doubt I could even stand up in today. But, *in general*, I like clearing and sorting – I could watch those weird videos of people tidying their wardrobes all day and do a home clear-out a

---

*Interestingly, studies have shown that multitasking also appears to affect our metacognition – that is, our ability to monitor our own performance. This essentially leads us to think we're doing a good job at something even if we're not, for example texting while driving.

†Most memorably when my parents grounded me for two weeks for walking down to Camden Lock at age 12 and getting a second hole pieced in my ear after being told not to. I just moved in to my grandparents' instead – my grandmother fed me chicken soup and took me shopping at C&A. Not quite what my parents had in mind, but an excellent 'grounded' experience for me!

couple of times a year myself. Clutter makes me uneasy, and I truly believe that, when it comes to feeling less overwhelmed, we should never underestimate the impact of a good old-fashioned clear-out on the brain (also, science agrees[5]). Our spaces are an extension of us, and by clearing them, we clear out ourselves too. Fewer things and less clutter equal less overwhelm on the eyes *and* the mind.

I recognise that not everyone is a natural de-clutterer, and I've worked with many clients who aren't either. In my experience you can train yourself to become more comfortable with it and there are numerous methods out there to help, from Marie Kondo to Swedish death cleaning. I won't, however, waste your time or my publisher's ink delving into them here – if you require well-defined guidance or a plan, seek out one of the million excellent, detailed blog posts out there. When you're ready, don't try to tackle everything at once as that might overwhelm your brain. Make it simple and doable by picking one place to start. Here are some ideas of where that could be . . .

- Wardrobe
- Fridge
- Documents
- Any room in your home
- Any drawer in any room in your home
- Any box in any drawer in any room in your home
- Digital devices
- Your inbox (not just in terms of opening and deleting unread emails but also unsubscribing from those that don't add to your life).

Next, move on to (or into) the real world . . . Make a list of the people you spend the most time with (family, friends, colleagues, etc.) and ask yourself the following . . .

FOUR QUESTIONS TO AUDIT YOUR RELATIONSHIPS

1. Is this a balanced, healthy relationship? (That is: 'Does this person respect my time, refrain from talking about me behind my back, listen to me and avoid only going on about themselves?')

2. Does this person bring me joy? (That is: 'Am I excited to see them? Do I look forward to the time we spend together? Do I feel uplifted after I see them?')
3. Is this person good for me? (That is: 'Does this person support my choices and give me honest feedback? Do the activities we do together fit my desired lifestyle?')
4. Does this person lift me up? (That is: 'Does this person help me learn and develop, and support my growth? Am I the best version of myself when around them?')

I'm not saying immediately cut anyone out who doesn't meet these criteria (although if you find someone *very* toxic, then I recommend doing so, if possible). Rather, I'm inviting you to examine the relationships in your life: to consider the idea that we are the average of the five people we spend the most time with, and think deeply as to how you can better surround yourself with people who (as much as possible) nourish rather than drain you. While some of my hardest relationships and friendships have taught me a huge amount about myself and how I want to show up in the world (and I'd never change that), I see a sharp difference between a person who challenges you (good thing) and a person who drags you down (less good thing). Conflict and adversity are how we build resilience and develop as people, but there's a limit – a line that only you can discover and draw for yourself. There's that famous saying about how someone can be in your life for a reason, a season or a lifetime. Don't cling to the reason or season relationships if they're no longer working for you. Let your answers to the four questions above, and how you *feel* about your answers, guide your next steps.

Bear in mind, however, that when you establish boundaries around your time and energy (particularly if you haven't done much of that before), not everyone will like it. As I wrote in Chapter 3: Saying No, part of setting boundaries is being okay with others not agreeing with your behaviour or actions, of being prepared to potentially disappoint them. The two questions to ask yourself are:

1. Do *I* like my behaviour or actions?
2. In not setting boundaries, am I disappointing *myself*?[*]

---

[*] Remember, an outward yes can easily be an inward no and vice versa.

Life is a push–pull between the things we want to do and those we don't, between the people we wish to see and those we wish to see . . . less. We all have obligations, and I'm not recommending you ignore people or ruthlessly cut them out from your life. Rather, I'm inviting you to press *unsubscribe* on certain people and/or their issues; to seek out the boundaries that will make the *biggest* difference to your overwhelm or stress. Establish them, and then be kind but firm in maintaining them (Chapter 3: Saying No will help with this). Remember: the boundary doesn't have to last for ever; it can be a temporary measure until you feel less overwhelmed or the relationship morphs into something more positive. In the meantime, remind yourself that it's there to protect your most precious resources: your time, energy and attention. It's there to protect *you*.

Once we've tackled the obvious but impactful external factors that add to our sense of overwhelm – app notifications, other people's toxic behaviours, clutter and so on – it's time to turn the mirror inwards, to look at how our *own* thoughts and habits are adding to our sense of overwhelm in life, aka . . .

CHANGING YOUR INTERNAL LIFE

In January 2021 the online 'wellness' influencers were out in force, pushing green juice, gluten-free pasta (remember spiralising courgette and calling it spaghetti? That was grim) and more supplements than one person could ever find the time to swallow. As someone recovering from an eating disorder,[*] while pregnant with my second child and trying to follow intuitive eating (IE), I found it toxic and scary. Also, my father was very unwell, which made me particularly conscious of our (read: *my*) capacity to obsess over the 'health' (often simply a cover for *thinness*) of our bodies while neglecting to consider that of our minds.

Of course, it's natural to feel a drive to overhaul your wellbeing in the new year after the excess of the holiday season. And I think in January 2021 the desire to 'get healthy' was stronger than ever, given we were still stumbling through lockdowns with their accompanying (legitimate) health fears and concerns. But emails were flooding my inbox from (well-meaning) PRs extorting the detoxing virtues of juice

---

[*] I think to some extent I'll always be in recovery, in the same way someone in AA might consider themselves in recovery for life.

cleanses, and all I wanted to reply was: *the body is good at detoxing itself! If it wasn't, we wouldn't have survived as a species – the liver does nothing but detox, 24/7. You know what's terrible at detoxing itself!? Your MIND.*

But instead of replying to any of them directly, I, in what some *might* call a passive aggressive move, wrote a blog post titled: 'Do you need a mental health detox?' The below is an expansion of that post, with all the additional things I've learned about the brain, stress and overwhelm over the past five years added in.*

DO YOU NEED A MENTAL HEALTH DETOX?

The brain, *your brain*, likes to hold on to thoughts.

No, obviously, not the ones you *actually* need such as the PIN for your credit card or the date of your anniversary – those it's more than happy to let go. What it likes to cling to, however, are the thoughts that cause us pain or worry. In evolutionary terms this makes sense: you stay alive by remembering what's painful – for example, a burn from a lit match leads you to avoid getting too close to fire when you encounter it in the future.

Works brilliantly with matches . . . but not always so well with our thoughts.

Many of us cling to thoughts and beliefs from negative experiences (break-ups, losses, trauma) long after we've made sense of the experience, learned from and processed it.† We also all have the general, habitual, pain-avoidant thought patterns‡ that develop through life – self-criticism, catastrophising or constant worry – which not only clutter our brain but can lead us to feel overwhelmed by even the smallest setback or concern. In my experience, these are not thoughts that your brain will easily 'detox' on its own. It needs a bit of help . . .

---

*Lest I get some flak for this, I feel I should mention I'm not against juice detoxes per say. I've done a five-day one in the middle of winter, which made me *absolutely* miserable, and a three-day one in June, which was fine. I know people who swear by them, but I don't think they're great for me right now as they seem to trigger the pathways in my brain around restriction. If you are keen to try one, please talk to your doctor or GP first.
†If you haven't yet processed something (and processing it doesn't mean never feeling sad or angry about it ever again) and it's been many years, this might be something to discuss with a trained professional who can help you move forward. See the Resources at the end of this book.
‡See the discussion of SITs in Chapter 1: Stress.

OVERWHELM

FOUR QUESTIONS TO AUDIT YOUR THOUGHTS

1. Do I frequently worry about things that haven't even happened yet, and probably never will?
2. Do I regularly catastrophise or blow things out of proportion?
3. Do I constantly obsess over what other people think of me? (E.g. replaying that time an unpleasant colleague slighted you in front of the office, or a friend didn't treat you kindly.)
4. Does a past relationship take up far too much of my brain/heart space?

If you answered yes to any of the above, you're not alone.

We *all* think *all* these thoughts, to some degree, some of the time. It's natural to worry about life and what others think of us.* In my experience, the key to not letting these unhelpful thought patterns bed down in your mind for good is relatively simple: challenge them, regularly. When we become more aware of our thoughts, when we shine a light to stop them festering in the dark or question their helpfulness and legitimacy, they begin to lose their strength.

We covered thought repatterning extensively in Chapter 1: Stress, so if you haven't yet read that section, I suggest taking a glance now. What I'll say here, though, in the context of better managing overwhelm, is that in order to do so, it's crucial to investigate any thoughts or beliefs that may be contributing to your feelings of overwhelm and look at how you can challenge and replace them. Remember, you can't control what's going to happen to you, what other people will say or do, or what life will pile on your plate. What you can control, however, is how you think about and approach your life. So, ask yourself:

1. Which thoughts are adding to my feelings of overwhelm?
2. Which thoughts would help lessen those feelings instead?

As I mention a few times in this book, I'm against *extreme* positive thinking – I think it can be toxic at best and dangerous at worst.

---

*We will explore the specific impact of our 'social brain' on our thoughts about relationships in Chapter 7: Rejection.

However, in my work as a positive psychology coach, I've seen first-hand the impact a balanced positive approach can make to someone's life, as well as to my own...

In September 2020, during the brief break between lockdowns, I found out I was pregnant with our second child. Five days later, my father collapsed on the kitchen floor in our home and was rushed to hospital. We weren't allowed to be with him because of COVID, but a few hours (that felt like days) later, his medical team called and told us they'd found a large mass in his brain. It was stage 4 glioblastoma, and the next few years of our lives became both chaotic and terrifying, with seizures and psychotic episodes and me often driving to my parents to greet emergency workers in the middle of the night.

It was a lot, by anyone's standards – to be pregnant and navigating this while also trying to parent my other child and keep my business afloat (plus, pandemic). My nervous system was in severe overdrive, with what felt like cortisol flooding my body at all times. I was barely sleeping; I couldn't think straight.

It was a challenging experience, to be growing a baby while losing a parent, and I wouldn't wish it on anyone. However, while it was hugely difficult, I began to notice after a few months that, however hard it may have been, I was making it worse, with my *thoughts*.

I was *constantly* telling myself that I was overwhelmed, that it was too much, that it wasn't fair. And the more I told myself that, the more it reinforced my reality and stopped me from finding solace in the quieter, joyful moments (of which there were many). Understandably, I'd worked myself up into a state. And, of course, those around me reinforced it; constant sympathy poured from all directions – friends, partner, colleagues, midwives and emergency responders alike. However, the more I told myself I was overwhelmed, the more overwhelmed I felt. I *knew* this from stress coaching – that constantly telling yourself you feel stressed is a great way to feel more stressed. I'd coached others for years using the principle that (to some degree) our thoughts create our reality, that our emotions are constructed. But I was too deep in my own experience (in my *pain*) to realise this at first...

When I *was* able to put down my thoughts of overwhelm, to say to myself: *life is a lot right now, but you have the tools to deal with it... What can I do to support you?* I fared better. I didn't ignore the pain, or the real-life stressors, but I stopped focusing on them quite so much. I gave them less airtime.

Now while my example is intense, it can easily be applied to the general overwhelm we all encounter: when the mental or physical load of life feels unbearably heavy, but you can't change your situation, my advice is to find the thoughts that will lighten the load.

THREE QUESTIONS TO ASK YOURSELF TO REDUCE OVERWHELM

1. Out of everything that's happening in my life right now, what will I still care about this time next year? (I.e. what is essential to my well-being, and what is superfluous?)
2. What can I do to support myself right now? (I.e. what do I need?)
3. What one thing could I take off my plate to make myself feel better?

I know that, when I'm feeling overwhelmed, these questions help me remember what's *actually* important. The answers make me feel held and give me a sense of agency and perspective. They help me realise that it doesn't matter if my to-do list falls apart and I feed my children pasta pesto for the nth time this week.* All that matters is finding a way to a place where (in the *future*) I feel and behave more like myself.

HABITS, RITUALS AND ROUTINES

Speaking of behaving like yourself, we can't look at overwhelm without glancing at the subject of habits . . . After all, our life is made up of our habits, rituals and routines – some of which lessen our sense of overwhelm, others that add to it. My daily meditation habit, for example, contributes to my feelings of wellbeing throughout the day (and also improves my focus which improves my productivity which means I get more done and therefore feel less overwhelmed – it has a positive ripple effect). Swiping through social media influencers' profiles, however, never fails to make me feel *more* overwhelmed as I compare my intermittently chaotic life to some perfectly curated version online. Make a list in your head or scribble down your regular habits, then ask yourself the following questions:

---

*Hot tip: Lowering your own standards is a great way to feel less overwhelmed!

PRIORITISE THIS

1. Is this habit good for me?
2. Is this habit aligned with my priorities, with what's important to me?
3. Do I enjoy this or am I doing it out of habit or social pressure?
4. Does this habit make my life feel busy in a positive or negative way?

You'll find clear guidance on how to change or create a habit in Chapter 2: Habits, so, as with thought-repatterning, I won't delve into it here. However, in essence, the aim of these four questions is to help you identify the regular behaviours and actions that may be contributing to your sense of overwhelm. In sum: when you catch yourself doing something simply because it's a habit, stop and consider whether it's helping you and/or if it's what you *actually* want to be doing in that moment.

Finally, since we're on the subject of habits, it's worth considering whether building a few of them into a daily routine might help ease feelings of overwhelm. Research shows that routine and rituals (i.e. doing a handful things in roughly the same order each day) can reduce stress and anxiety by providing structure, predictability and a sense of control. Anecdotally, I've seen this play out time and again: when clients establish even the most basic routine, their world tends to feel more manageable. A rough schedule can make daily life feel less hectic and minimise decision fatigue – the mental exhaustion that builds from having to make too many choices in a day – which lightens the load of overwhelm. You could also include here decision-saving habits such as laying out your clothes for the next day the night before or writing your to-do list for the following day at the end of the day.*

WHAT CAN I ADD?

When we're feeling overwhelmed, stressed or even mildly anxious, our natural instinct is to think about what to *take away* from life. What to eliminate to free up our time, energy or attention. And indeed, yes: so far I *have* asked you to focus on just that.

However, often the things we remove aren't actually the unhelpful things covered here, but instead are those that are keeping us mentally, emotionally, physically or spiritually afloat. We cancel plans with friends,

---

*For more on decision-making I strongly recommend Adrienne Adhami's book *Decisions That Matter*, which is included in the Resources section at the back.

skip the gym, miss bedtime with the kids, give up reading that novel . . . We do what we can to streamline life by taking away what feels 'extra' or burdensome. But, in doing so, we truly throw the baby out with the bathwater. The things that nourish your body and mind create the difference between understanding that your job has a lot of stressors and feeling stressed and overwhelmed by your job all the time. Movement-based practices, hobbies and supportive relationships have all been proven to be panaceas to stress and overwhelm.[6] So, although the majority of this chapter has focused on decluttering your mind and life, I now invite you to ask: *who or what do I need to cling on to or add back in?*

I work pro bono with a domestic violence charity, both one to one with the women and non-binary people who seek its services and in group settings giving stress-management talks to the case workers and volunteers that support them. In a recent workshop with the volunteers who answer the emergency call lines (an objectively emotionally challenging task), they asked for advice around how to switch off after a shift. I immediately spun the question round and asked: *what enables you to switch off?* Each of them gave a different answer, but they all revolved around the themes of movement, music or time with supportive friends/family. I then simply asked how often they were doing that thing, to which many replied not often. We then looked at how they could schedule in that thing (or a watered-down version of it) following a difficult call to help them reset.

What about you? Who and what helps recharge your batteries and restore your mental energy? What helps you switch off? *What do you need to add back in?*

IN THE MOMENT

While writing this chapter *I* became overwhelmed. (The irony!)

I had a deadline to meet, a workshop for two hundred people to deliver, coursework for my neuroscience training, a retreat to sell and plan, an issue to fix with my business bank account,* and, as if that wasn't enough, my son came down with a temperature and was off nursery for the week, while our nanny was away . . .

None of this is particularly shocking – life is busy and chaotic; we all have heavy workloads and kids, dogs, friends or selves that fall ill. Life will always behave just like life!

---

*A new addition to my skillset: I can now sing, in full, the hold music for Barclays' telephone helpline.

But the experience of feeling overwhelmed while writing about how to feel less overwhelmed got me thinking about what I do to manage overwhelm *in the moment*. When the advice of 'declutter your inbox and detox your thoughts' doesn't land, because the mere suggestion just adds to the mental and logistical load of living.

So, if life has come at you hard and you can't change that and need an immediate solution, let me offer what I ask myself when in that boat... First: *what's the top priority?* And second: *what's the one thought or action I can prioritise in this moment to make myself feel better?**

This is what makes me feel *immediately* less overwhelmed. This is how I control my little corner of the world the best I can, while knowing that I have little control in the world at large. I think: *low effort, high impact*. I ask myself: what's the *one thing* you can take off or add to your plate that would change how you feel? What would have the biggest effect on your health and wellbeing, on your ability to show up for yourself and your family? How can you *undo your to-do list*,† to create space in the moment so you can think and act with better clarity going forward? *What can you do?*

And now... what to do when it feels like you have *two* top priorities?

What if you're staring at a pair of same-sized golf balls, and you can't for the life of you figure out which one to place in the jar first?

My advice is this: focus on both as best you can, but choose one to make *slightly* more important *just for now*. Remind yourself it won't hold that position for the rest of your life – as I mentioned in the Introduction, this is the essence of *seasonal balance*: letting one thing take the lead for a while, without assuming it always will. Remember: balance is unbalance.

This is something I have to do with my children from time to time. For a few weeks, work might become the slightly bigger golf ball – even though my children are, and always will be, my ultimate priority. Even though I would drop everything for them in a heartbeat, sometimes, honestly, they come a gentle second. That's *my* version of balance. And while I feel guilty about it sometimes, I try to soften those feelings by reminding myself that I'm showing my kids something important: what it means to be a real person with competing priorities, wants

---

*I'm aware there are *a lot* of questions in this chapter ... However, interrogating ourselves – probing our thoughts, relationships and habits – is the *best* system I've found for creating change.
†Remember: It's there to serve you, not the other way around.

OVERWHELM

and responsibilities. When broadcaster, presenter, author, media polymath (and all-round wonderful person and friend) Amol Rajan came on *Priorities* back in 2020, he spoke of the 'The Four Hobs of Life' theory,* which I find immensely helpful to draw on in times in like this. The theory likens life to a stove with four burners representing family, friends, health and work, and it suggests that to be successful in one area you need to sacrifice another (and to be world-class, maybe even two). In life, sometimes you *have* to turn down the heat on one of the burners to stop the whole thing from setting on fire.

So, if you're holding two golf balls, pick one.

Don't destroy yourself trying to force them both into the jar at the same time. Choose a lead, and a close second. And if later you realise you picked the wrong one – something that happens to all of us – be kind to yourself. Say sorry if you need to, adjust where you can, learn from that experience and aim to do it differently next time.

It feels like every day we are bombarded with a million things, presented with ever more complex challenges at a near relentless pace. There's no way we can respond to or deal with them all. It's completely normal to sometimes feel overwhelmed by the stress and competing responsibilities in your life. One of the keys to robust mental health is accepting that sometimes everything *will* seem like too much. Sometimes it *will* feel as if you're not on top of your priorities, as if your jar is full of sand.

Short-term overwhelm is to be expected and can generally be managed and overcome using the techniques in this chapter, as well as *rest*. However, overwhelm shouldn't be your default. If it's persistent (i.e. lasts more than a few months), it can lead to burnout, and chronic overwhelm will require more than this book can offer. In those cases, I'd recommend personalised support.† And, whatever you do, try to focus on kind and supportive thoughts – negative self-criticism is not only more likely to add to your sense of overwhelm, but also, from a neuro-biological perspective, it interrupts the neural networks in your brain that can help you figure out how to best navigate a busy and challenging time.[7]

As I wrote in the Introduction, while each chapter in this book is its own one-man show, the others serve as supporting actors. If your

---

*It's officially known as the Four Burners theory and is attributed to humourist David Sedaris, who popularised it in a 2009 *New Yorker* article.
†You'll find Resources to help with this at the back of this book.

feelings of overwhelm are related to boundaries, Chapter 3: Saying No, will be of help. If they're stress related, Chapter 1: Stress, will be your first point of call. If you struggle to start or complete tasks and are overwhelmed by that, then the next chapter – Chapter 5: Procrastination – will help you understand and curb your procrastination and work more effectively and smarter, to gain some control over your brain, your inbox and your life.

Finally, for the past eight years I've had a reminder on my phone that pops up every day at 11 a.m. It reads: *you have time to do everything that's important to you.*

I definitely don't always feel that way, but it's a good reminder of what's essential and what can safely fall by the wayside.

So, for now, forget the sand and prioritise your golf balls. Ask yourself: what's the *one thing* can I do or think in this moment to feel better?

And then do it.

PRIORITISE THIS

- Overwhelm is a natural response to a world your brain wasn't built for.
- You can't prioritise everything; focus on what really matters.
- Multitasking drains your energy and increases overwhelm.
- Simplify your life: look at your phone noise, clutter and any boundaries that need strengthening.
- Challenge the thoughts that make everything feel too much.
- Pick a lead priority – balance can be seasonal.
- Instead of just cutting back, add in what restores you.

PRACTICES TO HELP WITH OVERWHELM

THE PRIORITIES MATRIX

I did not, sadly, name or come up with this tool. But it is one of my favourites – in fact, it's written on a Post-it note that's permanently stuck to wall in my office (I can see it right now). Sometimes referred to as the 'Eisenhower Matrix' – because US president Dwight Eisenhower came up with it – this simple yet effective technique helps with two of the most common struggles we all face: decision fatigue and prioritisation.

As you'll see in the image below, the matrix is divided into four quadrants that categorise tasks based on **urgency** and **importance**. Grab a piece of paper, draw out the grid, and start sorting your own tasks and commitments into each square.*

Important–Urgent	Urgent–Not Important
Important–Not Urgent	Not Important–Not Urgent

For example, for my day today: writing this book sits in Important–Urgent (top left quadrant), planning something longer-term like updating my website falls in Important–Not Urgent (lower left), buying my kids' toothpaste falls in Urgent–Not Important (top right). And if something falls into my Not Important–Not Urgent (bottom right) then I either delegate it or take it off my to-do list altogether.

---

*Or download a free one from the Prioritise This website.

Once your matrix is filled in, use it to guide your workflow – roughly in the order you'd expect:

1. **Urgent–Important:** do these first. Now, ideally. These are the tasks that move the needle *and* need immediate attention. If you've been putting any of these off, start here.
2. **Not Important–Not Urgent:** these are often time-fillers, distractions or tasks done out of obligation or habit. Delegate if you can. If not, let them go.
3. **Urgent–Not Important:** these tend to be the small-but-loud things – emails, errands, requests from others. Batch and move through these quickly, so they don't drain your energy or distract you from what matters most.
4. **Important–Not Urgent:** this is the quadrant I want you to really pay attention to. It's where big ideas, meaningful goals and longer-term priorities linger, often for far too long. These are the things you *say* you want to do but never quite get around to. And the longer you don't prioritise them, the easier it is for other, more urgent (but less important) things to take their place.

So, ask yourself:

- If this really matters to me, how can I bring more urgency to it?
- Could I carve out an hour a day for the next two weeks?
- What might shift if I did?

If it's a priority to you, find a way to *prioritise it*.

BRAIN DUMP

From unconscious beliefs about the world to a simple grocery list, we accumulate a remarkable amount of mental clutter over the course of a day, a week . . . and a lifetime! And at some point, it all starts to feel like too much.

One of the best ways to reduce that feeling is also one of the simplest: write it down. (And by that, I mean physically write – on paper. If you insist, use a Word document, but try not to use your phone.) Whether it's a problem you're struggling to make sense of, a goal that you're scared to pursue or a child's weekly schedule, getting it down offers a sense of clarity and serves as a pressure valve for your life.

In coaching we call this technique a 'brain dump'. Think of it like those celebrity 'What's in my bag?' videos. You tip out the contents of your mind in the same way they dump out the contents of their (let's be honest, *highly* curated) handbags. (Just less lipstick sponsorship, more mental clarity.)

This practice helps make sense not only of your to-do list but also of more abstract thoughts and worries. It stops you feeling like you have to keep track of everything in your head and brings actuality to half-formed plans and ideas. It helps you tackle your concerns, reduce stress and cognitive overload, free up brainpower and relax your mind. So, the next time you feel overwhelmed, grab a piece of paper and tip that bag upside down.

How it works:

1. Grab a pen and paper.
2. Choose your focus: a specific goal or task (a looming work project), a general topic (turning 30) or something persistent that bothers you (your inbox, a tricky co-worker).
3. Write down everything swirling around in your head about that topic. Stressors, thoughts, worries, tasks, half-baked ideas – get down all the mental clutter.
4. Keep writing until you feel like you can breathe a bit easier.
5. Now, either look at your list, identify what's leading to feelings of overwhelm (the biggest stressor) and make an actionable plan.
6. Or, do nothing! Sometimes just acknowledging what's there is enough to take the weight out of it.

BODY SHAKE

This may sound like something you'd order at a fast-food restaurant, but it's actually a somatic practice that works brilliantly for overwhelm, stress and general moments of emotional discomfort or dysregulation. It's also ideal for when you're struggling to wake up or feel sluggish in the middle of the day.

Rooted in Qigong (a traditional Chinese mind-body practice), the idea is to clear energetic and emotional blockages quickly – shaking things out, quite literally. I use it when I feel like I'm embodying that *Cambridge Dictionary* definition of overwhelm: BE TOO MUCH.

I first learned it from an 80-year-old Irish shiatsu master named Betty, when we lived in neighbouring huts on a beach in India. She was one of the most inspiring, fascinating people I've ever met – sharp, grounded and full of life. She practised this every morning, and looked and moved like someone at least 30 years younger – so I feel like there's definitely something there . . .

How it works:

- Stand with your back straight and feet hip-width apart, arms relaxed by your sides.
- Keeping your body soft, begin to gently bounce your knees, allowing the movement to ripple through the rest of your body.
- Gradually let the shake grow – still keeping your feet on the floor – letting your arms swing loosely from side to side as you bounce.
- Continue for around three minutes. Then stop, close your eyes and be still for a few breaths. Notice how you feel.

SHOULD I QUIT?

If you're wrestling with whether to give up something – a goal, a project, habit or commitment that's contributing to your overwhelm – a classic pros and cons list can be surprisingly helpful. Think of this as the grown-up version of the one you made in your teens when deciding whether to go on a date.

Pick the situation you're unsure about and work through the grid (or sketch it on a piece of paper). Make sure you fill in all eight quadrants, taking care to include both short- and long-term consequences. Be honest, be specific, and take your time to weigh up the real-life costs and benefits – on your energy, priorities and wellbeing.

Should I continue or quit _____?

(e.g. job, relationship, diet plan, drinking, exercise regime)

Extra practices – Worry window and Letting Go meditation – can both be found at www.prioritisethis.com/practices.

OVERWHELM

CONTINUE	QUIT
Benefits – immediate	Benefits – immediate
Benefits – long term	Benefits – long term
Costs – immediate	Costs – immediate
Costs – long term	Costs – long term

CHAPTER 5

Procrastination

• • •

'Hold every hour in your grasp. Lay hold of today's task, and you will not need to depend so much upon tomorrow's. While we are postponing, life speeds by.'

Seneca the Younger, Moral Letters to Lucilius

The first chapter I wrote in this book was Chapter 3: Saying No. My motivation was fairly straightforward – my most-read blog post to date is on the subject, clients often arrive with questions around boundaries and it's consistently one of my most requested corporate talks. I figured: *give the people what they want.*

The second chapter I'm writing is this one. And my reasoning here is similar – I'm *giving myself what I need.* Because while I am, by nature, an organised person – someone who likes to get things done, to not let others down and, as I've mentioned, *loves* a to-do list, I can still procrastinate with the best of them if given half a chance.

Case in point: this book. I was first approached about writing it in January 2022, almost three years to the day from when I'm sitting here typing now. There are valid reasons for the delay – the original publisher was bought out, and then my father became terminally ill, which didn't leave me in the headspace to write a book of this kind (or, frankly, of any kind).

But, honestly, I hid behind all that for too long. I found other important projects to focus on (search and ye will always find) while sidestepping the one that mattered most, because 1) it required a huge amount of work and 2) it had the biggest potential for failure.*

I'm glad I'm writing this book now, instead of then. I've gained more qualifications, worked with more clients and companies, launched a new business, experienced wins, faced failures ... I'm more equipped to write it today than I was three years ago – *I have more to give.*

However, I also don't want it to be *another* three years before it's complete. So, this is where I'm starting. And who knows? Maybe you're starting here too – perhaps even because you know you *should* start with habits but can't face that yet and so have decided to use this chapter on procrastination to ... procrastinate. If so, I applaud your ingenuity. Using procrastination to overcome procrastination is solid strategy.

We all procrastinate. It's a deeply human experience that's been around as long as we have. Aristotle used the word *akrasia* (which translates roughly as 'weakness of will') to describe that all-too-familiar experience of knowing what you *should* be doing but not doing it. That gap (or Mariana Trench-sized abyss) between intention and action.

The word 'procrastination' comes from the Latin *procrastinatus*, meaning 'till the next day'. To procrastinate literally means to put something off until tomorrow. But as we know, 'tomorrow' can take days, weeks, months, even years to arrive. If it arrives at all ...

At its core, procrastination usually arises from either a difficultly managing time or emotions (or, often, a combination of the two). Frequently, it's a way to regulate emotion – we avoid a task because it makes us feel anxious, overwhelmed, intimidated, bored, inadequate and so on. We prioritise short-term emotional relief over any potential future gains.

However, although procrastination may *initially* help us feel better, in the long run this approach increases stress.† [1] Any relief is short-lived; the task doesn't disappear. So, while we may *think* we're giving ourselves a break, all we're really doing is kicking that proverbial can down the road – until one can becomes many, and we're dragging them up a steep hill.‡

---

*There's a whole chapter on failure in this book, but since the fear of it is so interwoven with procrastination, we'll go into it here too. What fun!

† It's also linked to higher levels of depression and anxiety, although much more research is needed in this area, and it's all a bit chicken and egg – am I depressed because I keep procrastinating or am I procrastinating because I'm depressed? Like most things, it's often both.

‡ I'm thinking of the collection of cans that used to be tied to wedding cars here.

PROCRASTINATION

Sometimes we even procrastinate *knowingly*, despite being conscious of the consequences. We ignore a parking ticket, even though it'll cost us more later. This is simple avoidant self-soothing. It's just that, in turn, it becomes self-defeating . . .

A little procrastination is completely normal. You're not AI – you're human. And under certain conditions, it can be healthy, even helpful. However, it can also cost you in the long term. If you want to live a life aligned with your priorities and achieve your goals,* then learning to (mostly) curb your procrastination is vital.

This chapter will help you stop putting off what matters. We'll look at why we procrastinate (hint: it's your neurobiology) as well as the emotional habits that keep it going, and a wide range of tools to interrupt the cycle so that you can move forward.

And that range truly is wide. My experience with thousands of people (including many with neurodivergent brains) has taught me that, when it comes to procrastination, while a certain tool may be great for one person, it can be useless for another. That's why I've thrown the whole toolkit in here, and I feel certain that whatever your way of thinking, you'll find at least one, if not many more, that work for you.

WHY DO WE PROCRASTINATE?

Because we're lazy!

No, I'm kidding, obviously.

Procrastination has little to do with laziness. It isn't a sign of incompetence, or that you're not trying hard enough. The reality is, our brains are predisposed towards it.

Despite all those diagrams showing its various parts, your brain doesn't operate in neat, isolated compartments. It works through a network of systems and conversations, and these – just like conversations in real life – often have competing priorities. When it comes to procrastination, you're dealing with a long-standing internal debate between two opposing forces: 1) your brain wants immediate gratification – it prioritises pleasure and avoids pain, no matter the long-term consequences;

---

*Or just get things done!

and 2) it wants to plan ahead, regulate your impulses and make thoughtful choices that serve your life goals.

These forces are in constant conversation (and battle) – it's basically a broadsheet editor arguing with a tabloid one. They *fundamentally* believe in different things – one wants you to feel better right now (as in, five minutes ago); the other wants you to wade through discomfort in pursuit of long-term rewards.

And, ultimately, your brain's biological preferences mean that, in the battle, the instant gratification side is stacked. As you may recall from earlier chapters, your brain's two main priorities, aside from the not inconsequential one of staying alive, are to avoid discomfort and conserve energy – procrastination does both.

But, of course, evolutionary biology is just one piece of the puzzle. While we may be predisposed to procrastinate, how that tendency plays out is shaped by many factors – recent studies even found that your DNA could play a part.[2] That said, any possible 'procrastinating gene' is relevant (as with many other genes) only insofar as to the extent that any environmental factors in your life amplify or de-amplify it. In other words: how nurture affects nature. Whether you begin an important project as it's handed to you or the night before it's due is influenced by your upbringing, personality, neurodiversity, capacity for emotional regulation, the environment you exist in and even the fundamental building blocks of good brain health – sleep, nutrition, movement, connection and so on.

For example, take a moment to consider the norms around procrastination in your childhood? Were deadlines expected or ignored? What about now? Do you surround yourself with people who take action quickly or who always need 'just one more day'?* Cultural and social influences set an internal baseline for what's considered 'acceptable' behaviour. *Where does yours lie?*

Yet you're still an individual – and there are many personal, relatable reasons you might procrastinate, such as:

- **You feel bored.** The task doesn't spark your interest or feels too repetitive.
- **You feel intimidated.** You're not sure you have the skills or knowledge to pull it off.

---

* I know from a study of one (myself) that if I'm around friends who are tidy and do what they say they're going to do when they say they're going to do it, then I'm more likely to behave that way too.

PROCRASTINATION

- **You lack faith.** The goal feels out of reach or impossible, so you can't muster any strength to commit to it.
- **You feel anxious or scared.** Fear of failure, of judgement or of getting it wrong will all lead your brain to shy away.
- **You're a perfectionist.** If it can't be done 'right', it doesn't feel worth starting at all.*
- **You're a joy seeker.** If your priority in life is fun, dull or effortful tasks will always be shoved down the list.
- **You're overstimulated or distracted.** Your phone, your routine, your friends, your games, your cluttered desk. Too much input will wreck your focus.
- **You've created a habit.** Your brain has simply learned this loop. Which also means you can *unlearn* it.

The conditions for procrastination are perfect when an unpleasant task meets a perfectionist who is high in impulsivity and low in self-discipline. Yet, as I said at the beginning of the chapter, we *all* procrastinate. It's as unavoidable as death and taxes;† only the *degree* varies. In general, adults procrastinate less than children and students,[3] thanks in part to a fully matured prefrontal cortex – a brain area that significantly impacts thinking, planning and reasoning, all essential for combatting procrastination. As we age, emotional regulation, coping skills, conscientiousness and time perception all improve (as anyone over the age of 20 will know, the older we become the more we appreciate that time is limited).‡

However, there's also an important distinction to be made between a person who procrastinates – that is, every single human alive – and someone who is a *chronic procrastinator*, which experts believe make up between 20 and 25 percent of the population.§ [4] If you think that may be you, common signs include: procrastinating across many areas of life (work, admin, school, social, home), frequently putting things off and missing deadlines (daily or near daily), finding it hard to focus or follow through (even when you care about something), not learning

---

*Truth: nothing is ever perfect at the beginning, or at the end.
†Two other things we tend to desperately try to put off!
‡Younger people, including teenagers, tend to have a more abstract understanding of time. My children, who haven't quite grasped the concept yet, believe 'five minutes' is longer than 'one hour', which currently mostly works in my favour.
§This statistic rises to as high as 75 percent when applied to university students.

from past experiences,* and finally, possibly struggling with poor sleep, irregular eating patterns or general dysregulation.

In essence, chronic procrastination is the long-term tendency to *always* postpone things, rather than the tendency to postpone things for long periods of time. I may avoid my taxes until the last minute,† but since I do most everything else on time, I am simply procrastinating *on my taxes*. It's natural to postpone unwanted tasks now and then; always doing so indicates a chronic pattern.

If you fall into that category, this chapter can help. However, if you feel your procrastination is interfering with your relationships, work or wellbeing, you may benefit from additional support. Research has shown CBT (cognitive behavioural therapy) and CBC (cognitive behavioural coaching) to be effective for chronic procrastination.[5] If this resonates, see the Resources at the back of this book.

But, for now, keep reading. The next section is all about how to take action, even (or *especially*) when it feels impossible. Please know: you don't need to fix everything overnight, you just need to start *somewhere*.

THE ROLLERCOASTER

Before we dive into the tools and techniques to tackle procrastination (chronic or otherwise), let's briefly return to a simple but important driver of change we touched on earlier: *habit loops*.

As with *any* repeated behaviour, the more you procrastinate, the more entrenched a habit it becomes. The neural pathways strengthen – a loop forms when your brain starts linking 'I'll do it tomorrow' with momentary relief.

If you've already read Chapter 2: Habits, you'll recall the neurological structure of habit loops – *cue–craving–response–reward* – and how they can be rewired. Procrastination, too, can be unlearned. Sometimes all it takes is a single interruption to begin building a new loop, and,

---

*I think this point is particularly interesting – generally as humans we learn from our mistakes and reassess our approach accordingly. But for chronic procrastinators that feedback loop seems to be disrupted since the damage or stress that results from a delay doesn't teach them to start earlier next time. One explanation for this behavioural paradox relates to the *emotional component* of procrastination; that is, by always trying to relieve stress and discomfort in the moment, chronic procrastinators never quite figure out how to wade through that discomfort and relieve task-related stress in the long run.
†True story.

honestly, the simple act of telling yourself 'I am ready for a new, positive habit loop' is a good a place to start as any . . .

One of my clients arrived at a session clearly overwhelmed – his thoughts were scattered, and he was visibly anxious. After ten minutes of going around in circles, I asked, 'Is something weighing on you more than usual today?'

He paused, then admitted, 'There's this form I need to fill out for my child's school. Every time I think about it, I get anxious. So I keep putting it off. Now they've emailed me three times, and I'm worried they'll think I don't care.'

It was a classic example: the form felt intimidating which led him to put it off, but the longer he avoided it, the heavier it felt *and* the more he reinforced the idea that it was too much to handle. Yet the form was important for his child's education; it *needed* to be filled out.

'Shall we do it now?' I asked.

He hesitated. 'No. I'd be wasting your time and our session.'

'You're here because you want to feel more grounded and productive and less stressed,' I said. 'What could we do right now that might help achieve that?'

'Fill out the bloody form,' he replied, smiling.

So we did. Yes, there were stumbling blocks – forgotten passwords, broken links, the usual bureaucracy. But, by the end of the session, it was done. 'It was so big in my head,' he said. 'I always thought that at some point I'd want to do it, that I'd find the time.[*] But I never did. I feel so relieved. I feel so happy.'

That moment of doing the thing and feeling better afterwards created a new loop. One where the *reward* of completing the task (relief, pride, joy) outweighed the fleeting, *short-term relief* of avoidance.[†] He'd broken the cycle and, with it, unlocked a dopamine hit from the action itself.

After that, when faced with a task of that kind, he used his memory to fuel his motivation: *if I do this, I'll feel that again.* He created a new, *positive* habit loop.

---

[*] Studies have shown that we expect tasks to be less demanding or effortful in the future as opposed to the present, also known as *affecting forecasting*, and some neurocomputational work has linked this cognitive bias to activity signalled in the dorsomedial prefrontal cortex (https://www.nature.com/articles/s41467-022-33119-w).

[†] After all, the temporary relief we feel from not doing something is always replaced by a stronger anxiety over not having done it.

So, here's one suggestion for when you find yourself procrastinating: recall the last time you finally did the thing you'd been avoiding. Sit with how it felt, anchor yourself in the *relief*.

In essence, build a new loop. Then another. And another. Until what once felt like a painful struggle becomes akin to second nature. Before long, you'll find you've got a rollercoaster of good actions and positive choices looping through your mind.

HOW TO *ACTUALLY* STOP PROCRASTINATING

Now that we've covered the why, let's look at the *how*. Below is a full toolkit of techniques, grouped into four categories. You don't need to try them all – just pick the ones that resonate and experiment to find your personal formula. Remember: the more often you interrupt your procrastination loop, the easier it'll become to form a new one. Grab a highlighter, let's see what works for you . . .

1. REWIRE YOUR MINDSET
These strategies will help you change the way you see both the task *and* yourself.

Use mindfulness
Of course, we start with awareness – after all, if we're not aware of a behaviour, how can we ever expect to change it? Mindfulness here simply means noticing how, when and why you procrastinate. Observe what comes up – anxiety, dread, boredom, the sudden urge to clean the kitchen cupboards . . . Whatever it is, don't judge it. Just watch with compassion. And then remind yourself: *I am the one prioritising procrastination – which means I have the power to change it.*

Lower the bar
When something feels intimidating, or when you have perfectionist tendencies, your brain will do its best to protect you from it. So, remove the fear and overwhelm by lowering the bar. I do this when I'm writing a new talk: I don't set out to impress every single one of the hundreds of people who will be listening. That feels *terrifying*. I aim for just one (hypothetical)

person* to take away something useful from it. That's enough. Make it easy to start, *then*, when you feel ready, raise the bar accordingly.

Find your why
The final principle of *The Priorities Method*® can help here. Why is a *why* so helpful? Well, by forming a connection or ascribing meaning to a task, you're more likely to feel inspired to do it. Ask yourself: *what will it give to me or someone I love?* One client of mine used her family as motivation for putting off work tasks, saying to herself: 'I'm doing this now so I can be present with them later.' That was her why. Find yours, use it to move forward.

Consider your priorities
Yes, there will *always* be a priorities pointer . . . What are your priorities? And, crucially, what are you prioritising when you procrastinate? If kindness is a priority, know it's unkind to avoid something that's important to you. If creativity matters, honour it by making space for your projects and ideas. The more you align your actions with your priorities, the better you'll feel and the less you'll procrastinate.

Question your thoughts
For everyone, certain thoughts and mindsets can be obstacles to getting things done. Use the questions and exercises in Chapter 1: Stress to investigate the SITs that are holding you back and the SATs you can replace them with that'll drive you forward instead. A question I always ask procrastinating clients is whether they *think* they perform better under stress. Often, their answer is yes, which is when I let them know that studies show that, while we like to think this is the case, the opposite is true.[6] Intense stress doesn't make us perform better.

2. BUILD BETTER HABITS
These strategies will help you interrupt the loop and start building a new one.

---

*I once listened to a podcast with the comedian Katherine Ryan where she said that she doesn't like bread, and whenever she finds out that someone doesn't like her comedy, she says to herself: 'I don't like bread, but that doesn't make bread bad; lots of people love bread but not *everybody*.' I really liked it as a reminder that some people will *always* not like what you do, no matter what.

One brick at a time

The bigger and more intimidating the project, the quicker your brain will panic and run in the opposite direction. Make it easier to register by breaking it into smaller tasks. When I sit to write this book, I don't tell myself, 'Write the book! 80,000 words, written perfectly – now go!' – because, no thank you. I say: 'Write 1,000 words today.' Or: 'Sketch out three bullet points this morning.' I take away the fear by focusing on the next tiny step, and then the one after that. Remember: your brain doesn't care how small a task is – it'll still give you a hit of dopamine when you complete it. Use that. In time, feelings of satisfaction and pride will start to replace fear or stress, which will spur you to keep going. Basically: *build the wall one brick at a time.*

The One-Minute and Ten-Minute rules

Two rules, both great for bypassing the mental stand-off between you and a task. *The One-Minute rule* says that if something takes less than one minute to complete, then do it as soon as it comes up. Think: an email that needs replying to, a bill that demands paying, a kid's lunchbox that requires filling and so on. Don't think, just act. *The Ten-Minute rule*, on the other hand, is for the scarier, bigger stuff. Commit to doing something for ten minutes, that's it. Surely you can do anything for ten minutes? If it's awful, put the task down when your ten minutes is up, and try it again tomorrow. If you find momentum, however, *keep going.*

The 3-2-1-Go technique

This countdown-style technique involves picking three simple tasks that you've been avoiding or tend to avoid, setting a two-minute timer, and working on one of them for one minute. If inclined, say '3-2-1-go' to yourself to get you started. Then use the fact that you've begun to keep going: 'I've already unpacked half the dishwasher, might as well do the rest!' It works more often than you'd think. Repeat for each of your three chosen tasks.

Eat that frog

This method, from professional development coach Brian Tracy's 2001 book, *Eat That Frog!*, states that if you have to do something difficult or intimidating, it's best to do it first thing – before your willpower disappears.* Tracy argues that developing a lifelong habit of doing this is the key to reaching high levels of performance. Now I don't know if I'm anywhere near that but I do always guard my mornings for what matters most.† Your frog might be a presentation at work, an overflowing sink at home or a difficult conversation with a friend. The longer you put off important or challenging tasks, the harder and heavier they become. So, whatever it is, *prioritise* it, that way it won't hang over you all day.‡

Start somewhere else
Can't face or feeling stuck with a certain project? Do something else entirely, as long as it's still *productive*. Make the bed, clear your inbox, don't hit snooze (procrastination 101). It sounds unrelated, but each time you act, you lay non-procrastinating neural networks in your brain and reinforce a sense of self-capability. Sometimes taking action *anywhere* is what helps you take action where it really counts.

3. OPTIMISE YOUR ENVIRONMENT AND YOUR TIME
Make your surroundings and the hours of the day work *for* you, not *against* you.

Minimise distractions
Your brain *loves* anything that'll provide it with a quick, easy, dopamine-fuelled escape, and as we all know, our phones and computers are *full* of them. Remove temptation – mute notifications, shut tabs, use noise-cancelling headphones – do whatever it takes to create even just

---

*The title references a quote from American novelist Mark Twain: 'If it's your job to eat a frog, it's best to do it first thing in the morning. And if it's your job to eat two frogs, it's best to eat the biggest one first.' Let's not dwell too long on the obvious question – why exactly *is* it your job to eat a frog? – just to say that this is one of more than 70 books Tracy has written on productivity so he knows a thing or two about the subject. (Or really likes writing books.)

†In terms of natural circadian rhythm, most people experience their highest levels of energy and concentration in the morning, making that the optimum time for frog eating. I definitely fall into that category – by 8 p.m. I'm for all intents and purposes useless. Yet a small percentage of people experience their peak later in the day, so for them the morning may be better suited to smaller, less demanding tasks. There's an 'Energy tracking' exercise at the end of this chapter to help you understand your own rhythm.

‡Plus, by doing the tough stuff first, you're showing yourself that you *can* do hard things (positive thought *and* habit loop) and setting yourself up for less procrastination throughout the day and beyond.

a few distraction-free minutes.* And remember, your focus 'loop' will grow stronger the more you use it.

Task batching and time blocking

Two complimentary, excellent techniques . . . With task batching you group similar tasks together and tackle them all at once. This reduces the constant mental switching that comes from jumping between different kinds of work and makes it easier to push through the jobs you're tempted to avoid. (I often combine it with what I call a 'timed coffee break': make a tea or coffee, then clear as many small tasks as you can in the time it takes to drink it.) Time blocking takes this a step further by scheduling your day into set chunks – from projects and admin to exercise, errands, even downtime. The idea is to map out your day or week in advance, then assign each block according to what matters most. It helps to match your tasks to your energy levels: high-focus work when you're sharpest, lighter jobs when you're not. Once it's in the calendar, you just follow the plan rather than constantly debating what to do next. (On this, personally, I prefer a flexible approach, so I block out some periods while leaving others free and open. Also, sometimes I set it weekly, instead of daily – for example deciding I need to fit in a certain number of writing hours across the week.)

Create pressure but not stress

Honestly, this is part of why coaching works. Clients don't want to let me (or themselves, especially if they've paid) down. *Accountability works.* You can create this pressure for yourself – tell a friend your plan, make a commitment, sign up for something. Make it so you *have* to do it. Take the *stick* approach . . .

Create a reward system

. . . Or, use the carrot. After all, the brain loves bribery . . . It could be a sweet (simple, but works for me) or for something less dentist-wrath-incurring, maybe a hot bath, coffee/wine with a friend, an episode of your favourite TV show . . . anything that makes you feel good. You can also use less tangible rewards, such as focusing on the degree you'll

---

*The more you can declutter your life, the fewer distractions you'll have, full stop – if you haven't already read Chapter 4: Overwhelm, it can help with this.

earn, the project you'll finish, the peace of mind you'll gain – make the future feel real to inspire you to act now.

4. SUPPORT YOUR SYSTEM
Because it's hard to do the right thing when you don't feel quite right yourself.

Prioritise your health
Sleep, hydration, food, movement, connection – i.e. the basics that improve brain and body health and make life easier. 'Perfect' health doesn't exist, so just do what you can with what you've got. Remember: *control the controllable.* You may have no power over your child waking you up repeatedly the night before a 7 a.m. workday start. But you can drink a ton of water, make nourishing food choices, take a break outside in the sunshine (clouds, if you're in the UK). You can call a loved one, not necessarily to complain about how exhausted or annoyed you feel, but to chat, to see if a moment of connection can foster a better state of mind. Health is the scaffolding for your life. Build it.

Body doubling
This works particularly well for ADHD brains, but, honestly, anyone can benefit from it. All it means is doing the task while someone else is present – physically or virtually. They don't have to help or speak; they're just *there*. As to the earlier example of my client, having someone nearby while you do something makes you more likely to do it. Try it with a willing friend or family member, call them and say, 'I'm going to do this while you're on the phone with me.' It works.

Meditation or stillness
As a meditation teacher, I, of course, believe in its benefits, but I also know it's not for everyone. So, let's call this *stillness*. You don't need to be sitting cross-legged up a mountain – just a few quiet minutes, a moment to carve out space in your brain, downshift your nervous system and give your prefrontal cortex (PFC) a boost. (FYI: meditation has been shown to increase grey matter in the PFC as well as improve conversations between different parts of the brain,[7] which translates to helping curb procrastination.) Your PFC contributes to

your ability to override impulse and stay focused, and it needs calm to work properly. Stillness is how you can offer it that.

FINALLY . . . JUST F*CKING START
It doesn't have a category, because it's a category all on its own . . .

I don't know if that famous adage 'Starting is the hardest step' is true – I've certainly started something and been *shocked* at how challenging it's become. But I do know that, if you don't start, *there are no other steps*. None. So, you may as well start and find out! Don't overthink; don't let the task or project build up in your mind; rip off the plaster. Begin. Often the thing you've been avoiding isn't so horrific once you get started. But even if it *is*, at least now you're facing it.

OKAY, BUT WHAT ABOUT MOTIVATION?

Yes, great question!

Motivation! Isn't it brilliant?! That inspiring drive! The feeling we get when we're prepped and ready and engaged and . . .

Except if you've read Chapter 2: Habits, you already know that motivation is, at best, *fleeting*. In general (I'd estimate a scientifically un-rigorous 90 percent of the time), it *follows* action, not the other way round. I know this to be true as a coach, and I know it to be true as a *person*. Many of the things I do for my mental and physical health I often don't initially want to. I get up early most weekday mornings to have some time to myself before the children are up. I don't do this because I hate lying in bed. I love lying in bed! I do it because I know that *if* I do it, I'm a better person for the rest of the day. I'm happier, healthier, less stressed and better equipped to deal with life's curveballs.

And yet knowing this *still* doesn't always motivate me to get out of bed when my alarm goes off and it's January, freezing cold and pitch-black outside. I feel far more motivated to go back to sleep. But I don't,* because I know that motivation won't come. I know I just have to do it. Once I'm up and dressed, with a warm cup of tea,

---

*Mostly – I'm not rigid on this; if I've had a late night or a bad night's sleep I'll do a quick calculation as to what'll set me up best for the day, an extra hour in bed or my normal routine, and then play it accordingly.

hopefully it kicks in, although, honestly, sometimes it doesn't come at all.*

We often *think* that we will feel like doing something later or tomorrow. That while our present self doesn't feel inspired to act, our future self *definitely* will. *That* version of me *will* want to do it! But the eternal hope we place on tomorrow's motivation – also called 'affective forecasting', where we predict how we expect to feel in the future – rarely arrives. Motivation is not a reason to not do something; whether you *feel* like it must often be put aside.

I have a story about my daughter that inspires me on this topic. When she was four, she had a minor operation under general anaesthetic. Waking up, she was distraught, clutching her throat, which hurt from the breathing tube. My husband and I did everything to soothe her – yogurt, ice lollies – nothing worked.

Then a nurse appeared. Instead of more comfort food, she said briskly: 'Put that yogurt down, darling. What you need is a sandwich. That'll sort you out.'

A sandwich! I was horrified. Bread like cardboard for a sore throat? But she explained: 'Easy things won't help her heal. She needs something a bit tough.'

Sure enough, minutes after eating the bread (crust and all) our daughter stopped crying.

That simple act of wisdom reminded me of the saying: *hard now, easy later. Easy now, hard later.*

You've got to push yourself to do hard things, because the more you do, the more you'll know that you *can*. As with my daughter's example, for a long time the cure for back pain was rest. Nowadays, however, experts recommend the opposite – doing as much light movement as possible.

What's true for the physical body is true for the mind – doing the hard thing, going beyond your comfort zone, is what helps us develop and grow. Ideally, once you do the hard thing (*eat the sandwich*), some motivation and momentum follows.

But, if it doesn't, then, sorry, you have to keep going regardless. That's the way life works.

You are the motivation. Remember that.

---

*Something that can help me build motivation is the mindset shift of swapping 'I *have* to get up and meditate/exercise' to 'I *get* to get up and do this' or 'I have a body that is healthy and able to wake up early. I am so lucky to be in a body that can move, in a home where I can lay out a yoga mat, in a space that I feel safe.' And so on . . .

PRIORITISE THIS

PRODUCTIVE PROCRASTINATION

I mentioned at the beginning of the chapter that I think procrastination can sometimes be helpful, that it can serve a purpose. And it can. However, appreciating when an action (or non-action) is helping you prepare versus when it's just plain old simple procrastination is only for you to know.

I play 15 minutes of piano in the morning before I sit at my desk, which I know *prepares* me for work. It warms up my fingers for the keyboard and my eyes for the computer, and clears my mind. I experience a micro-win plus a few failures,* and I'm still learning, which means I show myself I can do hard things. If I'm lucky, I might even enter a flow state and be able to carry some of that energy into my workday. I also play when I've been sitting at a screen for too long or to reset after a challenging client session. Some may see playing piano in the middle of the day as procrastinating – and indeed it has the potential to be – but for me it's the opposite.

Now, I appreciate that very few people work from an office with a piano and, if they did, it's unlikely their co-workers would take kindly to an impromptu 90s EDM jam.† But what's your equivalent of my piano? What's your *productive, positive* procrastinating tool? A walk, calling a friend, a moment of breathwork, drawing/doodling . . . ? My husband loves a Rubik's Cube, one of my clients enjoys colouring books, another a run with her dog.

What prepares or resets you?

DO THE THING

It's clear that some people, due to a combination of nature and nurture, are more likely to procrastinate. However, whatever your resting point, your brain has an incredible capacity for plasticity and change. It's constantly making sense of past experiences and current data to work out what's going on, what might happen next and what best to do now. Use this to your advantage.

You *can* change your behaviour, even if it takes time and even though there will be setbacks. Remember: the pain from procrastinating on

---

*Which is excellent for brain plasticity, as I go into in detail in Chapter 6: Failure.
† If so, I want to work in that office.

something is generally more severe than the discomfort from going for it. Also, remember that as you acquire the skill of not procrastinating, you'll create a habit loop, so that in time it'll take less brain power to do it, rather than put it off.

If it helps, tell yourself that, in order to be kind to your future self, you *have* to stop compromising long-term aims for quick bursts of short-term relief. Time-management strategies aside (of which there are plenty in this chapter) curbing procrastination ultimately comes down to *emotional regulation*. If you want to get things done in life, you have to take responsibility for your actions and wade through some negative emotions along the way.

The better you can sit with and tolerate those difficult feelings, the better you will regulate your system and increase your productivity. Focusing on your emotional wellbeing and general health makes a difference. And, crucially, if you do procrastinate, don't beat yourself up. Be kind and forgiving – because you deserve that much, but also because self-forgiveness and kindness have been proven to help reduce procrastination.[8] Even if you've procrastinated for years on something, you can still start any time. There is always time.

Ultimately: *it's in the hard work that we get stuff done*. Please don't not do the hard things that matter to you. It doesn't need to be perfect – aim for the attainable (70 out of 100?), as you can always come back and improve it later. Or the next time. Or the time after that . . .

Something I always have to remind myself of in the planning stages of any project – a workshop, an article, this book – is that the research and planning are *not* the finished product. Yes, they are important. Yet, ultimately, it doesn't matter how many months I spend developing a workshop, if I don't *create* it, I'll never stand up on stage and deliver it. And though an article needs to be well thought out and researched, no publication will accept (let alone pay for) my notes on a subject.

Thinking about doing the thing is not doing the thing.
Researching the thing is not doing the thing.
Planning the thing is not doing the thing.
Making notes on the thing is not doing the thing.
Only doing the thing is doing the thing.
Go do the thing.

PRIORITISE THIS

- Procrastination is normal and expected.
- It occurs because your brain prefers short-term rewards over long-term gains.
- You can create positive or negative habit loops around procrastination.
- Not procrastinating is an act of kindness to yourself and to others.
- Effective approaches for curbing procrastination involve a combination of emotional regulation and time management strategies.
- Experiment with different strategies from the four categories to see what works for you.
- Remember: you can do hard things (*eat the sandwich*).
- Only by doing the thing will the thing get done!

PRACTICES TO HELP WITH PROCRASTINATION

On the next pages (and online) you'll find a range of techniques that help curb procrastination and improve productivity and focus. Many are complementary and can be used in tandem – it's really just a case (as always!) of uncovering what works best for you.

All these exercises will help you switch on the 'Executive Control Network' in your brain, which is responsible for complex thoughts, decision-making and planning, and the more you do them the stronger this network will become. Finally, as you've probably gathered by now, I believe the idea of increasing our productivity only matters when it increases our life satisfaction overall. Less 'how can I fit as much into my hours on this earth as possible' and more 'how can I arrange my time so that I have more of it for the people and things I truly love'.

TRACKING ENERGY LEVELS

An obsession with self-optimisation isn't healthy, but this tool is a simple way to follow that adage: 'work smarter, not harder'.*
By tracking your energy levels, you can begin to plan your day – insofar as you're able – around them, which can free up your time and energy. Think of it as swimming with the tide, rather than against it.

Use the table on the next page (or download it from the Prioritise This website) to mark your energy at each waking hour. You decide how to assess this – mental sharpness, productivity, physical stamina or something else. Try it a few times across different days or weeks, since hormones, sleep and many other factors all play a role.

Once you've got a good picture, use it to support yourself. Stop berating yourself for the dips and instead acknowledge and adapt. Depending on the control you have over your time, shift to keeping your 'peak' hours for demanding work, and move

---

*If that adage appeals, I recommend picking up a copy of entrepreneur Emily Austen's book *Smarter*.

meetings, easy-win tasks or errands to the times you have low energy and are probably more prone to procrastinate.

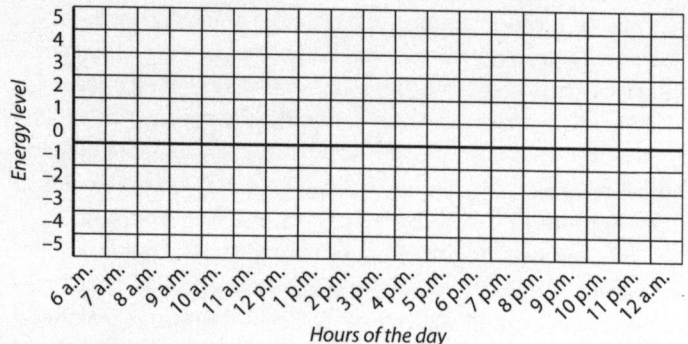

Hours of the day
Tracking energy levels

Instructions: give a number between 5 and –5 to your performance every hour (0 = average). Mark it on the graph and join them up at the end of the day to work out your energy cycle.

TIME LOGGING

Time logging is similar to energy tracking, but instead of noting energy, you record how you spend your time. It can be a bit of a shock, since it reveals just how many hours disappear into scrolling or small distractions. But knowledge is power. If you end the day wondering: 'Where on earth did that day go?' this tool will show you. By logging your activities and establishing a baseline, you'll see where you overestimate or underestimate tasks, spot procrastination patterns and begin to build a schedule that feels realistic and productive. This is turn will reduce the negative emotions you feel around your least productive times of the day, leading to less procrastination overall. FYI: track just your workday or include 'leisure' time for a more well-rounded picture.

How it works:

- You'll need a notebook (or Word document/notes app) and a timer – make sure you keep it with you for the whole day.
- Beginning with your first activity, write down the start and end time – that is, log the amount of time it takes.
- Include a short description of each activity. For example: '9–9.35 a.m.: Checked and responded to emails'. This is your 'data'.

- Every time you switch tasks, note it down. Be honest and meticulous.
- Once you're done, put all the data into a spreadsheet program (such as Excel or Google Sheets) and arrange it so that you can see the total amount of time you spend on each activity.
- Look at it as a whole and you should be able to see where your time is being lost as well as the times of the day when you're most likely to procrastinate.
- Use any insights to make changes, but don't make too many changes all at once. Slow and steady wins the race.

THE ABC METHOD

The ABC method, developed by Alan Lakein,[9] is one I particularly connect with because it involves *prioritising*, which as you know, I'm a *little* obsessed with. It's simple, useful and flexible, and I use it with clients and myself all the time.

How it works:

- Take a look at all of your tasks/projects for the day and/or week.
- Write them down somewhere using either paper, a Word document or a digital tool like Asana.
- Categorise your most important, urgent, highest-priority tasks or items under A.
- Categorise your tasks that need to be completed soon but aren't urgent or the highest priority under B.
- Finally, pop the least important things (your lowest-level priorities) under C.
- Then, work through your day or week prioritising everything in category A followed by B and finally C.

Go to the Prioritise This website for an extra Self-motivation visualisation.

CHAPTER 6

Failure

● ● ●

'The world breaks everyone and afterward many are strong at the broken places.'

Ernest Hemingway, A Farewell to Arms[1]

In no particular order, here's a non-exhaustive list of things I've failed at: my twenties, holding a handstand away from the wall, AS level biology, being happy, my driving test the first *and* second time, getting into Oxford, selling out *The Priorities Method Journal* in the time I thought I would, being any good at chess, getting a book agent the first time I tried, getting a book agent the second time I tried, eating, having a 'proper' university experience, launching my Substack, primary school, learning Spanish beyond the basic conversational level, finishing writing a work of fiction,* getting onto an MSc in behavioural economics, my online video membership platform 'Mindful Moment', being a good girlfriend/friend/daughter/sister/parent, hiring people, firing people, the monkey bars.

Failure, as with all the topics in this book, is universal. Every single person has failed in some way, probably many ways, both big and small. It's an inevitable part of being alive in this world.

---

* It was chick lit. I wrote 60,000 words before abandoning it. It's probably for the best.

It's also subjective – some of my 'failures' are based on my own perception, rather than any universal idea of what it means to succeed. Outwardly my twenties appeared successful, but inwardly I was unwell and a part of me feels that affected how I experienced those years. And no, I didn't *actually* fail primary school – imagine, 'You didn't use the Play-Doh properly, you're out!' – but I did attend six schools before the age of nine, despite never moving house. There are also failures on my list that I now view as successes – I was asked at my Oxford interview if I'd consider not taking a gap year and joining that year instead. I said no and while I don't know whether a yes would have secured me a place, I do believe the immense pressure of an institution like that would have sent my precarious mental health off a cliff. So, in retrospect, I see that failure as a win . . .

The point is, while we clearly all experience failure, we don't all experience it the same way. Now, as I'm sure you've heard a million times, failure is how we learn, it's how our brain makes sense of the world. It's also how we build resilience: through experiencing setbacks and developing methods for coping with them we bolster our ability to bounce back from challenging times. And it's true, failure *does* have the potential to create momentum, to propel us forward – as the writer Samuel Beckett so eloquently wrote, we can indeed 'Fail again. Fail better.'

And yet, while this outlook is deeply inspirational, it's also a little divorced from reality. Because it is *very* hard for most people, while in the midst of a failure, to embrace the motivational article viewpoint of 'Failure is the key to your success!' Failure, in whatever form it arrives, feels awful in the moment (and often for a long time afterwards). If things were as simple as knowing you should 'Fail forward!' and being able to do that every time, then we wouldn't find failure so tough and I wouldn't need to write this chapter.

Failure is not a measure of who you are, nor an indicator of what will happen to you or what you will do later in life.[*] But it is a fundamental part of living, one that affects us deeply. We have an inbuilt survival instinct which drives us to avoid failure and seek success. Moreover, failure is complex and not all failures are created equal, which is why I find the 'fail forward' idea occasionally jarring, at odds with the actuality of life.

My aim for this chapter is to avoid a lofty, divorced-from-reality lecture on 'How to fail better!', and instead empower you to navigate

---

[*] Henry Ford, Walt Disney, Steve Jobs, Thomas Edison and Oprah are just a few of the iconic figures who faced epic failure before achieving near-unimaginable success.

the *real-life* experience of failure. To enable you to not fear it so much, to maintain perspective, avoid feelings of discouragement and view failure as *possible* to grow from. Ultimately, to discover how to take the pain and learnings and use them to strengthen your resolve to find the momentum to go again.

> ## FAILURE MYTHS
>
> We all carry unspoken (inaccurate) beliefs that shape how we experience life, and failure is no different. Here's a few worth challenging:
>
> 1. **'Failure defines who I am.'** No, it does not. It defines what happened, not you as a person. A setback doesn't undo everything that came before (or all that's still to come).
> 2. **'Everyone else is doing better than me.'** You're likely comparing your behind-the-scenes to their highlights reel. People rarely showcase their fails, so you end up thinking you're the only one falling short. You're not.
> 3. **'I'll never recover from this.'** It feels like that in the moment, of course it does. But you will. Humans are wired for adaptation – remember all the things you've already overcome that once felt impossible.
> 4. **'If I fail, it means I shouldn't have tried.'** The opposite is true. Trying and failing means you were brave enough to go for something. That's a strength, not a weakness.
> 5. **'Failing means I'm not good enough.'** This one stings, I know. But failing doesn't mean you're not good enough. It can mean you're still learning, or it wasn't the right time, or luck didn't favour you. You're worthy, regardless.

HOW WE LEARN

Failure gets a bad rap – understandably, because it makes you feel like sh*t. But it is how we learn. I don't mean this in some 'Live Laugh Love' embroider-it-on-a-cushion-to-make-yourself-feel-better kind of way; I mean it's *literally* how your brain makes sense of the world, what enables you to develop and grow. We try, we fail, we adjust, we try, we fail, we adjust and so on, until (hopefully) we succeed. The strongest visual example of this process is watching a baby learning to crawl – they put one leg there, an elbow there and then fall flat on their face repeatedly until their brain (hopefully) gets the correct sequence of things and they're off.* Having taken up piano again after a casual 25-year hiatus, I fail repeatedly at hitting the right key at the right time, until eventually . . . I don't.

Your brain is essentially a giant prediction machine, using past experiences to predict future outcomes – when you try something new, your brain draws on what it already knows and experiments to find the 'correct' answer.† What's wild is that your brain is wired to detect failure and misses within *milliseconds* – a specific brain region (the cingulate cortex) flags the mistake before you're even aware of it. This response is called an ERN, or 'error-related negativity',[2] and it happens incredibly quickly (within fractions of a second) with your awareness coming slightly later, once the rest of your brain is alerted to the mistake. Over time, as you make mistakes and adjust accordingly, new neural connections form, which is your brain's way of saying: *something's off, what do I need to learn?* (In fact, research shows that after a mistake, your brain responds by slowing you down (also known as post-error slowing, or PES) – not because something's wrong with you, but because it's giving you more time to respond better next time.[3]

Scientific studies have shown that we all have different sized ERNs. Your individual ERN increases with age, meaning it's weakest in children – which is connected to the cingulate cortex not developing fully until your late twenties. In real-world terms, this means that a region of your brain that's crucial in learning from mistakes may not be able to help you do so until later in life. Not a reason to condone questionable behaviour in the young, but perhaps good to bear in mind if you're struggling with a teen who seems to almost purposefully not be learning from their mistakes.[4] ‡

---

* And as a parent, you never rest again.
† Sometimes it does this very successfully; at others . . . less so!
‡ If you're wondering whether a larger ERN is useful, the results are mixed. One study found that university students with larger ERNs were likely to have higher grades, suggesting an increased ability to learn from a mistake. However, another found that people with developed ERNs experience more anxiety, raising questions around whether an outsized ERN suggests the brain is overreacting to a failure, blowing the situation out of proportion – something we know is always unhelpful in life!

So, how the brain navigates mistakes *is* how the brain develops. However, if failure is such a crucial part of how we learn, then why does it hurt so much? Why doesn't it feel *good* instead?

Our pain reaction is rooted in evolutionary biology – for our primordial ancestors living in the wild, a misstep or failure could have meant injury, death or ostracisation from the tribe (which also would have spelled death). If you're trying to avoid a predator, a mistake would be lethal, to be avoided at all costs.

Many of the opportunities for 'failure' today are not deadly; they're far less tangible, with minimal connection to our *literal* survival. Nonetheless, we still have this natural *fear* of failure.* And this is further compounded by the negative emotions failure elicits (and we prefer to avoid) – disappointment, shame, embarrassment, anger, frustration, sadness, regret, confusion and so on – as well as perceived, cultural norms around 'success' and 'winning'. Additionally, we all like to hold a positive image of our 'self' (both internally in terms of what we think of ourselves and externally in terms of what others think of us) and failing can impact this. When we fail at something – an exam, job interview, work project, competition, relationship – our self-image suffers. We all want to 'succeed' in life, but sometimes the fear of *not* succeeding is what holds us back.

And so we have this push–pull relationship with failure. On the one hand, it's fundamental to how we develop, each miss bringing us closer to our desired outcome. On the other, we fear and are conditioned to avoid it. Recognising this undulating process in your brain is the first step to understanding and better managing failure in your day-to-day life. The painful feelings you experience with failure are part of what your brain does to help you succeed in the future.

FORTUNA

In 2018 I taught a six-week meditation, mindfulness and stress-reduction course at an exclusive private members' club in Mayfair, a very smart area in central London. As one might imagine, the members had few concerns around financial security – externally their lives were ones of extreme privilege. Internally, however, they struggled with the same stuff

---

*The most extreme form has the brilliant name 'atychiphobia' and sadly severely affects the ability of sufferers to function well in daily life.

we all do. Money may soften the edges of life, but it doesn't take away insecurity, overwhelm, imposter syndrome, stress or any of the rest.

In our final session, I focused on the power of our thoughts – similar stuff to what's in Chapter 1: Stress, the water–rock analogy and so on. Members often hung back after sessions to chat to me, and that week I noticed a smartly dressed man in his early thirties patiently waiting. He'd been a 'model student' – attending every week, engaging with the topics and so on. 'What about failure?' he asked when everyone else had left. 'How can you feel less stressed about that?' After gentle questioning, I gathered his company was on the verge of collapse, that everything he'd been working on and towards for the past six years was about to crumble. He viewed it all as his fault, even though it sounded as though there were (as there almost always are) circumstances completely outside of his control that were making the business hard to sustain.

In our modern, secular lives it's common to believe that our successes and failures are our own. There is *so much* opportunity in today's world, and the accompanying messaging is clear – it's up to *you* to make the most of it. Fail, and it's squarely on you!

The ancient Greeks, however, took a different perspective. They believed life is random, defined not by an individual's grit and determination (though both were encouraged) but rather by chance and luck. And I've got to say, I agree. I know people who've worked hard on a brilliant project to have it fail due to no fault of their own. I also know those who've put in the bare minimum but had huge success come their way. I'm not saying don't work hard – clearly the more you dedicate your energy, attention and focus to something the more primed you'll be if luck does come your way. However, while fortune clearly favours the prepared, failure isn't always your fault.* You didn't manifest it; you didn't welcome it. In all likelihood you could have made some different (read: better) decisions along the way . . . but isn't that the case for us all?

Back to the members' club and the man who wanted to feel less 'stressed' about the failure of his business. I mentioned some of the above as well as the fact that if he didn't feel stressed that would be concerning – his stress was a natural reaction and it showed how much he cared about what he'd built. I suggested he try the Zone of Control (see Chapter 1: Stress). Finally, we spoke about the vast gulf between how we speak to ourselves versus those we care for, about the flexibility, forgiveness and compassion that we too often fail to apply

---

*Yes, by the same admission, sometimes our successes aren't ours to claim either!

inwardly. Obviously, a ten-minute conversation didn't make this man's complex feelings around failure disappear, but it did let in a crack of light that helped lessen the mental burden and enable him to see the situation more clearly.

So, this is your reminder to remember the ancient Greeks and their constant offerings to the goddess Tyche (the Romans called her Fortuna), whom they believed controlled their luck. You don't need to adhere to their polytheistic belief system and I don't think a lack of agency – *It's in the hands of the gods!* – is a valid excuse for everything that doesn't go our way. But, while ensuring that you accept responsibility for something that *is* your fault, remember also to give yourself a break when it's not.

THE REASONS YOU MAY FEAR FAILURE

Psychologists have identified a number of traits and circumstances that influence how we feel about failure. These include:

- **Perfectionism:** your desire to make everything 'perfect' prevents you from even starting a task or going after a goal. You set yourself impossibly high standards and live in fear of not meeting them. You equate performance with self-worth and view failure as a sign of being worthless.[5] The higher your standards, the harder it can feel to risk falling short.
- **External pressures:** you feel overwhelmed by the expectations placed on you by others – you don't want to disappoint anyone (parent, friend, boss, etc.) or feel judged for not achieving the standards they expect of you.
- **Low self-worth:** you rely on external validation (achievement/success) for your self-worth and fear not meeting the standards that you use to prove your worth so you avoid situations where someone could think negatively of you or your abilities. You don't feel confident enough to fail.
- **Upbringing and/or wider social values:** you grew up with a primary caregiver, peer group or community who feared failure, handled it badly or taught you that failing was wrong and you've learned to believe the same.

- **Experiences:** you once encountered a traumatic failure (e.g. forgetting your lines in a school play and feeling humiliated) and your brain now tries to avoid feeling those painful emotions again.
- **You care:** you feel deeply about something, it matters to you a lot, and you don't want to feel disappointed by it or feel the shame that you may experience following a failure.[6]

The following four questions combine deep reflection with action-orientated guidance. They will help lessen overwhelm, improve objectivity and leave you more able to plan a way forward. They may also help you identify fears, thought patterns and limiting beliefs you weren't aware of. Ask yourself:

1. What am I really afraid of?
2. What do I care about? Sometimes your fear stops you from living in a way that is aligned with your priorities and values. What's meaningful to you?
3. What's the best possible outcome?
4. How will I recover if I fail?

FIVE BENEFITS OF FAILURE

Society has not traditionally encouraged a positive view of failure, conditioning us to avoid it where possible. I believe things are changing (and see it in my children's school's approach), which is clearly for the good, as one of the common threads seen in people who thrive after failure is that they seek the positive. I'll put my hand up and say: *this is not always easy to do.* Sometimes you don't want or don't have the energy to look for the bright side. I truly get that. I'm not asking you to deny your negative feelings – wallow in them for as long as you need. Just don't stay there for ever. When you're ready to prioritise the positive, here are five benefits of failing to help you on your way . . .

1. **Enhanced resilience:** picking yourself up after a failure is hard, but by doing it, neural connections signalling that you *can* form in your brain, reducing your fear of failure and making you less likely to view it as ruinous the next time. Every failure you face and overcome has the potential to make you stronger and spur you on, and this resilience will begin to show up in other areas of your life too.

2. **Emotional regulation:** failure forces you to confront difficult (*universal*) feelings such as disappointment, shame, embarrassment and frustration. If you can learn how to cope with these feelings in a constructive way, you'll feel better equipped to recover from setbacks and manage challenging emotions overall as well.
3. **Improved neural connectivity:** as I mentioned above, when you make a mistake your brain has to work hard to figure out what went wrong and how to fix it. The more you do this, the more you prune and strengthen your brain networks around 'learning' and 'improving'. Failure imprints lessons in your mind, making the 'lessons' hard to forget. In essence, it advances your brain!
4. **Common humanity:** someone who experiences success after success can easily feel like a hero (*and separated from the rest*) until one little failure brings everything crashing down... Ultimately, we all struggle with failure – embrace this universality of experience and the closer you'll feel to others who you know have experienced it too. (Yes, it can have the opposite affect when it feels like everyone is succeeding except you – we'll come on to this in a moment.)
5. **Increases self-efficacy:** while failure can negatively affect belief in one's ability ('I failed X, so clearly I'll also fail Y!'), the resilience and emotional regulation that develops from repeatedly picking yourself up after a failure actually leads to an increase in self-efficacy overall.

20 WAYS TO *ACTUALLY* OVERCOME YOUR FEAR OF FAILURE AND FAIL FORWARD

It's a long list, I know! The idea here is to have something for everyone; let's give it a go...

1. **Normalise mistakes.** Pencils have erasers. Ink fades. Insert other writing-related analogies here... The point is, *mistakes are part of living*. Reminding yourself that small failures are normal in your day-to-day life will help you bring that same energy to the bigger ones when they occur. Also, google famous failures – there are literally hundreds of inspiring stories out there. Go and seek them.
2. **Analyse what went wrong.** You may be desperate to stick your head in the sand post-failure, but that's proven to be the worst thing to do.[7] To learn from your failure, face it head-on. Don't dwell on what went wrong; rather, reflect on what happened and what part

you had to play versus what was outside your control. Zoom out and take a bird's-eye view* to gain insight and understanding and use them to do better next time.

3. **Perceive yourself as able to learn.** Studies have shown that possessing a *learning* mindset is one of the best indicators for handling and moving on from failure.[8] If you already always view missteps as an opportunity for learning, then great!† But, if like most of us humans you can struggle to make that connection, especially immediately following a real-life failure, focus on your *general* capacity to learn and grow instead.

4. **Focus on what you do well.** Confidence tends to take a hit post-failure, but this can be softened by focusing on what you *can* do well. Remind yourself of your skills and abilities or concentrate on a different area of your life. For example, if you've had a failure at work, focus on what you do well at work outside of this failure (*I am punctual, I support my colleagues,* etc.) or, alternatively, on the strengths you have in another area altogether, such as your friendships.

5. **Own your fear.** If you are scared of failing, recognise that. Not accepting your fear gives it free rein to show up in other, creatively unhelpful ways in life. And know that fear doesn't always mean thinking a project is too big; it can be more subtle – like the lawyer I worked with who wanted to write poetry but was afraid her colleagues would mock her.‡ That type of fear (the social kind) taps into our *need to belong*, but give in to it, and you end up failing *yourself*. Find someone trusted who you can talk to about your fears – seek empathy and encouragement as you confront and accept them.

6. **Focus on what you can control.** If you're struggling with the fear of failure, start by trying the Zone of Control practice (Chapter 1: Stress). This will help you identify which aspects of a task or project are within your control, and then you can map out for yourself how to focus more on them and less on what you can't control.

---

* Some studies suggest it's beneficial to practise 'self-distancing' by thinking about yourself in the third person – e.g. 'Why did Lily fail?' I don't love this approach (it makes me cringe); however, self-distancing was found by psychologist Ethan Kross to help soften our emotional reactions and make failure feel less threatening to our ego/sense of self. If it resonates, it's worth a try.
† If so, why are you even reading this chapter?!
‡ They might have – still not a reason not to do something . . .

7. **Foster a growth mindset.** A growth mindset is the idea that you approach yourself and any projects as possessing the capacity for progress and evolution. Approach challenges with curiosity, view them as opportunities and you'll find yourself more willing to overcome your fear, to adapt and grow. (Turn to Chapter 9: Moving Forward for more on a growth mindset.)
8. **Develop your failure muscle.** If failure terrifies you, improve your resistance by allowing yourself to repeatedly fail and try again, but in non-pressured spaces. Start small and give yourself permission to take manageable risks – for example, try a new skill or cook a meal that feels intimidating. Experiencing small failures helps grow your muscle for navigating bigger ones.
9. **Think of the potential positives.** When we're scared to try and fail, we naturally think about what could go wrong or what we could lose. Flip your thinking around and focus instead on what could go *right* and what you could *win*. Focus on the (on *your*) future potential.
10. **Lean on your community.** As I repeatedly mentioned in Chapter 1: Stress, social connections are *crucial* for stress prevention and management. And failure *is* stressful. When we're down we need support, so lean on yours. Discuss your failure with people you trust, those who will give you positive advice (there is a time and place for healthy criticism, this is not it). You will feel less burdened and chances are they'll have stories about their own failures too, which will make you feel more connected and less alone. (Bonus points if you can offer advice around the failure to someone in a similar position as you – one study found this to be one of the most effective ways to 'fail forward'.[9])
11. **Remember your priorities.** Reminding yourself of the principles, people and things that you deem most important is an effective way to bring perspective to any mistake, failure or miss. Spend a moment reflecting on your priorities, write them down if inclined and then focus on them instead. (P.S. Sometimes when we've failed or made a mistake it may be that we've gone against our priorities. Do not berate yourself but do consider why they are meaningful and how you can use them to help you through.)
12. **Don't identify with your failure.** You are not the sum of your failure, even though I know it can feel that way. Unless you need to (i.e. it *was* your fault, and it'd be helpful to reflect on that), try not

to take the failure personally. Seek objectivity and distance, separate yourself (and your self-worth) from it as much as you can by reminding yourself that you are much more (*and* much more complex) than this one moment or thing. Repeat after me: *failure is not a measure of my value as a person.*

13. **Think: temporary.** Failure is a loss, yes. However, avoid looking at the loss as something permanent and it'll feel less overwhelming. It's one moment in a long life full of moments, of ups and downs. If you can think of it as temporary, it'll be easier for you to move forward (onward, upward, sideways or any other direction). Remember: almost every 'overnight' success was years in the making.

14. **Set new goals or projects.** This isn't rocket science; I appreciate that many people do this instinctively, but bringing conscious thought and intention to setting new goals for yourself can dampen feelings of disappointment. Seek out the dopamine hit your brain awards you for setting a goal (see Chapter 9: Moving Forward). It could be within the area that you've 'failed' or in a different one – a well-trodden path after the end of a relationship ends is to book a holiday with friends or set an inspiring fitness goal. (Yes, I have done both those things.)

15. **Develop a ritual.** There have been a few recent, interesting studies around rituals and failure. In short, rituals modulate the ERN response, decreasing the brain's sensitivity to errors. This has been shown to help rewire your brain to better handle challenges, meaning you're less emotionally engaged by setbacks and can maintain focus and calm.[10] Rituals could include: a morning walk, a face massage, a few push-ups. Rituals can be leaned on post-failure, but they're also preventative, helping your mental health remain robust overall.

16. **Be okay with discomfort.** Now I'll preface this by saying that I remember how jarring I found this kind of advice when I was going through a difficult time in life. If you feel that way right now, then ignore it (the same goes for every other word in this book!). But I do think the *general* idea of embracing discomfort is an important one to get on board with. Much of life *is* uncomfortable, and being okay with the discomfort, knowing that it's part of a full and rich life, helps not only build resilience and persistence but also improve self-efficacy.

17. **Anticipate a bit of failure.** Are the manifesters going to hate me for this?! Maybe. But the reality is that anticipating failure can be useful. All good businesses prepare for it while simultaneously going after their dreams and goals (or, you know, sales targets), and I think *sometimes* it can be helpful for us to do the same. If you have a deep fear of failure, confronting it head on can help. Know that if you are trying something for the first time, it's unlikely to be perfect (watch out for the fear of failure meets perfectionism loop[11]). Accept that failure *is* possible, and you'll be more likely to see it for what it tends to be – a bump in the road. Sure, some bumps feel like mountains, but whatever the size, this approach makes you less likely to be completely thrown and more likely to quickly pick yourself up again. Don't *always* anticipate failure, rather: *hope for the best, plan for the worst*. Try the Coping visualisation at the end of the chapter – imagine the worst outcomes and plan how you'll deal with them to reduce fear and worry.

18. **Get comfortable with rejection.** Failure and rejection are deeply interlinked, and we often fear failure simply because of the potential for rejection. I won't go into detail here, since the following chapter is dedicated solely to that topic, I'll just say that the more comfortable you can be with rejection, the more comfortable you'll find yourself with failure too.

19. **Move your body.** As I wrote in Chapter 1: Stress, one of the best ways to complete the stress response cycle (which comes into play with failure) is to move. Your body is built to move, so if you are able to, *move it*. Doesn't matter how or when, just find some form of movement or exercise that you enjoy and can stick with, and use it to help your body process those stress hormones.

20. **Try again. Or quit!** I'm really covering the bases here, but we do only have two options following a failure – give up or try again. It's important to try again, to not be discouraged by a failure the first (or even second or third time round). Yet it's also important to know when to call it quits, to not have such an inflated sense of self that it will eventually destroy you. Only you'll know which course is right for you in the moment, but if unsure, I'd suggest (no surprise here) considering your priorities ... What's important to you about this failure or success? Does continuing to try align with your priorities, or will it actually negatively impact them instead?

PRIORITISE THIS

MY FATHER

When I play a new piece on the piano or try a challenging posture in yoga, I feel connected to the learning process of failing. I'm presciently aware of the triggering of neural pathways that help my brain to adapt, adjust and come back stronger. Of failing repeatedly until I succeed. And I'm sure you can think of examples of your own where failure feels like constructive, useful feedback.

However, there is a difference between failing to kick the ball into a net as you learn to play football as a child and missing a penalty shot at the World Cup. When you miss the net as a kid, your brain builds new connections that help it avoid doing so again. When you miss the penalty as an adult, your brain may do the same, but the experience is different. Yes, failure can propel us forward – it can help us become smarter, more resilient and better prepared for future challenges. But it's also painful and this pain and/or feelings of shame have been proven to have the potential to hold us back.[12] I don't say this to scare you, I say it to warn you – to be conscious of whether you find yourself running away or burying your head in the sand, ostrich style, after failure. I'm sure we can agree that that's not a great way to learn; it's a great way to get stuck.

Nobody likes failing. It hurts, it feels embarrassing, it shifts our sense of self (which can take a while to find again). And though it clearly serves a purpose, the reality is that sometimes we fail and feel like we've learned a huge lesson whereas at others we're left baffled as to the possible message. When you're struggling to see a failure as positive, my advice is to treat yourself with compassion. To prioritise people and environments that encourage living through trial and error. To know that though that failure could mean the end of one thing, there are *always* other options in life (even if they're not your first, or even second, choice). If you can, prioritise thoughts around what you learned. If you can't, don't force yourself. Wait a few days or weeks and then try again. Acknowledge the pain and disappointment, but also acknowledge the learning, say to yourself: *my brain loves a challenge. This is a challenge. This is my brain developing.*

And, ultimately, that adage of 'Never try and you'll never know' is *true*. Failure and success go hand in hand – never attempt something and you'll never have the chance to succeed at it. As Winston Churchill is commonly believed to have said: 'Success is not final, failure is not fatal: it is the courage to continue that counts.' Finding that courage is hard, but just like a baby learning to crawl, the more you fall down, the better you get at picking yourself up again. Sometimes you have to be afraid and do it anyway, for it's often in the actual doing of the thing that the confidence comes. Whether in your career, personal life or studies, you ultimately become stronger and more resilient as a result of failure, even though it rarely feels that way at the time. Failure rewires your brain, making it easier to not be defeated by setbacks and to find the motivation to dust yourself off and go again.

I'll end this chapter with a story about my father. My intimidatingly intelligent father, who got the highest possible first for his master's degree, wrote multiple long, detail-heavy books, and whom I honestly never knew to forget a fact or (let's face it, sometimes useless!) piece of information in his life. This man . . . *failed* his O level English.[*]

Completely and utterly failed.

But! Thirty-odd years later, when I was a teenager, the *same* board that failed him used an article he'd written as sample material in the *same* exam. They used his writing to help other young minds learn how to write.

I don't know if this is an example of failing forward. But I do know that this experience was part of the tone in my house growing up: *failure wasn't something to be avoided*. It didn't define us, and it definitely didn't mean the end of something. It was just part of life.

Failure isn't a reflection of who you are or what you are capable of. It doesn't always mean the end of something. It definitely doesn't mean the end of you.

PRIORITISE THIS

- Failure is an inevitable part of life.
- Your fear of failure is rooted in evolutionary biology.
- Failure is not a measure of who you are, nor an indicator of what will happen to you or what you will do later in life.
- Your brain is a giant prediction machine – failure is how we learn.

---

[*]The old version of the General Certificate in Secondary Education (GCSE), an almost UK-wide qualification typically taken by students at age 15 or 16.

PRIORITISE THIS

- There are benefits to failure – it builds resilience and a sense of common humanity, and improves self-efficacy, emotional regulation and improved neural connectivity.
- Take responsibility for your actions but also remember that sometimes failure is not your fault and may have nothing to do with you.
- There are so many different ways to support yourself through failure; use them.

PRACTICES TO HELP WITH FAILURE

POSITIVE FAILURE REMINISCING

This exercise helps you to remember failures that haven't negatively impacted your life and so prime your brain to fear failure less and improve your mindset.

How it works:

- Bring to mind a time that you failed at something, but the consequences were not dire or impactful to your life. Perhaps they were even positive, as with my Oxford example.
- Spend a minute thinking about that time.
- Get lost in your positive thoughts about how you navigated that failure and came out stronger or more aware of yourself or whatever other benefits you experienced – lessons the failure taught you or the unexpected directions it sent you in.
- Notice how you feel afterwards.
- Use this as motivation to help you overcome what's happening now.

COPING VISUALISATION

This technique is often used for stress management, and is brilliant when you're facing a situation that feels worrying or overwhelming. However, because it encourages you to imagine coping with a feared scenario, I've also found it very helpful for overcoming fear of failure too. The practice challenges the negative and/or stress-inducing thoughts or imagery that hold you back, and by seeking a 'middle ground', it gives your brain a realistic and accessible alternative way of thinking. Manifestation fans may not love it – we're imagining the worst, after all! But the purpose isn't to dwell there; it's to imagine the worst happening and then imagine moving through it.

How it works:

- Think of a future situation in which you are scared of failing or making a mistake.
- Consider the aspects of the situation that you are fearful about. What is it that scares you? Why does it matter so much if you

fail? What is the alternative? Note it down either in your mind or on paper/your phone.
- As you consider the situation, imagine yourself failing and how you will cope with that failure. Explain to yourself that it won't be as bad as you might imagine. That even if you fail, it's just one failure, just one moment in your life.
- Repeat to yourself that if you don't try, you will never know.
- Carefully visualise yourself in the feared situation. Slowly picture or talk yourself through coping with this failure or mistake, and then through recovering from it, of picking yourself up. Of going again in the future.
- Repeat this three or four times.
- Practise these last two steps daily or whenever your mind feels frozen by the fear of failure or making a mistake.

FYI: when we use this technique for stress management, the aim shifts. Negative images and thoughts about a stressful situation can raise our stress levels further, creating a self-fulfilling prophecy. If we have little confidence about an event, jumping straight to imagining mastering it is often too big of a mental leap, and also doesn't prepare us for the possibility that we might not, hence why we focus on 'coping' instead.

For an extra Overcoming Difficulty meditation practice, go to the Prioritise This website.

CHAPTER 7

Rejection

• • •

'You can be the ripest, juiciest peach in the world, and there's still going to be somebody who hates peaches.'

Dita Von Teese

I first tried to get an agent for this book in 2020.

It wasn't *exactly* the same one – the name was different, the content more somatic, less neuroscience-y – but the aim was identical: to help people like you and me better navigate the chaos of modern life.

I'd been working on the book for six months, the idea had come to me in the fugue state of early motherhood, and I felt ready to get it out there. I wrote a solid proposal which included sample chapters, market analysis and details around how I would promote the book (something all agents and publishers like to hear!), asked friends in the industry to look it over, and extensively researched agents to see who'd be a good fit.

At the beginning of January, I emailed 12 agencies with my proposal, explaining I was seeking representation.

Two weeks later the first reply arrived: 'Thank you very much for your submission. Unfortunately, this is not one for us, but please keep in mind that other agencies may feel differently.'

No agencies felt differently.

By the end of February, it had been rejected by them all and I was crushed. I am no stranger to professional rejection – I'd say on average

I get one commission for every ten articles I pitch to magazines and probably two out of five gigs from corporate workshop proposals I'm asked to submit. This level of rejection in my work life (as well as having had my fair share in my personal too) has, *generally*, hardened me. I've built up the capacity over the years – exposure therapy some might call it – to view most rejections as redirection.

This time was different. It didn't feel like the book had been rejected; it felt like *I* had been rejected. Early motherhood had flayed me emotionally thin, and this felt deeply personal.

Yet, in fortuitous timing, I'd recently been commissioned by *Vogue* to write a detailed feature (one of the rare ones that *wasn't* rejected) titled 'How to Overcome Rejection'. I won't say that I reread the piece and suddenly felt fine and was never affected by rejection again, because that's not what happened.

However, I did find that leaning on that article, as well as the extensive additional research that hadn't gone in (there's only so much one can say within an SEO-friendly 1,000-word limit), the wisdom of the experts I'd interviewed (such as psychotherapist Sara Rourke and coach Nicky Clinch) and my training in mindfulness and stress management, enabled me to crawl out of the hole I'd found myself in. (Shortly after, COVID hit and we all found ourselves in an *entirely* different kind of hole.)

The goal in life is not to avoid rejection.

Rejection is inevitable, it happens to us all – not just once, but many times over. And, while it can be deeply painful (for reasons I'll go into in a moment), it's a crucial part of developing as a person.[*] Rejection fosters learning, understanding and awareness. It keeps life in perspective, builds empathy and offers opportunity for growth and change.

My aim for this chapter is to help you become more comfortable with rejection. To discover how to take it less personally, reframe it as redirection and use it to build your resilience and drive. It's difficult, sometimes impossible, to have any control over what other people do or what happens to us in life. What we can control, however, is how we *respond*. Whether it's something big (a break-up) or something small (a colleague not following you on Instagram), as you make your way through these pages, you'll discover what's most helpful to you and build a toolkit in line with that. The learnings, coping strategies and

---

[*] Show me someone who's barely encountered rejection and I'll show you someone with narcissistic tendencies.

practices in this chapter won't necessarily take away the sting of rejection, but they will provide a soothing balm. Ultimately, they'll ensure that, when you find yourself in a rejection-related hole, you'll be able to crawl your way out too.

WHAT IS REJECTION?

There are too many definitions of rejection for me to rely on a dictionary here, so I'll broadly sum it up as *the act of being pushed away from someone or something.* However, as we all know from personal experience, when it happens to *you*, it feels like much more than that.

The painful emotions that accompany being rejected, excluded, scorned or ignored are complex – it's common to experience some combination of hurt, sadness, depression, anxiety, disappointment, distress, dejection, worthlessness, fear, shame or anger, among others. It's even not uncommon to experience physical responses to rejection, such as nausea, cramps or chest pain (also known as broken-heart syndrome). Rejection can be debilitating and life altering, and in fact many psychologists tie the experience closely to that of grief, of *living with loss*.[*]

Rejection occurs in every area of life – work, school, home, hobbies, relationships, friendships, social networks – and we can incur it from both people we love and respect, as well as perfect strangers. It can be individual, such as not being invited to a party that all your friends are going to, or collective, such as when the UK voted yes on Brexit and spurned the EU. We can feel rejected on any and every aspect of our 'self' – from our looks to our personality, intelligence, capability, talent, social standing and more.

There are, of course, the big rejections – a partner's infidelity, being fired from a job, not getting into your university of choice. But there's also the subtler pain of smaller ones, of being snubbed by a friend of a friend or ghosted after a first date. These ones, though smaller, can have a grinding effect over time, and, in our modern world, there now exist a myriad of tiny (but far from insignificant) ways that we can feel excluded or ignored in the digital sphere. The expansion of smartphones, dating apps, social media platforms and even email has created rife conditions for potential emotional wounding from hundreds, if not thousands, of people hour-to-hour, day-to-day. A potential date

---

[*] You may even experience some the five stages commonly associated with loss and grief: denial, anger, bargaining, depression and acceptance.

not replying to a message, a colleague not cc'ing you into an email, an unchecked comment on a WhatsApp group . . . It's death by a thousand digital paper cuts.

Naturally, the pain of a rejection depends on the depth of your relationship to the person or outcome. But while it's easy to make sense of the hurt of a rejected university application, it's harder to understand the painful effect of a friend never liking your videos on TikTok.

So, why do we care when that happens? Why do we care about being rejected *at all*?

THE SOCIAL BRAIN

From an evolutionary standpoint, pain (whether physical or mental) is necessary – it's a warning system that helps keep us alive. Our extreme emotional response to rejection and personal disappointment is simply part of this . . .

One of our deepest, most primal needs as human beings is to be accepted and to belong.[1] We are fundamentally social creatures, and our craving to connect likely developed through evolution. Our primordial ancestors lived and hunted in tribes, because in harsh environments with dangerous predators this maximised their chances of success and survival. Individuals who integrated with the group and formed close bonds with others were more likely to be 'popular', and therefore to reproduce and survive. Those who did not were likely to be abandoned or exiled, which, 200,000 years ago, meant death. The danger associated with ostracisation formed an innate fear of rejection in our ancestors, which has been passed down to us.

This neuro-biological drive to connect with others is in fact so strong that multiple studies have found little difference, in terms of brain activity, between social rejection and physical pain.[2] A broken leg and the hurt caused by being ghosted on a dating app are processed similarly by your brain – it doesn't know the difference between the two.* Studies have even shown that taking a pain blocker such as paracetamol can make a rejection feel less painful (though

---

*Take a moment here to consider the intense pain of being *cancelled*, of mass rejection . . . I've written about cancel culture over the years but have never come to any firm conclusion as to whether I think it's good (people being held accountable for their actions) or bad (deeply aggressive and isolating, sometimes disproportionately so). What do you think?

I absolutely don't suggest popping a pill whenever you anticipate being spurned).[3]

Moreover, we actually remember emotional pain for longer and in more detail than physical pain. I, for one, can't remember the physical pain of breaking my finger when I was 27, but I can clearly remember the agony and shame of being embarrassed in front of my peer group as a teenager. Furthermore, social situations and rejections are layered and nuanced (annoyingly, there's rarely just one 'answer' or 'solution' to hand) and our brain helps us traverse this complexity by reliving and analysing scenarios, trying to make them make sense (even if, as is often the case, it can't). This 'helpful' instinct is what leads us to lie awake all night obsessing over something we may or may not have said in a social situation, regardless of whether doing that actually makes us feel worse.

Experiencing strong feelings after a rejection is natural – it's how your social brain processes and recovers from a threat to your sense of belonging. And, in the same way you may not be able to prevent the pain or shock of a sprained ankle, your psychological pain reaction to rejection often isn't under your control either. What you *can* control, however, is how you navigate your feelings of loss, how you treat yourself and how you respond to your pain . . .

GHOSTED/SNUBBED/SPIRALS

As I repeat more than a few times in this book, our experience of a situation is greatly influenced by *our reaction* to it. We can't control how other people are going to treat us or what will happen to us in this often seemingly indiscriminate world. What we *can* control, however, is how we respond.

There are many ways to respond to rejection; some of which make *everything* worse.

When we react with hostility, rumination, negative self-talk or by withdrawing from others, we simply set ourselves up for more pain – multiple studies have linked these responses to a wide range of health concerns such as depression, loneliness, physical wellbeing problems and relationship issues.[4]

Let's look at how this can play out in three case studies . . .

1. A young woman I worked with was 'ghosted' after several dates with a man she'd met on a dating app. Before he disappeared, she

wasn't that sure about him, but the pain of the rejection led her to put him on a pedestal with self-critical thoughts such as 'He's amazing ... I'm not good enough for him ... I'm not good enough for anyone' flooding her brain. She outwardly used the anecdote of being ghosted to make her friends laugh, and she swore off the apps.

2. A corporate client felt snubbed and ignored by his boss. While they were not friends, they had a good working relationship and he felt valued and respected. Each morning his boss would stop by his desk to say hello. However, for a few days she'd walked straight to her office without even a glance. He catastrophised the situation and concluded that he'd done something wrong and was going to get fired. He started feeling angry and hostile towards her.

3. A completely random person that I've just made up finds herself in thought spirals every time a friend doesn't reply swiftly to a text message. She assumes that the lack of reply means they don't like her anymore. She starts worrying that maybe no one actually likes her ... ?

Now you don't need a single coaching qualification to know that these reactions (though perhaps *instinctive*) are unhelpful. Indeed, the people in these examples *knew* their responses were harmful; it was what to *do* about it that they struggled with. As I mention in the Introduction, knowledge doesn't always translate to action, and can sometimes even have the opposite effect with *too much* knowledge leading to apathy and inaction. Most people have a reasonable amount of self-awareness – they know they should think or behave differently; it's the *how* they get stuck on.

There are, however, much healthier, more effective and productive ways to respond to rejection. There are thoughts, behaviours and solution-focused coping strategies that, when *prioritised*, can transform your experience. Let's explore them ...

YOUR FOUR-PART STRATEGY TO RECOVER AND THRIVE AFTER REJECTION

1. EMOTIONAL FIRST AID

The first strategy after rejection is to provide yourself with immediate support for both your body and mind. Here are some ideas on how to do just that ...

Try mindfulness

As you will have gathered if you've read any of the preceding chapters, I believe mindfulness is the best first step for emotional recovery, laying solid ground for whatever follows . . . After a perceived rejection, step back and notice what you're thinking, feeling and experiencing. Do this without judgement and with compassion. Keep your focus in the present, trying not to fixate on the past or future. I am aware that this may feel like the last thing you want to do, however studies have found that mindfulness can help you more easily navigate rejection – providing space from the pain and improving a sense of connection that helps with recovery.[5]

Feel your feelings

As with most situations in life, one of the worst things you can do following a rejection is deny your feelings. By pushing them away, you make it harder for yourself to overcome them, so recognise and allow yourself to *feel* them without criticism (no mentally beating yourself up, please!). This practice will enable you to move through your emotions and process the pain of the rejection with greater ease. However, equally, don't wallow in your feelings. If you focus on finding fault in the situation or with another person, you may find your pain cemented by a sense of entitlement and blame. Be wary of *overindulging* in your pain – it can create a victim mentality which ultimately makes it harder to move on.

Focus on self-care

I know it's dull and I'm a broken record, but *do it*. Pay attention to the basic building blocks of your health (sleep, nutrition, etc.). Prioritise activities and people that support your wellbeing and foster a sense of ease, connection and/or relief. This might include movement, music, hobbies, meditation and so on – anything that nourishes and stabilises you.

Act don't react

It can be difficult to think clearly after a rejection on account of your brain having been hijacked by your feelings, but if possible, take a moment (or 50) to think through your response. You may want to react immediately, but instead attempt to first focus on the points above – these will help calm your system and enable you to better process the rejection. From that place of *relative* calm, you can decide how best to act and move forward.

2. SHIFT YOUR PERSPECTIVE
The second strategy is to challenge any unhelpful stories your brain is telling you and see how you can replace them with helpful ones.

Differentiate *being* rejected from *feeling* rejected
Some of the instances in which we *feel* rejected, we haven't been, so be wary of interpreting neutral or non-reactions from others as rejection when that's not the case. For example, a lower number of likes than usual on a social media post could easily be down to the algorithm, rather than your actual followers. Or a colleague who hasn't responded to an email isn't ignoring you, but is stressed and will reply in time. Often, a rejection has little to do with you and more to do with the other person or circumstance, so don't always assume it's personal. Ask yourself: *am I being overly sensitive? Are there are other factors I haven't considered? Am I taking this personally without enough information?*

Check your thoughts
On a similar note, it's essential to keep an eye on your *thoughts*, since the thoughts that pop up when you're feeling strong emotions (such as after a rejection) are not always the most accurate or helpful ones. Are they kind or unkind? Rational or irrational? Helpful or unhelpful? Can you think of ways to challenge, change or distract them?* Be wary of descending into a state of comparison – rejection becomes more painful when compared to other people's successes, so please, step away from your ex's new partner's social media accounts.

Review the experience, not yourself
While it's helpful to review a rejection and consider how things could have gone differently (*and* acknowledge the part you may have played), it's unhelpful to analyse your personality or who you are as an individual. As you examine the experience, focus on your actions and those of others, rather than *who* you are. Stay away from self-blaming, try not to internalise the experience, recognise that it's a temporary setback and not a permanent reflection of your abilities or self-worth. Practise self-compassion, avoid self-criticism, give yourself the empathy you'd offer a good friend.

---

*Refer to Chapter 1: Stress for more guidance on this.

REJECTION

Spread your self-worth thinly
My beliefs around self-worth align with my (probably stronger!) beliefs around Marmite – they are both linchpins of a good life, and they must both be thinly spread. The more you can scatter your sense of self-worth and identity across a wide range of areas – work, family, friends, hobbies, etc. – the more resilient you'll be after a rejection, or any disappointment. If, however, you wrap your identity around one aspect (e.g. your career) a rejection in that area (such as one bad job interview) will be felt as a *threat* to your sense of identity. Think about the ways you define yourself, then focus on building up all the pillars of your life, so that if one comes crashing down, you have plenty more to help you stay upright.

3. REBUILD THROUGH CONNECTION AND REFLECTION
The third strategy looks at how you can regain your sense of self as well as your connection to yourself and others.

Focus on your strengths
Reminding yourself of your strengths and achievements, positive qualities and past successes will help provide some much-needed counterbalance to the negative feelings that accompany rejection. Make a list (written or in your head) of five to ten strengths and good qualities that you possess, then brainstorm how you can better apply them in your day-to-day life. For example, if honesty is a quality of yours then focus on engaging in open and honest conversations with your friends and loved ones.

Spend time with supportive people
Speaking of friends and loved ones . . . when you've encountered a rejection, your brain will be feeling socially 'unsafe'. Receiving love, compassion and support has been shown to repair that sense of belonging and help your brain feel safe again.[6] Connecting with others can help you feel included and give you the opportunity to share your pain – reach out to people who nourish you, stay away from those who don't. Confide in them and I guarantee they'll share their own experiences of rejection with you too. Remember, you're not alone.

Look for signs you're valued

Rejection can easily spiral into a self-fulfilling prophecy; if you're looking for it, you'll find small rejections absolutely everywhere – whether it's a colleague not including you in a meeting or a partner forgetting to plan a date night. If, however, you look for signs that you are *valued*, you're more likely to start seeing them everywhere instead. Don't let one rejection colour your view of every interaction; rather, focus on the signs that show you are appreciated and loved.

Consider your priorities

A rejection can easily throw you off track, particularly if it's connected to something you really wanted. Post-rejection is a good time to think about your priorities, to consider what's of meaning and value to you, and whether you are living in line with that. If a priority is compassion, ask whether you are treating yourself with compassion. If a priority is adventure, see how you can build more into life, to help align your days with what truly matters to you.

4. MOVE FORWARD WITH INTENTION

The final strategy is to look at how you can motivate yourself to grow and plan for the future. Often, this is best done after the emotional wave has passed (as you'll have more mental clarity), but if you have a solution-focused brain you may want to dive in sooner and use those negative feelings to help drive you forward.

Make an alternative plan

As I wrote earlier, not everyone is always ready to hear the advice of 'rejection is just redirection' immediately following a disappointment (me included!). However, when you *do* feel ready (or *almost* ready – sometimes you need a nudge) begin to prioritise thoughts around *redirection* and how rejection is a (painful) process of elimination. Remind yourself that your pain is a sign of how much you wanted something in the first place, of how much you *care*. What do the feelings mean? What's the goal underneath it all? What do you really want? After you've answered those questions, brainstorm possible solutions – such as engaging in a difficult conversation or focusing on different directions you could take. Are there any *new* opportunities you can embrace? Perhaps even ones that better align with your priorities, values and long-term goals? Create a new plan and then another one. Keep going with alternative plans until you get to a place that feels right for you.

Set helpful goals
Goal-setting works on the dopaminergic pathways of the brain and, in the right circumstances, can have a transformative impact on your wellbeing. Set achievable objectives for yourself in areas of your life unrelated to the rejection – for example, after a break-up, set an attainable career or health-related goal instead. This will help provide a sense of accomplishment and rebuild your confidence and self-worth. (Chapter 9: Moving Forward offers much advice here.)

See opportunities for growth
When you first experience a rejection, someone saying 'Wow, what a learning opportunity!' probably doesn't land very well. So use this approach only once you feel willing to hear that. But do use it, because rejection has a way of revealing things to us, of uncovering patterns of behaviour or thoughts that aren't necessarily of service or support. Ask yourself: *how can I grow as a person from this rejection?* Can you see how you would do things differently next time? Or, if you were particularly self-critical, can you investigate *why* you talked to yourself in that way and what you can do to change your inner voice so that it's more supportive next time?

BACK TO GHOSTED/SNUBBED/SPIRALS

Hopefully you can see how one or more of those strategies would work for you. If any felt particularly relevant, you could scribble a star or note next to it. It's easy in the moment of pain to forget the things that are helpful or useful to us – highlighting strategies now will make you more likely to put them into practice following a future rejection.

For now, though, let's jump back and see how we can apply these strategies and techniques to the three examples from earlier in the chapter . . .

1. I really felt for the young woman who was ghosted – it truly is a brutal experience, made worse by the lack of closure, and it can deeply affect self-worth. However, what we saw was that when she stopped pushing her feelings away, and instead allowed herself to feel

the disappointment she was masking, she was able to rebuild that sense of worth. We focused on self-care, made a list of her strengths and positive qualities (specifically, as a partner), challenged her self-critical thoughts using the 'Four life-changing questions' in Chapter 1: Stress, reviewed the experience (including her own input) and then set one achievable goal to give her morale a boost. When she felt ready, she went back to dating, armed with improved boundaries and a better understanding of herself and her needs.

2. Now I tell this corporate client story at almost every company workshop I deliver, because it's a perfect example of someone's 'social brain' fabricating an unhelpful, *incorrect* story. Our brain loves to make sense of a situation, but often it does so with wildly unreliable sources . . . On this occasion, eventually his boss called him into her office. 'You're getting fired today!' his inner voice shouted as he walked in, however, she didn't fire him. In fact, she told him she was having a difficult time with one of her children and was feeling overwhelmed, and then asked whether he could help by taking some of her workload. He wasn't being fired; he was being given *more* responsibility and trust. As is so often the case, it was *not about him*. Now, every time he assumes some perceived rejection is, he asks: what else could be at play? Instead of jumping to conclusions, he checks his thoughts and differentiates *being* rejected from *feeling* rejected, which saves him unnecessary stress and anxiety.

3. With this final case study, which is, you may have guessed, my own, I'll give you some backstory . . . By the age of eight I'd been to five schools. At my fifth* the small friendship group I'd formed turned against me. I don't know what made them turn, and it wasn't severe bullying, but I was excluded and ignored, and they were cruel (as little girls can be). I was *rejected* by the girls I thought were my best friends, and it was immensely painful. And, honestly, I think there's some part of me that's never quite got over that experience, that there are neural pathways around that early rejection that have made me overly sensitive to any potential adult ones (even though I have many amazing, loyal, life-enhancing friends who I trust one hundred percent with my life). And these days, I know I can do something about my brain, having taught myself over the past

---

*Which was also my second as my parents had taken me out and moved me to two others before putting me back into that one. Confused? Imagine eight-year-old me!

12–15 years to talk myself out of these emotional spirals. I differentiate *feeling* rejected from *being* rejected; assure myself these are old pathways in my social brain trying to keep me safe; check my thoughts; consider other potential factors at play; remind myself that situations in life have less to do with me than I think they do; try my best to *act* instead of *react*. And now, *most of the time*, I no longer spiral.

THE STORY THAT NO ONE COULD BEAT

With hindsight, I'm glad I'm writing this book now, rather than in 2020. I've learned so much over the past six years (both professionally and personally) which has made me better at my jobs and this book will be improved as a result. I genuinely see that particular rejection as a *good* thing; however, I'd be lying if I told you that it doesn't still sting a little if I dwell on it.

But of course it does. Evolution has bequeathed us a social brain, which responds with physical-like pain signals to any threat to our social acceptance, belonging or standing. Feeling hurt after a break-up, being ghosted or not getting the job of your dreams is to be expected. You can try experimenting with the techniques offered by Jia Jiang's website Rejection Therapy[*] to see if these dampen your response, yet, ultimately, your brain will almost always feel the pain of rejection because it's evolved to do so.

I believe, then, that it's finding ways to *process* our pain, to *support* ourselves and uncovering *constructive* ways to move forward that truly matters. It's learning to develop resilience and compassion towards the inevitable reality of rejection, difficulty and disappointment. And we do this over and over again, despite the pain, because we know that rejection, like failure, is part of the process of creating the life we want.

It's also a genuine opportunity for self-reflection and growth, since (infuriatingly) we tend to learn our best lessons in moments of pain and loss, rather than when life is ticking along. And, as we all know, distance and time can reveal that a certain rejection was good for you – I actually met my husband through a painful romantic rejection, so . . . there's an uplifting rejection-as-redirection story for you!

---

[*] www.rejectiontherapy.com. He also has a TED Talk if of interest: https://www.ted.com/talks/jia_jiang_what_i_learned_from_100_days_of_rejection

It can be helpful to make a bank of these types of stories of your own to draw on the next time you feel crushed by a rejection. You don't have to trust that everything happens for a reason (unless you do – in which case, great) but you do have to trust that you have the capacity to pick yourself up again. To know that, *at some point*, you will tell yourself that if you weren't right for that person or situation, then they weren't right for you either. That you will support yourself; that you will redirect yourself with each rejection to something better.

When it came to the book, I eventually managed to do just that . . . COVID hit shortly after, and I, like much of the world, had to pivot* my predominantly in-person business to online, while parenting a one-year-old, who, to *literally* keep us on our toes, learned to walk on the first day of the first lockdown. I started daily 'lives' on Instagram (remember when they were a thing?), where I shared the content of the book-that-wasn't-to-be with my audience there instead. I tried (unsuccessfully) to pitch it as a column,† before eventually building what became a successful four-week online course around it instead. I also started my podcast, *Priorities*, figuring that if a book wasn't on the cards, it was the perfect moment to go after a different long-time goal of mine.

That title of that podcast has since become my entire personality. I built my career around this concept of priorities and have had more success with it than I could have imagined in 2020 . . . It was a good redirection, even though it took five years for me to achieve the original goal of finding an agent (*Hi, Morwenna!*) and publishing the book.

Whether it's a friend, a romantic partner or a job, emotional attachments around rejection don't disappear instantly, especially if your feelings were deep or the connection was significant. Over time, however, their intensity will likely diminish, allowing you to move forward.‡ Try to let go of the factors that are outside of your control; the reasons behind other people's choices and actions are complex, and I think it's helpful to remember that, sometimes, the clear answers you so desperately want just might not be there. Show yourself kindness and grace, keep a bit of hope, set new goals. Don't shy away from social

---

*The word of the pandemic.
† FYI: it took me another four years before I secured one of those!
‡ If your feelings do not diminish and you're suffering intensely with a rejection, whether present or past, and have the means to talk to a mental health professional, I suggest doing so. See the Resources at the back of this book.

and professional risks because they might cause rejection – stay open to what life throws your way.

The late author and illustrator Dr Seuss (real name: Theodor Seuss Geisel) has sold more than 600 million copies of his books. Film adaptations of his work (*The Grinch* is a firm favourite in our home) have grossed over $1 billion at the box office. He is widely recognised as one of the most prolific and gifted children's writers of all time. And yet his first book, provisionally titled *A Story That No One Could Beat*, was a story that no one, at first, wanted – Geisel was rejected by every single publisher in Manhattan. He'd decided to give up and was planning to burn his drawings, when, luckily for him (and us), a chance encounter with an old classmate, recently appointed as an editor with a small left-wing press, changed everything and led to Geisel becoming the exceptional talent he is known as today (the book became *And to Think That I Saw It on Mulberry Street*). In my humble opinion, his books are unbeatable.

And I think you probably are too.

PRIORITISE THIS

- Our strong emotional reaction to rejection is based on our evolutionary need to belong to a group – that is, you have a social brain.
- Certain 'natural' responses to rejection are unhelpful and can make the painful feelings worse over time.
- There are four complimentary strategies we can take to recover and thrive after rejection.
- Differentiate being rejected from feeling rejected.
- Setting achievable goals can help you overcome a rejection more quickly.
- Prioritise thoughts and behaviours that support rebuilding your sense of belonging and acceptance.
- Accept and acknowledge your feelings, but respond to rejection by considering solutions and alternatives.

PRACTICES TO HELP WITH REJECTION

TIME TRIPPING

Originally coined by American psychologist Richard Lazarus in 1981, but perhaps better known by Stephen Palmer's* label of 'Time Projection Imagery', Time tripping† involves imagining how a situation or belief might look in the future. It's used in coaching to encourage a client to stop blowing a situation out of perspective or to 'de-awfulise' it,‡ to gain some perspective and reduce the intensity of any negative emotions. The technique, as with many in this book, helps demonstrate the lasting impact of our thoughts and beliefs on how we experience life. It's traditionally applied to stress, but is easily applied to rejection and failure too.

How it works:

- Choose a recent rejection that is painful or is still bothering you.
- Picture yourself three months from now. Visualise every aspect of your life. Can you see how your life would have grown positively around or in spite of the rejection? Is the rejection still as painful in the future as it is today? Will the memory and significance of the rejection have faded? Can you see yourself getting on with life?
- If yes, then do the same but six months from now and ask the same questions.
- If still yes, then keep 'tripping' forward – one year, 18 months, two years and so on – until you find a point in time where it no longer feels painful.

A COMPASSIONATE LETTER (OR EMAIL)

Strong evidence has been found to suggest that both offering and receiving compassion helps to regulate psychological distress, such as the pain of rejection,[7] and this simple exercise encourages you to do both! You'll be writing a letter to yourself from the perspective of a wise, compassionate person offering the suffering side of yourself kindness and support. This is most

---
*Founder-director of the Centre for Coaching and one of my tutors.
†I use the original name for the very simple reason that it's more fun.
‡See SITs and SATs in Chapter 1: Stress.

helpful for when you're in the depths of a painful rejection or are struggling to let go of a past disappointment.

How it works:

- Grab a pen and paper or open a new email (don't worry, you won't actually be sending it).
- With the rejection in mind, think about what you would say to a loved one who is suffering as you are. If you feel stuck, think of a wise person you know (or even someone famous) and imagine what they would say instead. Imagine how a compassionate person would try to help you make sense of this rejection and process it (the 'Strategies' section in this chapter can help).
- Start your letter by acknowledging the situation and your painful emotions, something along the lines of: 'I'm so sorry you're going through this, I know how hard it is to feel this way . . .' and so on.
- Include a reminder that everyone experiences rejection.
- Acknowledge the context of the rejection, any factors outside of your control and the actions of other people. If you believe your own behaviour played a part, mention that too, while retaining your self-compassion.
- Remind yourself of your strengths and good qualities, as well as your priorities and values.
- Consider any lessons to be learned and how you can use this letter to guide yourself to see opportunities for growth.
- If it feels appropriate, include suggestions or questions around future goals or alternative plans that will help you find redirection.
- When you've finished writing, read the letter or email out loud to yourself using a kind, compassionate voice.
- If this exercise resonates, try it more than once. One study found that doing it daily for a week improved feelings of depression.[8]

Go to the Prioritise This website for an extra Mountain meditation practice.

CHAPTER 8

Comparison

● ● ●

'The grass is not, in fact, always greener on the other side of the fence . . . It's greenest where it is watered.'

Robert Fulghum

As that world-famous, esteemed philosopher, the hookah-smoking caterpillar in Lewis Carroll's *Alice's Adventures in Wonderland*, once asked . . . *Who? Are? You?*

'I hardly know,' Alice shyly replied.

For many years, I sympathised with Alice – I didn't have a true grip on my 'self'. If using the *Merriam-Webster Collegiate Dictionary* definition of self-worth – 'a sense of one's own value as a human being'[1] – mine was non-existent. My external life may have been full and 'impressive', but my internal world was so warped that I was unable to see much value in myself. The consequence?

Comparison became my default.

I measured myself constantly – against friends, colleagues, strangers on the street, and, of course, random people online. Anyone who wandered into my line of sight became a benchmark, and, more often than not, I fell short.

I'm hardly alone in this. The fashion world, where I spent over a decade, is built on comparison. While the bi-annual fashion weeks may *in theory* be about showcasing the 'next big thing',[*] in reality they're about competition – on the runway, of course, but also in the audience, among the editors... Who's been seated where?[†] Who's wearing what? Who's been invited to which party? Who's got the best freebies? We were all sizing each other up, all the time, even those who claimed to be above it. (Spoiler: no one is.)

While this environment didn't help my relentless measuring-up, ultimately, it was my low self-worth that led me to either seek evidence to confirm my perceived shortcomings ('She's better than me') or try to prop myself up by putting others down ('At least I'm doing better than them'). Unsurprisingly, neither route worked.

The word 'comparison' comes from the Latin *comparāre*, meaning 'to bring or place together'. But that's not what we tend to do when we compare today. We don't place things together with curiosity or care – *we separate*, creating distance, hierarchies, winners and losers. We use comparison not to understand but to judge, even though, more often than not, the person we're truly judging is *ourselves*.

In itself, comparison is neutral – it's just noticing similarities or differences. The impact lies in *how* you compare:

- When you compare from a place of appreciation or inspiration, it can motivate you.
- When you compare from a place of judgement or lack, it can dismantle you.

Sounds simple, right? If only.

We are all living in a *comparison trap* – with a 2008 study finding that comparative thinking accounts for a staggering 12 percent of all our thoughts.[2] Comparison becomes a true 'problem', however, when it's constant, unconscious and/or tied to your self-worth. There's that well-known adage – *Comparison is the thief of joy* – which, while it may be spot-on, doesn't give the whole picture... 'Problematic' comparison steals more than joy. It filches contentment, connection and confidence and, left unchecked, builds unhelpful thought loops – cycles of self-judgement, resentment or superiority – that pull us further from our priorities and values and closer to anxiety, low self-worth or

---

[*] Insider secret: The 'next big thing' is almost always some kind of old thing dressed up anew with a higher price tag

[†] Your seat is a true mark of status; however, the real measure was whether an editor doing your exact job at another publication had a better seat. I've watched editors refuse their assigned seat or steal another editor's outright. It's a jungle out there.

performative behaviour. Ultimately, it holds us back from doing the things we want to do and becoming who we want to be.

My aim for this chapter isn't to pretend comparison is simple. It's not. And I won't be telling you that, after reading this, you'll never compare again. Rather, I'll show you how to improve your self-worth to help *shift how you view comparison* – to notice when it's holding you back and discover how to let it move you forward instead.

WHAT EVEN *IS* SELF-WORTH?

The self-worth theory of motivation, proposed by Martin V. Covington and others, posits that the highest human priority is the search for self acceptance. Building from this, research has found that around 50 percent of our feelings of self-worth seem to be inherited, while the other 50 percent are environmental.[3] Though the genetic influence or specifics of 'environmental' remain vague, it's useful to understand that, as always, both nature and nurture play a part. (And crucially, that with nurture, there's always scope for change.)

Self-worth is deeply personal – indeed, we each have our own set of parameters that help define it. However, if we use the broad *Merriam-Webster* definition to set those parameters, then the question to ask yourself becomes: *how do I define my value?*

There are many ways that we can, and do, measure our worthiness in life. More often than not, we use external markers – common touchstones we all rely on to compare ourselves to others (and ourselves to our former or future selves), such as how we look, how much we earn, what we do and who we know. And while it's normal and healthy to value and take pride in your achievements, accomplishments and appearance, completely basing your value – your self-worth – on anything outside of your control is not a great idea. What happens when you fail? Or lose your job? Or your looks fade? That foundation crumbles, your sense of self-worth disintegrating along with it.

I personally think of high self-worth as having a clear understanding of (and compassion for) who I am deep down inside, beneath all the layers I may present to the world. It means having internal faith that I'm of value, that I deserve empathy, kindness, love and respect regardless of what I do or don't achieve. That I am good enough, full stop.

What it doesn't mean, however, is holding an inflated sense of my own ability, or believing that I am always right. That would make me a narcissist.* And high self-worth is the opposite of narcissism. It's knowing that you do fail and make mistakes (sometimes really big ones). It's appreciating that you have weaknesses and faults and can be monumentally wrong about people and situations. It's understanding that you are far from perfect and likely to remain that way (i.e. human) for ever. High self-worth doesn't give you free rein to be a terrible person. It's about confronting your mistakes, failures or wrongdoings, and believing that, despite them (or perhaps even because of them), you remain worthy.

I will admit, it's easier to do this as an intellectual exercise than in real life – particularly in our modern world where the constant barrage of curated imagery via social media and advertising makes us believe we should look a certain way, own a lot of nice things and go on all sorts of Instagrammable holidays. We're more influenced by other people's lives than ever before; we can be made to feel lacking simply by glancing at our phone.

Attempting to be the best version of yourself is something I actively pursue, and it's my job to help others do the same, yet I feel there's something uniquely pernicious about life in the mid-2020s, whereby, thanks largely in part to social media, our world has become so competitive and comparative that we need to feel special just to feel half decent about ourselves. We all want to be 'above average', even though it's statistically impossible for us all to be so. But, still, we try. Often by comparing ourselves to others, so that – whether consciously or unconsciously – we puff ourselves up and put others down in order to feel superior, in order to raise our self-esteem.

Though this pursuit of superiority is rooted in our brain's understanding of societal hierarchies and survival, it's clearly an unstable foundation. Tie up your self-worth with improving the self and being the 'best' version of you (possibly, 'better' than others), and it becomes easy to move into a place of separation, isolation and, yes, narcissism. The other big question is: what happens to your mental health when you don't meet the standards you've set for yourself? Or even, let's say you do achieve your 'best' self: how do you hang on to it with life's inevitable ebbs and flows? The last thing you want is for your sense of

---

* P.S. If you've ever worried that you're a narcissist, you needn't – apparently the sheer act of worrying that you could be one makes you not one. True narcissists never concern themselves with such things.

self to be so unstable that it depends on any random success or failure to make or break you. Or that in the absence of constant, unwavering success you can't feel good about yourself. All that can easily lead to you avoiding situations that could create feelings of inadequacy or failure, which in essence could lead you to avoid *life itself.*

High self-worth isn't just a 'nice' thing to have; it impacts our ability to navigate much of modern life – if our self-worth is robust, we will better weather a romantic rejection, a failure at work or even just a stressful day. Brain scans have shown that high self-worth builds resilience, making us less likely to experience pain from common emotional wounds such as rejection or failure and more likely to bounce back from them quicker. On a neurochemical level, higher self-worth seems to lead to less cortisol being released into our bloodstream in a stressful situation which makes us both less vulnerable to anxiety and more able to cope with stress.

I don't believe there is an 'end' point with self-worth. You don't get to a certain place and that's it; you've got it for life. It's a continuous process, influenced and impacted by so much, particularly external changes – for instance the breakdown of a relationship or having a baby (every new mother I've known has experienced some sort of self-worth upheaval!). Developing robust self-worth is a lifelong relationship, one that will ebb and flow and, in all likelihood, that you'll need to work on for ever.

This is not a bad thing.

This is the nature of relationships, and the relationship you have with yourself (so clichéd but so true!) is the most important one you will ever have.

EIGHT WAYS TO IMPROVE YOUR SELF-WORTH

1. **Increase your self-understanding.** Imagine that everything you have is suddenly taken away from you (career, possessions, achievements, status, etc.). Ask: without all of that, who am I, what is important to me and what makes me of value? Can you understand who you are and what your worth is underneath all the layers?
2. **Reinforce your value as a being rather than a 'doing'.** Focus on the fact that you are valuable for who you are, not what you look like or what you do. Whenever you become

conscious of attaching yourself to external sources of validation, step back and create distance. Remind yourself of what does not determine your self-worth.

3. **Reaffirm your worth after a failure.** This is a good way to remain connected to yourself when something goes wrong. Choose a recent perceived failure and then jot down a list of the positive qualities you have that relate to the 'failure'. For example, after a painful break-up, note the qualities that make you a brilliant partner (e.g. loyalty, compassion, fun, naughtiness). Or, if you've failed to get a job you applied for, jot down the qualities that make you a good employee (responsible, punctual, team player, etc.).

4. **Do something for someone else.** It's my sincerest belief that in order to appreciate our own worth we also need to connect with the worth of others. And this is backed up by science! Studies consistently find that people who volunteer have higher levels of happiness and purpose.[4]

5. **Forgive yourself after you've messed up.** Allowing yourself to make mistakes is at the core of improving self-worth. Bring to mind a time that you've truly messed up – for example treating a friend badly. Spend a few moments thinking about it, then tell yourself that, yes, you didn't behave at your best, but you can't change the past. All you can do is apologise, if possible, and aim to do better next time. You are allowed to be forgiven; one mistake does not define who you are.

6. **Compare yourself to others, but not in the way you think.** Forget what society might value most – money, status, etc. – start judging people on their kindness, empathy, respect for others and how they treat those around them*. Compare yourself to those markers.

7. **Challenge your inner voice.** The voice inside your head is likely to be both the one you hear most often and the one you believe to be most true (it's literally *me* after all!) Unfortunately, when our self-worth is low, we damage it further by being self-critical, which leads us to feel even lower, which then leads to more negative thoughts. To help free yourself from this loop, use the thought-repatterning practices from

---

* Nothing is more telling about the kind of person you are than how you talk to staff in a restaurant or coffee shop!

Chapter 1: Stress to interrupt, challenge and replace your self-critical thoughts.

8. **Spread your sense of self-worth across all areas of your life.** While ideally your self-worth wouldn't be tied up with anything external, while we are working towards that place, know that one of the easiest and most actionable ways to protect it is by spreading your value across many areas – from work to relationships, home life, hobbies, spirituality/religion and so on. Ideally, connect with the underlayer of these – for example at work focus less on the promotion you received and more on how you supported the struggling new hire. Find your sources of worth, then integrate more of them into your life – just don't put all your eggs in one basket.

WHY DO WE COMPARE?

We can think of comparison in two ways – upward and downward:

Upward is when we compare ourselves to people we perceive as doing better – more successful, more attractive, more 'together'. It can be motivating if you possess high self-worth or a strong sense of autonomy, but, if not, can instead result in feelings of inadequacy or defeat.

Downward, meanwhile, is when we compare ourselves to people we perceive as doing worse. This can provide a temporary mood or ego boost, but also reinforces a scarcity mindset and a (fragile) sense of superiority.

Whether we like to admit it or not, we all sometimes puff ourselves up at the expense of others or shrink ourselves in response to how others appear to be doing. I'm not immune to it myself.

Yet, as with every topic in this book, comparison isn't just something we *do* – it's something we're *designed* for. A deeply ingrained human behaviour, it's rooted in our brain's understanding of social hierarchies and survival. From an evolutionary standpoint, comparison and envy[*] were once useful – determining where we stood in our group and how we could improve literally advanced society. It gave us the drive to seek out what others possess, and above all, helped us stay safe, secure and *alive*.

---

[*] In case you're unsure of the difference between envy and jealousy, *envy* is when you want what someone else has, while *jealousy* is the fear of losing what you already have to someone else.

And so, we are comparison creatures, with social brains designed to constantly scan and evaluate our environment through an interpersonal lens. In today's world, however, the frequency and scale of comparison has exploded, and this has led to what psychologists call *lifestyle envy* – a sharp rise in dissatisfaction not necessarily because our lives are bad, but because they don't appear to measure up.

Research supports this, showing that comparing ourselves to the top performers in any field increases our negative mindset.[4] The higher the bar we set based on others, the worse we tend to feel, and social media's endless curated content intensifies this. It is contextless (i.e. we have no actual idea what's going on behind the screen of someone's life), which reinforces not just comparison, but perfectionism – what has been dubbed the 'Instasham effect'.

Emotions like shame, rejection and jealousy exist only in the context of other people – they are *relational*. And, according to psychologist Leon Festinger's 1954 social comparison theory, we evaluate our value – our abilities, skills, attitudes, opinions and appearance – by comparing ourselves to the people around us. We use them as benchmarks, or reference points, to help us define and understand ourselves. Ultimately, Festinger proposed, we only learn who we are and what we're worth by measuring ourselves against others.

The impact of this social comparison is shaped by two key factors:

1. **Similarity** – we tend to compare ourselves more frequently to those who we perceive as similar to us, whether in age, profession, lifestyle or values.
2. **Relevance** – we're more likely to compare ourselves to others in areas that matter deeply to us, whether that's parenting, appearance, work success or creativity.

For much of human history, however, our reference point – the people we compared ourselves to – was minute: just family, neighbours and co-workers. Mass media changed all that. Through newspapers, magazines, television and film, we gained access to a new tier of people to compare ourselves with – celebrities, public figures, people living lives seemingly a million miles away from our own. But even then, their world felt separate – they were *there* and we were *here*.

Not anymore.

The internet has expanded our group to include every single person with an internet connection. Social media has given us a continuous (warped) window into the lives of others; whether it's our friends, family, celebrities or perfect strangers, we have other people's daily habits, meals, children, partners, outfits, careers, yoga poses, holidays, and everything in between, right there at our fingertips, at all times. Every scroll is an opportunity to compare, and thanks to algorithms designed to keep us scrolling, the content we see is curated and filtered, often quite literally, which means we're not comparing ourselves to reality, but rather to a carefully crafted version of it. (Moreover, the people and groups we are now faced with differ from us dramatically in terms of indicators such as wealth, status, power, physical appearance and fame, which leaves even more potential for us to compare ourselves negatively.) Even when people do share their challenges or failures, it's often in the service of an inspirational reframe – it's rare to see someone simply *being* in the mess of life, without eventually tying it up in some neat, aesthetically pleasing bow.

The result is that we assume everyone else is doing better than we are, that somehow, we're the *only one* failing to keep up.

And this constant measuring subtly, but deeply, shapes our sense of self. I've had more than one client come to me wishing to reshape their relationship with their 'self', and changing their relationship with comparison is one of the first places we start.

M, a freelance designer, was convinced she was falling behind. Every time she opened Instagram, she was hit with a wave of inadequacy – seeing peers winning awards, publishing books or getting invited to events she didn't even know about. 'I feel like I'm not doing enough,' she told me, 'even though I never seem to stop working.' When we looked deeper, it wasn't the achievements themselves she envied, but the perceived recognition and sense of belonging they seemed to signal. Once she realised that, she started to redefine success in terms of impact and creative satisfaction, instead of public recognition. That shift didn't stop her comparing overnight, but it did give her a better filter for deciding (and prioritising) what really mattered.

Interestingly, research has now revealed that social comparison activates the brain's reward system, specifically the ventral striatum – an area that lights up when we experience pleasure or success.[5] This suggests that outperforming others can be as rewarding to the brain as receiving a personal reward.* Our brain wants us to do well in life

---

*Yes, the opposite is also true.

and when we outpace someone else, it perceives this as a 'win'. This biological wiring can reinforce comparative behaviours, especially in competitive environments or online platforms that highlight metrics such as likes, shares or followers.

But, of course, just because something is biologically ingrained doesn't make it healthy or helpful. Our wiring towards comparison isn't inherently bad – it can drive ambition, creativity and personal growth. Friendly competition, for example, has been found to be highly effective in pushing people to exercise more.[6] However, constant social comparison can be dangerous, engendering a negative physiological response (you may recall from Chapter 7: Rejection that physical and social pain light up the *same* networks in the brain) that impacts, among other things, your cognition.[7] The algorithm takes us further away from ourselves, and it's important to be aware of the *how* and the *why* behind our comparisons. Are we using comparison as a tool to inspire and motivate, or to diminish ourselves? And can we get to a place where we can admire others' achievements without feeling like we're falling behind?

Five signs you're stuck in the comparison trap

Comparison can be subtle – it can shape your choices and affect your energy without you even realising it. Some signs it might be getting in your way include:

1. **You downplay your own achievements.** Instead of celebrating your own progress, you dismiss it as not enough.
2. **You struggle to start or finish things.** You put off starting something important or lose momentum halfway through because someone else already nailed it.
3. **You feel resentment towards people you love.** You may *want* to feel happy for your friend's promotion or your sibling's engagement, but you don't. You may even feel bitter, with their success seeming like it reflects your own perceived lack. (P.S. It doesn't.)
4. **You're living by someone else's script.** Instead of listening to what feels right to you on the inside, you chase what looks good from the outside and make choices based on other people's priorities or timelines, rather than your own.

5. **You constantly feel 'behind'.** No matter what you achieve, it *never* feels like enough. You measure your progress against other people's highlights, and as a result feel a constant, low- (or high-) grade sense of failure.

HOW TO MANAGE AND OVERCOME COMPARISON

In all likelihood, we will *never* stop comparing ourselves to others, so let's look at some of the processes that can help us use comparison to thrive. There's quite a few, so I've divided them into four sections. As always, pick the ones that resonate best with you.

SHIFT YOUR PERSPECTIVE
These strategies help reframe comparison from something harmful to something constructive by changing how you interpret it:

1. **Awareness is the first step.** Of course, it always is ... Comparison is deeply human but can also often be *unconscious*. Start by noticing when, why and how you compare. Ask: *what triggered this? How does it make me feel? What's the truth behind this thought?*

2. **Stop viewing life as a zero-sum game.** Just because they win, it doesn't mean you lose. Try to inch yourself away from a *scarcity* mindset ('There's not enough to go round') and towards an *abundance* one ('There's enough for everyone, including me') instead. Someone else having something doesn't mean there's less for you. Also, ultimately (once your basic food and safety needs are met), the most meaningful resources – joy, peace, love – aren't finite. Plenty of the important stuff to go round. (I know, I'm a complete hippy at heart.)

3. **Swap envy for insight.** Envy may be painful, but it can also be *useful*. Ask: *what is this envy trying to tell me about what I want or need?* Sometimes, the results can be surprising – for example, I had a client who drilled down into her feelings of envy for a social media influencer friend and then realised they were more about

the sense of freedom and confidence that her friend appeared to possess than her actual life. *That* she could work on, and *that* was her insight. *What's yours?* Let envy guide you towards the unmet needs and wants in your own life.

4. **Swap comparison for inspiration.** Building on from that idea, can you reframe someone else's success as proof of *possibility*, rather than a reflection of your inadequacy? Don't be discouraged, be inspired. Ask yourself: *what am I trying to achieve with this comparison? What can I learn from this?* Focus on the steps you can take to close the gap, instead of how far behind you feel. Be inspired by the big picture but seek learnings from the little things. For example, if you're comparing yourself to a friend who's an amazing runner, look at what habits or training/recovery plan they use and ask them for tips, *get inspired.*

BUILD INNER STABILITY

These tools focus on strengthening self-worth, identity, and emotional resilience so that comparison doesn't destabilise you:

1. **Know yourself and your priorities.** If you're constantly looking outward at others, it's impossible to tune in to your own priorities. Ask: *what truly matters to me? What are my values, priorities and goals?* That's why one of the most helpful practices is to *define your own version of success* (which the next chapter, Chapter 9: Moving Forward, will help you do). Return to it whenever you catch yourself drifting too far into someone else's world. Focus on your own instead.

2. **Listen to the stories you tell yourself.** As we covered in Chapter 1: Stress, our thoughts shape how we see ourselves and the world around us. And often, it's our thoughts and the narrative we create, rather than the reality, that actually hurts. Ask: *is this story I'm telling myself objectively true?* Learn to separate perception from reality, especially online. Much of Chapter 1 can help with this.

3. **Focus on *enoughness*.** Sometimes we need a bit of mediocrity, to favour imperfection and contentment over constant striving. Try the mindset of 'enough' – not *less than*, not *better than*, just *enough as I am.* It's important to strive, but know that you don't *always* have to outperform to be worthy.

4. **Practise gratitude.** Honestly, the advice of 'Be thankful' can sometimes grate, but reflecting on what you are grateful for, *no matter how small*, can also create a mental shift. Ask: *how much has a skill of my own improved over time? How much worse could a situation be than it is in reality? Who may see me as a role model right now?* Train your brain to see and seek the good.

5. **Tie comparison to identity, not outcome.** We tend to use comparison to measure what we've done (or not done). Instead, use it to nudge yourself towards who you want to *be*. When you find yourself comparing, ask: *what does this show me about the kind of person I want to become?* That shift from result to identity can help you stop obsessing over what someone *has* and start noticing what you *value* instead. In essence, let their life point you back to your own.

INTERRUPT THE HABIT LOOP

These are the behavioural tools and actions to take when you start falling into a comparison spiral:

1. **Watch your own behaviour (especially online).** If you don't want to feel stuck in an envy-inducing comparison trap, then ask yourself whether you often try to inspire envy in others. The more you can move away from that place of fuelling comparison and vanity, the less you'll feel in competition with others. Be wary of social media. Ask: *why am I posting? Why am I scrolling?*

2. **Change your environment.** We all know which comparison triggers – social media, again! – lead us to feel less than. Try to avoid situations and people that fuel those feelings; pay attention to *who* you follow online and *how* they make you feel. Ask yourself: *does this person inspire or deflate me? Am I learning from them, or losing myself?* Curate your digital and real-world spaces as best you can towards what uplifts, rather than drains – think, less self-doubt more self-reflection (see Chapters 3: Saying No and 4: Overwhelm for help here).

3. **Track your triggers.** Comparison tends to show up in the same, predictable places, so I recommend working out when you feel it most. Is it a certain time of day, a particular person, a mood, a scroll? Awareness doesn't always make it disappear, but it *does* give you options, and once you know your triggers, you'll be more easily able to pause, breathe or log out before the spiral truly kicks in.

4. **Ask what you're trying to achieve with this comparison.** Before you fall down the rabbit hole, ask yourself: *what am I actually hoping to get from this?* If you're seeking inspiration, then great, choose someone that lifts you up. But if you're looking for new ways to feel like a failure ... please, don't. Bring some conscious choice into the process, and remember that often the comparison isn't actually about *them* – it's about you.

STRENGTHEN CONNECTION AND SUPPORT
These emphasise the essential role of relationships and community in reducing harmful comparison:

1. **Celebrate everyone.** You don't need to shrink to lift others up, and vice versa, so celebrate your wins *and* others'. There's enough to go around – share your friends' names in a room full of opportunity and see how they then share yours too. We rise by lifting others.
2. **Build meaningful connections.** When you surround yourself with people who see you, celebrate you and who you trust, you stop needing to constantly measure up. Find your people and focus on nurturing those relationships. They're the ones that'll always say *your* name in a room of opportunity; they're the ones that matter.
3. **Remember shared humanity.** No matter how confident or polished someone may appear, they'll still have their own cross to bear. Everyone struggles, and most of the time, we don't really know what's going on behind the scenes in someone's life. Realising others are like us, with rich internal lives, is the basis for cultivating compassion and empathy (which, in turn, actually also helps us manage stress).

SIX HUNDRED AND SEVENTY-TWO HOURS

There is no reality (that I know of) where we stop comparing ourselves to others.

Social comparison plays a significant role in how we view and evaluate ourselves, how we interact with the world, *how we exist*. You will continue to look at other people – friends and strangers alike – and compare.

However, if we take the statistic from earlier (that we spend 12 percent of our day in comparative thought) and break it down, the real-life consequences are something like this ...

Assuming you sleep eight hours a night (we all wish!), that means 12 percent of your waking hours is one hour and fifty-two minutes.

That's almost two hours every day spent comparing yourself to others.

Fifty-six hours a month.

Six hundred and seventy-two hours a year.

I'm sure we can agree that that's far too much time to be wasting in endless comparison with others or your *past* self – who you used to be or what you used to look like. But while you may not be able to eliminate comparison, you can change *how you approach it and what you do with it*.

Other people will always be doing impressive, envy-inducing things. There will always be someone better at something than you. There will also always probably be someone worse at something than you.

They are not you. You are a different person, with a different (and equally brilliant) set of skills and abilities; embrace that. Redirect the energy you waste looking outwards towards yourself. Stop using external barometers to measure your self-worth, uncover your inner value with an internal barometer instead. Define yourself not by what you do but who you are and how you *live*. Try to disregard external factors (which you can't really control) and focus more on the things you can control, such as your thoughts or how you treat others (and yourself). Live according to your priorities, create a life that feels meaningful internally rather than one that just looks good externally. Evaluate and appraise your actions, question your behaviours so you can learn from your mistakes or failures, but don't conflate them with your personal worth. Seek out people and environments that are supportive – ones that validate your emotions and experiences. Build up your internal scaffolding, so that if something in your external life changes or goes wrong, everything doesn't come crashing down. Ask yourself: what can *I* do with what *I* have?

Ultimately, the time we spend comparing could instead be spent *creating*. Comparison not only steals your time but also your attention, focus and originality. We are wired to create, rather than just consume, and every moment reclaimed from comparison is time you could spend building something that's truly yours.

Be curious about what others are doing, but don't let it hold you back. Invite any comparison to reveal your priorities and values, to point you back to yourself. You're already enough, *and* there's room to grow. Two things can be true at the same time.

I know that I am happier when I'm not comparing myself to others, and I also know that I compare myself less when I'm happier. The more I focus on my own progression or version of success, the more I stay busy and keep my life (comfortably) full, the less inclined I am to look outward at others. I do a lot less comparison these days than when I worked in fashion, but the potential for it is very much there – the 'wellness' world is actually just as, if not more so, competitive than fashion. My penchant to compare is still there, I just (mostly) manage it; I don't feed the thoughts that drive it.

And to do that I have a personal motto that I repeat to myself when I'm feeling vulnerable to the comparison trap: *stay in your lane*. It reminds me to not get distracted by what others are doing, and to focus on myself instead.

Focus on *yourself* instead.

Define your own version of success, concentrate on your own priorities, live your own life. Remember: *the grass is greenest where it's watered*.

Go, water.

PRIORITISE THIS

- Comparison is human, it's *how* you do it that makes the difference.
- Don't compare your own life to someone else's carefully curated best moments.
- Low self-worth feeds comparison, strong foundations weaken it.
- High self-worth is about having a clear understanding of (and compassion for) who you are deep down inside.
- Spread your sense of self-worth thinly across all areas of your life.
- Envy can be a clue pointing to what you really want.
- You can't always stop comparing, but you can stop letting it dictate your life.
- The more connected you are to your own priorities, values and positive traits in the moment, the less you chase others' or past versions of yourself.

PRACTICES TO HELP WITH COMPARISON

THREE GOOD THINGS

Also known as 'Count your blessings', this positive psychology exercise is as simple it gets, yet it works – practices such as these have been repeatedly proven to improve mood and minimise negative comparison. The aim is to shift your attention inwards, away from other people's lives (on- and offline), and towards what's working in your own. Now, I don't love the word 'gratitude', but, let's be honest, this *is* a gratitude practice – just wrapped up in a different paper, which, for me, makes it land better. (I also have a section in the weekly overview of The Priorities Method Journal – 'Joyful Moments' – that riffs on this.)

How it works:

- At the end of your day spend a few minutes focusing on three good things that happened. What went well? What did you enjoy? What are you thankful for? It doesn't need to be anything big, in fact often the smaller the better – for me it's things like the pre-dawn birdsong, my health or a good cup of coffee.
- Write down each one (on phone, journal, scrap of paper) and include the reason/s it made you feel good. The *why* is important – it deepens your connection.
- Do this for a week, aiming for every or every other day.
- At the end of the week, look back at your notes. How do you feel? What do you notice?
- Try to do this practice four to five times a week for a month. After that, you can become less committed – once a week might be enough.
- Keep reflecting – look back and consider how you feel and what you notice. The impact of this practice lies not just in the doing but in the noticing – by observing good things, you'll reframe your mindset to see good things, and, somehow, more will then appear.

DO I ACTUALLY WANT THEIR LIFE?

This is a tool I sometimes use with clients – and myself – when comparison creeps in. When you find yourself feeling envious of someone, pause and ask: *do I actually want their life? All of it?*

Not just the moment you're seeing – the relationship, outfit or award – but the day-to-day behind it too. The sacrifices, stress, trade-offs, choices. Would you also be happy to give up your own life, including all the experiences and people it's filled with? Often, the answer is a clear no. Ask yourself: *what is it exactly that's leading me to feel this way?* Often, you don't actually want someone's life but rather a specific *feeling* that person represents: freedom, connection, confidence, calm and so on. Take that as the direction to move in – use your envy to sharpen your clarity, rather than feed your self-doubt.

WELLBEING CUPS

This is an exercise I use with clients to boost their sense of self-worth, motivation and happiness and minimise any negative comparison. It takes just a few minutes but seems to have a big impact.

How it works:

- Grab a piece of A4 paper and draw four cups (or wine glasses!), one in each quadrant of the paper.
- Then label them as: 1) Happiness/Joy/Contentment; 2) All the opposite of that; 3) Meaning/Purpose/Achievement; 4) All the opposite of that.
- Now write down the things/people/activities/thoughts that correspond to each of those cups. (FYI: some things will fall in more than one . . . my children, for example, bring me a lot of joy [cup 1] but they sometimes also bring me the complete opposite of that [cup 2]).
- Finally, have a think as to how you can spend more time filling up and drinking from cups 1 and 3, and how you can spill (or spit?) out some things from cups 2 and 4.

CHAPTER 9

Moving Forward

● ● ●

'If the ladder is not leaning against the right wall, every step we take just gets us to the wrong place faster.'

Stephen R. Covey

The story I shared in the Introduction – that moment in Paris when I realised the goal I'd been working towards for ten years wasn't actually what I wanted – well, it wasn't the first time this had happened. I had previous.

On paper, my job as features director of top UK fashion and arts magazines looked like a dream. But, honestly, it wasn't the job *I'd* always dreamed of. Much to the surprise of my creative family, I'd once wanted to be a human rights lawyer, with an eye on perhaps eventually becoming a diplomat. So, I studied politics and global health at undergrad, before embarking on a master's in human rights law.

Because I didn't have a law degree, I had to start my master's with something called 'pre-law', where, in as short a time as possible, you learn as much about the legal system as possible to get you up to speed.

I did *not* get up to speed.

Towards the end of those three weeks, midway through a lecture, I came face to face with how bad my memory truly is. While I can cram information and retain it in the short term (for, say, an exam), I can't keep it there. Much to my husband's constant entertainment,

I can watch a film and a few months later see the trailer and say: *'That looks great, we should watch it!'* On average I read a few books a month, but, if pressed, I could not with much detail or precision tell you what they were about.

There was no way I was going to get through the year, let alone an entire career in law, without constantly battling against my memory. I was never going to be as good as my peers with perfect recall, those who always had the right date or case number to hand. And I couldn't be a second-rate human rights lawyer, when people's lives were at stake. I got up, walked out of that lecture and never went back. (In a stroke of luck, or foresight, I hadn't yet paid my fees, so was able to extricate myself without much fallout.)

About five years later, while safely ensconced in the magazine world, I came across a book, *The 7 Habits of Highly Effective People*, by Stephen R. Covey. In it was the quote I opened this chapter with: 'If the ladder is not leaning against the right wall, every step we take just gets us to the wrong place faster.'[1]

It hit home hard.

While I don't regret studying politics (and have gone on to use parts of my degree in my work), my ladder was clearly up the wrong wall. Ever since then, I've kept the ladder analogy front of mind – not just in respect to work but also relationships,[*] friendships, even major life decisions. I think it's brilliant: a good reminder to reflect, question and actively engage with the direction our life takes.

After a few years of working as a coach, however, I began to view it differently, to wonder whether there was something missing. And this exploration ultimately led to the question that's defined my career: *what about the ground beneath it all?*

Because, if the foundation that underpins the wall or ladder is unstable, uneven or thin, you don't stand a chance. The ladder will never stay in place. The wall will shift and crack, perhaps even crumble.

Your priorities (and what you prioritise) are the ground beneath it all. They are the foundation on which your entire life is built and lived. If we don't work on creating a stable, authentic, strong foundation to our decisions and actions, we'll always be operating on shaky ground. We'll never quite find our feet.

---

[*]I've definitely still climbed up a few wrong walls in that area; I've always just managed to not fully scale the edge.

This aim of this final chapter is to help you place your feet on solid ground. Ground that will carry you through the good times and the bad, that will bolster your resilience and capacity, that will enable you to use the lessons from this book to move forward towards a life that feels meaningful to you. It's ostensibly a chapter about goals, but hopefully you'll discover it's about much more than that . . .

Let's go.

MENTAL TIME TRAVEL

So yes, we are going to talk about goals,* but, let me say now, we won't be setting them. If that's what you're after, I'd suggest picking up a copy of *The Priorities Method Journal* or joining me at a talk, workshop or course. And if you're thinking, *Wait, WTF, is this the upsell portion of the book?* It's not. You can set goals without me too. Anyone can, especially with an internet connection and access to the millions of blog posts out there on the subject. Goals are *easy* to set.

What's much harder is actually *achieving* them[†]. And harder *still* is doing that in a way that's aligned with what matters to you. So, given I have a word count to stick to, I think it'd be more beneficial if I share the practices and strategies that'll enable you to actually *move forward* and *fulfil* your goals instead. That's what I'm here to do.

Goal setting at its core is a form of mental time travel – a future-thinking task that involves taking your beliefs and past experiences and combining them with your current reality to create a picture – a 'representation' – of how you want your future to look and feel. You draw on your memory, observation, knowledge and imagination and use that 'data' to mentally project yourself forward.[2]

However, as psychologists Winona Cochran and Abraham Tesser note: 'a goal is a cognitive image of an ideal stored in memory for comparison to an actual state; a representation'.[3] In other words, a goal isn't just about a desired outcome, of something you want to achieve. It's a picture of how you think things should be, used as a way of evaluating where you're at right now.

---

*If you don't love the word 'goal', feel free to use an alternative instead – dream, target, agenda, objective, intention, destination, etc.
[†]Makes sense – if goals *were* easy to achieve, we wouldn't need to set them in the first place. We would just . . . do them.

Interestingly, neuroscience supports this too. The same brain regions involved in memory are also active when we envision future goals.[4] That's because imagining the future uses many of the same mechanisms as remembering the past – the brain sifts through past experiences, blends them with current knowledge and tries to simulate what might come next.*

Yet, the issue is that often, the information we feed into that simulation is . . . kind of bullsh*t. Whether your goals are long- or short-term, concrete or abstract, learning or results based, frequently the 'data' points we use to set them are the *wrong* ones. We build visions of the future based on other people's ideas, we let cultural norms, societal pressures or family expectations override our own instincts, or we just default to what we *think* we want – without questioning where those desires came from in the first place. And that all leads us to climb up a ladder that's leaning against the wrong wall.

In the next few pages, we'll take the time to map out and define your *own* version of success. One that's built on *your* data points and metrics, and based on *your* priorities.

We'll find the right wall for you.

YOUR PSP

What helps us define our own version of success and stick to our goals is prioritising a combination of clarity, intention and consistent action rooted in what we value. And all of these are made possible by focusing on three key pillars: your priorities, strengths and purpose – your *PSP*.

Let's look at each of these in turn:

1. MY PRIORITIES

This is your non-negotiable starting point,[†] After all, you cannot build a meaningful future or prioritise what matters to you until you understand *what* that actually is. Think about your life – the people you

---

Very interestingly, there is a persuasive hypothesis in neuroscience that the function of memory isn't to remember or look into the past at all. Rather, it's to use past data to drive us forward – to set goals and the like – and keep us safe. In other words, memory's purpose is forward planning.

†Which by this point in the book is, clearly, no huge shock.

spend time with and activities you spend time doing . . . Ask yourself the classic questions: *what brings me joy and meaning? When do I feel most aligned? What am I doing when I feel most like myself? What is important to me? (And what is* not *important to me?) What matters to me more than anything else in this world? What do I value?* These are the inquiries that'll help you to cut through the clutter and noise of life. They'll spotlight the values and principles that matter most, and highlight where your time, energy and attention are currently being spent, versus where you *wish* they were.

From this reflection, create a shortlist of around eight to ten core priorities. You'll find a list of common ones on the Prioritise This website (www.prioritisethis.com/corepriorities) – you may find yourself drawn to some or have your own entirely. Either way, that clarity will leave you better placed to create goals that are worth your effort.

2. MY STRENGTH

The second lens to look through is your strengths – what you're good at, *where you thrive*. Positive psychology coaching is grounded in the belief that aligning your goals and actions with your strengths leads to a more fulfilling life. For example, if honesty is a strength of yours, you'll thrive at work if surrounded by other honest people; if fun is a strength, then you'll be happiest when there are lots of opportunities for it in your life. Now, you may already have a good idea of your strengths; if not, I often recommend the VIA Character Strengths Survey (google it – it's free, this is not another upsell), which asks a series of questions to help determine your 'top', 'middle' and 'lower' strengths. It's not gospel,[*] but it is a helpful tool for recognising what you're naturally good at. Then, once you have your strengths in mind, the question becomes: *are they showing up in my life? How can I build more of them in? Are my goals aligned with my strengths? And if not, how can I make them more so?*

I have a client example here that I can share: L came to me dissatisfied with life, drained by her job at a large accountancy firm. Among other interventions, we looked at her strengths and it became clear that

---

[*] While questionnaires of this 'personality profile' type can be useful, I also suggest taking them with a pinch of salt. So much can influence how you respond to the questions on any given day, so they are clearly not always the most accurate representation of you. Secondly, don't get too attached to the results – they're there as guidance, not something for you to build your whole personality around.

a few of her top strengths (including humour) were nowhere to be seen in her day-to-day life. Through trial and error, we found a way to prioritise them. She (bravely) started doing stand-up which, although she reported to be 'hard and completely terrifying', made her very happy. And, interestingly, this feeling of happiness and connection to one of her top strengths rippled out and led her to feel more content at work. The goal with L could have been to help her quit and find a new job (and indeed initially we did discuss that), but in the end, by expanding life outside work, her job then felt more tolerable, and she felt more satisfied with life overall.

Discover your strengths, and find a way to integrate them into your life and work. (If you're responsible for a team, do the same for each of them too – you'll find it positively impacts dynamics and increases productivity.) Aligning with your strengths can genuinely be transformative, but don't always assume it's an overhaul you need. Much like with L, it may just be about connecting to and prioritising what's already there instead.

3. MY PURPOSE

As Viktor Frankl wrote in his seminal work *Man's Search for Meaning*, 'The meaning of life differs from man to man, from day to day and from hour to hour. What matters therefore is not the meaning of life in general but rather the specific meaning of a person's life at a given moment.'[5]

Purpose – the tendency to seek and derive meaning from our experiences – plays a central role in goal setting. It helps us choose a direction and gives us something to return to when life gets hard. But when I wrote the section in *The Priorities Method Journal* on purpose, I somehow forgot to include a very important message, one that I never normally fail to mention: *you don't have to find meaning in everything.*

Purpose helps you define your own version of success and set goals that stick. However, it also doesn't always have to be that deep. Possessing a sense of intentionality, of goal directedness, doesn't require a big, grand gesture. It can just be about showing up for yourself or someone you love, with a bit of presence or intention. Think of the 'why' principle of *The Priorities Method*®, and consider how even the smallest 'why' can have an outsized impact.

Purpose is also not, as to Frankl's quote, static. It evolves, shifts and changes as we change. One year, your purpose might be to care for someone you love, the next, it could be to start again. Both are valid and carry meaning, as long as they mean something to you.

And research even shows that a sense of purpose isn't just psychologically grounding; it's *neuroprotective*, meaning it supports long-term brain health and is correlated with better physical health outcomes overall.[6] It acts as a buffer – keeping us anchored, especially when things get tough or don't go our way.

If you're not sure where to start, maybe it's worth considering the most common sources of overarching meaning:[*]

- Pursuing meaningful goals or leaving a legacy.
- Contributing to something larger than yourself (religious, spiritual or otherwise).
- Deep, loving connections with others.

You may draw from one, two or all three. Or you might find purpose in something else altogether. Just ask yourself: *what brings me meaning? When do I feel most aligned with myself and/or the world?*

Whatever it is – if it matters (and makes sense) to you, it's enough.

MIND OVER MIND

When your three pillars of priorities, strengths and purpose are clearly defined, moving forward – with your goals, your life, or both – becomes easier. They form the *foundation* beneath the ladder and the wall, and ensure that whatever comes next is built on solid, authentic, intentional ground. And honestly, when that's the case, your chances of creating goals that not only *matter* but also *materialise* are higher.

Now, with that foundation in place, the next step is to explore three evidence-based mindset strategies that can help you stay aligned and forward-facing . . .

1. THINK PROCESS OVER OUTCOME

The language (and culture) around goals is predominantly *outcome-orientated*: 'Crush it!', 'Smash them!', 'Be unstoppable!' and so on . . . Truthfully, I used to echo this narrative and sentiment myself; these days, however, I think it misses the point.

---

[*] I know I just said it doesn't have to be that deep, and these are very deep. Both things can be true, or as my friend Boo likes to say: 'The only thing consistent about me is my inconsistency.'

Because while, yes, on one level the aim of setting goals *is* to achieve them, on another, it's not. When a goal is rooted in your PSPs, the experience of pursuing it – the *process* – becomes meaningful in its own right. And the upside of this is that it then doesn't feel so raw if you don't 'smash' that goal,* while any met goal becomes the cherry on top of the experience of moving forward in a way that reflects what matters to you.

And, while sometimes tunnel vision, outcome-orientated, life-altering goals can be great, they don't always integrate the full picture of life, of the demands, constraints and responsibilities that can derail even the best laid plans. *Process-orientated* goals, however, are more adaptable – they allow for all that life throws at you. They keep you moving forward, even when the path isn't linear or clear (or is absolutely strewn with rubbish). And rather than feeling demotivated or downcast when you fail to meet a goal, instead you are connected with the learning process – with growth and development, with staying on track with your priorities, regardless of the outcome. Which is itself a kind of success.

If you've read Chapter 6: Failure, you'll know that I'm no stranger to things not going to plan. And while, obviously, I don't *love* missing a target when I set one for myself, it doesn't throw me in the way it once did. Failing to reach my goals doesn't feel like failure; what feels like failure is failing to stay on track with my priorities. I don't measure success solely by whether a goal was hit; I measure it by the choices I've made and whether I've honoured what's important to me. That's my win, and I hope it'll become yours too.

2. KNOW YOUR MOTIVATION STYLE

As I've mentioned throughout the book, motivation is famously unreliable. However, what makes it less so is understanding what uniquely drives you, also known as your 'motivation style'. Styles vary from person to person, from day to day and from one goal to the next, and while there are many, here are five I often work with:

- **Achievement-orientated:** you're driven by the desire to excel and love a clear target. You are competitive and thrive on recognition for your achievements.

---

*I feel I should caveat this with *most of the time.* There can be instances where everything is aligned and you don't meet a goal that is important to you and that is not an enjoyable experience.

- **Affiliation-orientated:** you care most about building and maintaining relationships. You're motivated by a sense of belonging and social connection.
- **Power-orientated:** you're driven by the desire to influence and control your environment or others. You seek leadership roles and enjoy making decisions.
- **Purpose-orientated:** you are motivated by a deep sense of meaning and personal values. You want your efforts to make a positive impact on the world around you.
- **Joy-orientated:** you are led by what feels good. Motivation comes through pleasure, curiosity, creativity or joy.

Knowing your motivation style helps you set goals that work *with* your natural drives, rather than against them. For example, if you're affiliation-orientated, working towards a solo achievement might feel unmotivating unless you bring others in. Or, if you're joy-orientated, serious goals that don't allow for any creativity may leave you feeling stuck.

If you haven't yet read the section on intrinsic and extrinsic motivation in Chapter 2: Habits, I recommend flipping back to it now – it's a helpful topic that builds on this. Both types can be helpful depending on the circumstance; experiment to see which one works best in any given circumstance to give your motivation a boost.

3. FOCUS ON MOMENTUM

Often, what derails a goal isn't the lack of desire or ability; it's the absence of momentum. Sometimes this is created by fear, when a task feels too big, overwhelming or anxiety inducing.* At other times, it's a lapse (holiday, illness, a life curveball) that derails a routine, and then not doing something for a few days (or let's be honest, weeks or months) takes you out of the groove.

Luckily though, bringing back or creating momentum is also simple. Because even the *smallest* action can create motion – you know how it goes . . . Take a step, followed by another and another, and very quickly you start to build something.† You can do this in a few ways. First, remove friction by breaking down large goals into manageable,

---

* As we all know, stress, anxiety and worry tend to be highest before we act on something – without action, all we *can* do is worry and stress.
† Or as that Chinese proverb more eloquently puts it: 'A journey of a thousand miles begins with a single step.'

less overwhelming steps. Second, stack small wins, in any area of your life, and then *celebrate* when you meet them to build that drive. Third, seek support and accountability, enlist the help of others to ensure you stay on track. Fourth, imagine (or visualise) success, to keep your brain engaged in the process. And finally, regularly assess and refine your goals, to help you stay aligned with what's working.

Consistency and repetition create momentum – they reinforce progress, which builds confidence and belief, not just in the goal, but in yourself. The more you begin to influence the outcome, the more your fear or worry will lessen, which in turn creates momentum . . . In essence, momentum builds motivation and motivation builds momentum. That cycle, once you're in it, can move you closer to wherever it is you want to be.

THE STRUGGLE TO MOVE FORWARD

Okay, but what about when you feel completely stuck? When life has thrown a curveball and you can't get off the sofa, let alone move forward in life? When you're trapped in the past or obsessing about the future, not living anywhere near the present moment (*your actual life*) at all? This next section is for you. It's a combination of action-orientated and mindset-focused exercises and practices that complement and support everything we've looked at so far. I've written it based on the idea that when we feel stuck, we may believe 'Things should be different', yet in order to move forward, we must believe 'Things don't have to be different for me to feel better.' I'm not invalidating your emotions or experience, just suggesting that if we always wait for the outside world to change how we feel for the better, we can end up waiting a long time.

TEN WAYS TO GET UNSTUCK AND MOVE FORWARD

1. **Accept the situation, allow your feelings in.** It's understandable to feel the drive to reject where you are right now, but sometimes when we think we're running away from something, it's really just a circle and (surprise!) we're running back towards more of the same. Acknowledge and accept the situation – you're not resigning to your fate, you're just recognising that this is where you're at now.

Feel whatever it is you're feeling – ignoring your negative emotions will only lead to more feelings of stuckness down the line. Be conscious of any goal-blocking emotions, such as stress, shame or anxiety. Don't judge them; give them some breathing room to just be.

2. **Create a positive want loop.** When we are experiencing what we don't want, our natural instinct is to judge it and concentrate on what we don't have. If, however, you can draw on your positive inner resources (which I appreciate may be running low) to focus on what you *do* want instead, you're more likely to build the positive emotions that'll help you move forward.* Don't ignore your (valid) emotions (see point above) or sugarcoat a difficult situation, just think *solution rather than problem.* Create a positive wanting loop that drives you forward, rather than holds you back.

3. **Work on something,** *anything,* **often.** Focus on committing your time (not much of it, 1–10 minutes) on a task or goal for six days a week. It doesn't matter what you pick, it doesn't have to be the goal you're feeling stuck on, it could be something else entirely. Whatever it is, with repetition and consistency, you will improve (not in a straight line and not 1 percent every day because, although that's a great marketing slogan, mathematically or anecdotally it doesn't hold up). But it will happen, and crucially, when you see progress, and/or feel immersed in the process, you'll start to feel you can move forward in the area you feel stuck too.

4. **Create 'aha!' moments.** An 'aha!' or 'eureka!' moment is when a creative insight occurs, and a previously elusive solution becomes clear. This strategy is linked to unconscious processes in your brain, where the mind makes connections after periods of contemplation or distraction. This isn't about forcing yourself to come up with ideas; it's about giving your subconscious and intuition a chance to steer the ship for a moment. Creative insight can be enhanced by a number of protocols, including: low cognitive tasks (e.g. sorting through your desktop), taking a shower/bath or sauna, going for a walk or gentle swim, or experiencing a positive emotion (e.g. listening to a funny podcast).

5. **Celebrate yourself.** When feelings of stuckness feel as if they're tipping into thoughts about what you have, or what you do, as 'not

---

*The section on using envy as insight in Chapter 8: Comparison is useful for this too.

good enough', now is the time to double down on self-support. You need yourself more than ever, and the more you *can* see value in yourself, the more you'll naturally see it in your life and endeavours too. Build yourself up from there, ultimately seeking an inner state where you can celebrate yourself not based just on what you've accomplished, but *who you are.*

6. **Try something new or do something old in a new way.** Take yourself from inaction to action by shaking up your brain with something novel. Start a new hobby (anything will do) or practise an old habit in a new way (e.g. if you're a musician, try playing a different style of music). Both of these will naturally make your brain pay more attention and give you mini tasks and challenges to overcome, which in turn will make you feel satisfied which, as we know by now, creates momentum. (As to the point above, celebrate these attempts as well – note down when you enjoyed yourself and why/how you're proud of yourself for trying something new.)

7. **Do something for someone else.** One of the best, proven approaches for getting out of a rut (and increasing life satisfaction overall) is to turn your focus outward. Stop thinking about yourself and your own troubles or concerns and instead think about how you can help someone else. Because of our social brains, part of our wellbeing comes from contribution, from feeling useful to others. Shift yourself from the perspective of self-interest to: *how can I serve and support the people around me?*

8. **Focus on how you want to feel.** The physical world clearly has an impact on our emotional world, but we can also instigate inner change that either amplifies or de-amplifies that. So, forget for a moment what you *want*, and instead ask: *how do I want to feel?* Don't demand specific answers, rather think broadly – for example, I want to feel supported and connected or I want to feel worthy and valued. Ask yourself: *what advice would I give to someone I love in this same situation? How can I get myself closer to how I want to feel?*

9. **Think of yourself as a plane.** Imagine your life is like a plane's flight path. The plane may have a destination, but to get there it doesn't follow a straight line. In fact, if you overlay the actual path a plane takes with the straight line the pilot is 'supposed' to be following, you'd see it's very *wavy*. Although both lines end up at the same place, they only cross briefly along the way. Flying a plane is a constant series of adjustments – watching the monitors, being

aware of conditions around you and tweaking your direction. You end up in the right place eventually, but for around 90 percent of the time you're heading in the wrong direction. The path of the plane corrects itself overall, and so can yours.

10. **Redefine winning.** If you're feeling stuck and demotivated by your lack of progress towards a goal, this approach will reduce your frustration and reignite some motivation and momentum. Instead of focusing on the initial goal you set for yourself, redefine what it means to 'win'. Ask yourself: *what is it that's frustrating me? What are the obstacles to change?* Then ask: *what are ten other options for definitions of winning that will satisfy me?* Brainstorm (no stupid answers here; in fact the whole point is to come up with filter-less ideas which may seem a bit mad) and then pick one or two that you can use as your goalpost instead.

GROWTH VERSUS FIXED MINDSET

We can move through life thinking our abilities are either malleable or set in stone – what psychologist Carol Dweck coined as a growth or fixed mindset. A fixed mindset sees intelligence and talent as innate – you're either born with it or not – so failure feels like confirmation of your limits ('I'm just not good at this'). A growth mindset, on the other hand, is the belief that your abilities can be developed through effort, learning and persistence; you don't assume you're brilliant at everything but stay open to improvement ('This is hard right now, but what can I learn from this?'). These mindsets are worth keeping in mind when you're stuck or afraid to try something, since moving forward often looks far from pretty – trying and failing, trying again, even moving backwards – and a growth mindset reminds you it's the movement that counts.

PRESENT YOU VERSUS FUTURE YOU

In life there is almost always a toss-up between a 'present' and 'future' version of our self. Present You wants to drink all the tequila; Future You will have to deal with the consequences. Present You wants to stay in bed; Future You knows you'll feel better if you get up and on with your day. It's natural to put short-term needs and desires ahead of what we know will be good for us in the long term. This tendency is called present bias, and some studies have suggested that we do this because we cognitively struggle to perceive our future selves as ourselves – in fact, we perceive them in the same way we perceive total strangers. (Isn't the brain weird?)

Sometimes, for the win, Present and Future You align – for example, you enjoy a walk in the moment and Future You benefits from the health positives. Seek out these magic concentric circles in your life, and prioritise them whenever you can. But also know that, at other times, the choice can be more complex: Present Me wants to stay out late dancing with my friends, but Future Me knows I'll be exhausted tomorrow. BUT Future Future Me knows that the recovery will be worth the memories.*

Here are three questions that will help you make good choices going forward:

1. What are my long-term priorities?
2. What does Future Me feel is important?
3. How can Present Me better support that?

RESILIENCE

Life is full of difficult situations, challenging choices, setbacks, failures and stressful days (or years) – many of which can impact us in some way for the rest of our lives. The difference between moving forward through these, and getting subsumed by them, depends on multiple elements, but a key one is our ability to get back up after a fall: our *resilience*.

Resilience is a dynamic process, a positive adaptation of the mind, that emerges through adversity. It involves the capacity to return to a state of calm, or where we feel like ourselves, following a difficult or painful experience. In the context of goals and moving forward in life, resilience is vital – it's what enables us to pick ourselves up off the ground and go again.

---

*In *The Priorities Method Journal* there's an exercise that invites you to imagine you're 90-ish years old and looking back on your life. It encourages you to zoom out and away from present you, and think more about your bigger, lifetime priorities, to understand for yourself what you value and desire in the long term. It can be helpful with this.

There are a few differing theories around resilience; however, ultimately, I believe it is shaped both by our individual characteristics (genes, temperament, personality) and the environment we are raised in (family, community and surroundings as well as broader cultural influences). Resilience is the result of a combination of protective factors, and while there are some things we can't change, such as our genes, there are others that we can.

No matter our starting point, we can all develop habits, skills and attitudes that support us in building resilience and enhance mental toughness. There are a couple of crucial factors that can help, such as strong supportive relationships with others,* autonomy, a sense of purpose, identifying our strengths and values, having a high capacity for emotional regulation, a belief that we can bounce back and confidence that's built from taking on challenges. Luckily, coaching, and much of this book, helps you do all of that – from challenging your thoughts in Chapter 1: Stress, to confronting your procrastination in Chapter 5: Procrastination, to developing your resistance to failure and rejection in Chapters 6: Failure and 7: Rejection. In one way, this *is* a book about resilience. So, I'd recommend flipping back through the chapters and seeing which topics resonate. Which ones lead you to feel stronger, more settled in yourself and able to achieve? That's your personal resilience coaching plan right there.

TOMORROW MIGHT BE DIFFERENT

Fun fact: 80 percent of New Year's resolutions fail within a month.[7]

But of course they do. A few hundred years ago the pressures and expectations the typical person (you and I) might have had were fairly basic: provide for yourself and your family, be good at your work (which would have been whatever your parents did), stay alive. Today though, our goals, expectations and opportunities are tenfold and rarely so clear-cut.

In this world of plenty, it can be hard to move forward. My hope is that this chapter has given you more clarity about how to do just that – about how to approach your goals so that if you are a New Year's resolution kind of person, then you either find yourself in the small

---

*This can be summed up with the line of questioning: *Is this a threat to me? How will I cope?* versus *Is this a threat to us? How will we cope?* There's safety in numbers, always.

percentage who succeed, or feel okay within yourself if you don't. And if you're not the resolutions type, then you can at least now see a new path for yourself, one aligned with what's important to you.

Ultimately, the only reason we want to change anything in life is because we believe that the change will make us feel better. Our ability to imagine the future – to envisage that things can change (that *we* can change), is a highly sophisticated function. Our capacity to envision, set and achieve goals is astounding. And the fact that we can do this while staying (relatively) positive is something that's both ingrained in us as humans, and that we need to cling on to, whatever life throws our way. The more we can rely on helpful processes, as well as our resilience and cognitive reserve, the more we will remain invested in the idea that things could change. That tomorrow might be different, in a good (perhaps even *staggeringly* so) way.

Goals serve as an excellent motivator and compass: your brain likes them, your dopaminergic pathways like them (remember, dopamine is the molecule of *more*, of driving you forward). They have an energising function and can positively impact your wellbeing,[*] bringing purpose and meaning to your life through their very existence. Your brain loves little more than having something to look forward to – imagining, planning and anticipating events and experiences lights up the reward system and makes us feel happy.[†] So plan, set, strive.

But remember that *moving forward* is far more important than any arbitrary goal you might set. As Albert Einstein once said: 'A calm and modest life brings more happiness than the pursuit of success combined with constant restlessness.' Einstein may not be known as a modest underachiever himself, but his sentiment remains good – finding a balance between accomplishment and wellbeing, between striving and resting, is key. If your goal is to run a marathon and you injure yourself, the best way you can support that goal is by remaining flexible and kind towards yourself – by taking an approach that redefines winning as recovery instead.

Ultimately, goals without self-knowledge can feel empty and meaningless, and even *accidentally* move you further away from the life you want to live. Lean on your priorities, strengths and purpose

---

[*] There are several studies that prove the positive impact of goals and future thinking on people with clinical depression. See, for example, https://www.tandfonline.com/doi/full/10.1080/03007995.2024.2313108#abstract

[†] More so, even, than doing the actual thing we've planned! Studies show that we feel happiest about a holiday one day before we go on that holiday. Anticipation is king.

(your *intrinsic* motivators), as these set you up to create lasting change. Think about the big picture of your goals and your life, but also zoom in and ask: *am I prioritising daily what will move me closer to where I want to be?*

Do all that, and you'll find you have your ladder leaning against the right wall, with solid ground underneath, and the determination to scale to the top.

PRIORITISE THIS

- Define your own version of success.
- Goals built on priorities, strengths and purpose are more meaningful and achievable.
- Prioritise process over outcome.
- Find your motivation style to help you on track.
- Focus on momentum to help drive you forward.
- Bolster your resilience and cognitive reserve through life.
- Consider Future You, not just Present You.

PRACTICES TO HELP WITH MOVING FORWARD

LIFE COACHING AUDIT

This exercise sums up the saying 'You can't change what you don't acknowledge'. In essence, it's a check-in, designed to help you see your life more clearly by assessing both where you're at and where you'd like to be. The aim is not to fix everything all at once, but rather to identify the areas of your life that feel aligned versus those that feel less so, and then use that knowledge to create change. It can be done anytime, during moments of relative calm as well as when you're in a 'What the hell am I doing with my life?!' state of mind. Either way, it'll help you recentre your priorities and move forward with intention.

How it works:

1. Grab some paper and write down each of the following headings, leaving space underneath: work/career, relationships, friendships, health, finances, creativity, meaning, home, hobbies (plus any others relevant to you, e.g. parenting or studies).
2. For each area, ask yourself: *what is going well?* and *what would I like to change?*
3. Don't judge your answers – this is about paying attention and understanding your life, not casting opinion. Jot your answers down under each heading.
4. Once you've finished, ask: *which area, if I changed it, would have the biggest positive impact on my life?*
5. Use your answer to decide where your energy would be best spent over the next few days/weeks/months – that is, which area of your life you need to *prioritise*.
6. It may be that you tackle two areas at once, but I wouldn't recommend more than that. Remember, *if everything is a priority, nothing is*! You'll also find that when you enact change in one area, the others shift for the better too. If not, once you feel you've focused enough on one area, move on to the next, and so on . . .

POSITIVE CHANGE MEDITATION

Imagine a glass jar full of water and mud that you're carrying around all day. The longer you carry it, the more shaken up and cloudy it becomes. But when you set that jar down, the mud falls to the bottom and the water becomes clear. That's exactly what you're doing with your mind during this exercise – putting down the jar so that the 'mud' (i.e. your thoughts and worries) can settle and you can see your life more clearly. You can do this meditation sitting or standing, with the eyes open or closed. And if you'd rather listen to the instructions, scan the QR code below.

How it works:

1. Take a deep breath in through your nose and exhale gently through your mouth. Repeat this a few times.
2. Now, breathe as you normally would but bring your full awareness to the physical sensation of your breath as it moves in and out of your body. Notice the rising and falling of your abdomen and chest, and the feeling of the breath as it travels through your body.
3. Every time your mind wanders – it will, it loves to do that – guide it back to your breath.
4. Continue like this for a few minutes – visualise or imagine the jar and remember that you're putting everything down so that you can see your life more clearly.
5. Now, remind yourself that we are all human and imperfect, and that sometimes our behaviour, or circumstances outside of our control, take us away from how we want to live. There is always space for positive change in life.
6. Finally, say to yourself three times – in your head or out loud – 'I am open to change. I am ready to move forward.'
7. Take a deep breath in through your nose, sigh it out of your mouth and decide how to continue with your day.

THE BUG PYRAMID

The perfect place to be with a goal is *uncomfortable*. Huge, unattainable goals can lead to a loss of willpower, while small, easy ones destroy motivation. The sweet spot for effort and investment is to sit *uncomfortably* at the edge of comfort. Enter: the big uncomfortable goal* (a BUG, if you will).

Whether it's a university project, a marathon or a five-year business plan, a BUG is scary, and this fear can prevent even the most motivated among us from starting something. So, in order to *actually* achieve it, it's best to break it down. In doing so, you make the goal less intimidating and more manageable and palatable to your brain.

How it works:

1. Draw a pyramid on a piece of paper, with your BUG written at the top. Let's use the example of launching a new purpose-led business.
2. Then, at the very bottom of the pyramid, write the habits and priorities that'll keep you on track, such as not getting distracted by your competitors as a habit or 'contribution' as a priority.
3. Next, jot down inside the pyramid the micro-goals that you need to achieve before you can get to this BUG. As with the example above, these could be: design logo, purchase website, set up website, create PR plan, set up five potential client calls, etc. Write these in the order that they need to be done, so purchase website would go lower down in the pyramid than set up website, potential client calls would go towards the top and so on.
4. Work through the pyramid from the bottom up, keeping your habits and priorities in mind and continuously breaking down your BUG until there is always something on there that feels like an attainable goal for you to work on on any given day.
5. You know the drill – Build the wall, one brick at a time.

Head to the Prioritise This website to download a free BUG worksheet.

---

*For help with choosing a BUG, refer to goal frameworks such as SMART – which can be found on the Prioritise This website or in *The Priorities Method Journal*.

Final Thoughts

'To exist is to change, to change is to mature, to mature is to go on creating oneself endlessly.'

Henri Bergson, Creative Evolution

Imagine there's a bank that every single morning deposits £86,400 into your account.*

The amount doesn't carry over from day to day – it appears first thing and disappears overnight. There's no overdraft, so you can't borrow or spend any more than you have. And you can't save a single penny; there's no way to compound it or squirrel it away.

Each day you must use it, or it's lost.

Gone, for ever.

We all have a bank – it's called *time*.

Each morning you are credited with 86,400 seconds, and each night the slate is wiped clean. No amount is carried over from day to day. You can't beg, borrow or steal from yesterday or tomorrow. You can't take out a loan. There's no overdraft.

The time you have is the time you have.

Every day, every hour, every minute, every second of our lives we make complex assessments and decisions about what to do with our time. Some we are aware of – you've chosen to read this book for example (brilliant decision). Others come from our subconscious, happen automatically or are second-nature habits, shaped through time – mindlessly scrolling through social media, for example (in my experience, *less* brilliant).

Whether you are conscious of it or not, your brain is constantly appraising the world around you, searching to understand and allocate your resources (time, energy, attention) according to what it regards as

---

*Sounds like a phenomenal bank, I know.

more important than another. From the thoughts you think and actions you take, to the habits you practise and people you spend time with, you are perpetually making choices about what to prioritise. About how to assign your personal reserves. And this, in turn, ultimately creates *you*.

What you prioritise *becomes* your life.

Now you may think the purpose of me ending the book with this bank–time analogy is to encourage you to *make every second count*. To urge you to go out and seize the day; to appreciate all that you have and never take another moment for granted ever again.

And sure, if you'd like to do that – and can keep the *carpe diem* momentum going ad infinitum – then, of course, go ahead. (While you're at it, please take one of those precious moments to write and let me how you do it; I'd love to find out!*) But I suspect that, if you spend your time desperately trying to wring every last moment out of life, you'll find you've wrung out the joy, spontaneity and peace from it too.

I'm not here to tell you to make the most of every minute of your life. It's your life, and I think (within reason and the law) that you should do with it as you please. That you should seek out what you believe is important, chase what brings you meaning and joy (as well as bring those things to others), and then put them first.

What I'm here to do, what I hope this book has done, is show you another way of living. One where you prioritise the thoughts, behaviours, people and things that move you closer towards the life you want. One where you appreciate that every single day, hour, minute or second you have the opportunity to prioritise something that will help you navigate this unruly modern world even just a fraction better. One that honours the fact that just because someone else has it worse doesn't mean your experience isn't valid – you can be living a safe, comfortable life and still find yourself overwhelmed by your thoughts, feelings or emotions. You can still have a bad day that leaves you feeling like sh*t.

On my bad days, the lessons I've learned in my work show up when I need them most – if I'm trying to change a habit, I'll find myself thinking about reward prediction error. If I'm deep in a thought spiral, I'll focus on Socratic questioning. The coaching and the science are great anchors, and they've literally changed my life. But honestly, though it all becomes easier the more you do it, improving your life *is*

---

*hello@lilysilverton.com

FINAL THOUGHTS

hard. And just in case I haven't made it abundantly clear throughout the book: I do not have it all figured out. I struggle with every single one of the topics included here, and more.

Ultimately, we live in a cure rather than a prevention society, always waiting until the cracks become canyons. Taking the time to support yourself by prioritising the health of your mind, body and nervous system *before* you fall to the bottom is really what this work is about.

Annoyingly, no one else can do it for you except you, but you don't need to overhaul your entire life – think small pivots, tiny habits, a new mindset here or there. Play the hand you have while also creating a different story for yourself along the way. Learn to be with your difficult emotions. Take the time to value the positive stuff (don't worry, you know your brain will remember the negative all on its own!). Connect with your priorities and the people and things that matter. Stop measuring your days by degree of productivity; rate them by degree of *presence* instead.

Whatever you do, don't expect a straight line – life has lapses and curveballs, some of which you'll anticipate and others you'll never see coming. There will be moments when you don't believe in yourself, in your abilities or capacity to change, as well as times when it will feel much easier to remain stressed and rushed, because that's been your default for so long. When it does feel like you're swimming against a truly vicious tide, try asking yourself these final three questions:

1. Is this [INSERT HABIT/THOUGHT/PERSON] serving me?
2. What empowering decisions do I need to make right now?
3. How can I deal with this moment better?

Don't give up. Keep going, make changes, and then monitor and evaluate so you can adjust what's not working while doing more of what does. Remember that when you drive down a road and it's closed, you don't just get out and abandon your car. *You find another route.* We expect life to be easy and then when it's not – which is a lot of the time – we feel demotivated, as if things are unfair. No matter how painful or unfair an experience is, you can still look for the thoughts and actions that'll help you move through it – this is behavioural and cognitive flexibility at work, and this is the crux of everything I do. Now that you've read this book, you will always be able to find another route. And if that one doesn't work, then another, and another, and so on, until you find your way out.

As I've been saying throughout this book, stay mentally and socially active. Not just once in a while, but *regularly*. Keep the activities in your life complex and varied, so that they challenge your mind. Make sure they're enjoyable, as that will make you stick with them. See your friends *and* meet new people. Keep learning* and educating yourself on what you do know, as well as what you don't since the brain truly benefits by having to tackle something unfamiliar. Travel, explore, get out of your comfort zone. Don't ever fully retire or, if you do, keep setting yourself novel projects and goals to go after. Goals themselves are neuroprotective – providing a certain amount of tolerance to the damage that occurs to your brain as you age.

While nobody is going to read this (or any) book and immediately become their ideal self, my hope is that the shared knowledge I've put here will help you better adapt and create for yourself a more harmonious life. This book isn't about knowing the next step; it's about knowing that you won't abandon yourself no matter where the next step takes you. No matter where life takes you.

Ultimately, life will feel calmer not because *it* becomes less chaotic, but because *you* become less chaotic.† And it's my hope that you and your (mildly) chaotic self now have a few more tools in your toolbox to create a buffer between your brain and the beautiful insanity of being a person in this world. That you have become more of an expert on your solutions, rather than your problems.

Do what you can, with what you've got.

And remember that the most effective strategy, intervention or practice is *the one that you will do*. Latch on to just one thing from this book.

Prioritise *that*.

And you're on the right track.

---

*Studies interestingly show that mentally demanding professions, like doctors or air traffic controllers, continuously build cognitive reserve throughout their life, which protects their mental function in later life.
†But still with a small dose of chaos, because that's important too.

Resources

READING LIST

Below is a non-exhaustive list of the self-development, psychology and neuroscience books that I've read and found truly helpful over the years. Let's be honest, many of these kinds of books get abandoned after a few chapters (side note: if you've read *Prioritise This* to the end then a heartfelt *THANK YOU*). I am not immune to doing this myself, but all of these I've read in their entirety (some even more than once) . . . They are keepers.

Adrienne Adhami, *Decisions That Matter*. Cornerstone Press, 2025.
Oliver Burkeman, *Four Thousand Weeks: Time Management for Mortals*. Vintage, 2022.
James Clear, *Atomic Habits*. Random House Business, 2018.
Elizabeth Day, *How to Fail*. Fourth Estate, 2019.
Paul Dolan, *Happiness by Design: Finding Pleasure and Purpose in Everyday Life*. Penguin, 2015.
Charles Duhigg, *The Power of Habit: Why We Do What We Do, and How to Change*. Penguin, 2025.
Carol S. Dweck, *Mindset: Changing the Way You Think to Fulfil Your Potential*. Robinson, 2017.
Edith Eger, *The Choice: A True Story of Hope*. Penguin, 2024.
Lisa Feldman Barret, *Seven and a Half Lessons about the Brain*. Picador, 2021.
BJ Fogg, *Tiny Habits: The Small Changes That Change Everything*. Penguin, 2019.
Victor Frankl, *Man's Search for Meaning*. Penguin, 2004.
Mo Gawdat, *Solve for Happy: Engineer Your Path to Joy*. Bluebird, 2019.
Elizabeth Gilbert, *Big Magic: Creative Living Beyond Fear*. Bloomsbury, 2016.
Ryan Holiday and and Stephen Hanselman, *The Daily Stoic: 366 Meditations on Wisdom, Perseverance, and the Art of Living*. Profile Books, 2016.
Julia Hotz, *The Connection Cure: The Prescriptive Power of Movement, Nature, Art, Service, and Belonging*. Headline Home, 2024.
Lucy Jones, *Matrescence: On the Metamorphosis of Pregnancy, Childbirth and Motherhood*. Penguin, 2024.
Sarah McKay, *Brain Health for Dummies*. For Dummies, 2024.

Sarah McKay, *Demystifying The Female Brain: A Neuroscientist Explores Health, Hormones and Happiness*. Orion Spring, 2018.
Katy Milkman, *How to Change: The Science of Getting to Where You Want to Be*. Vermilion, 2022.
Suzy Reading, *How to Be Selfish*. Vermilion, 2025.
Angela Scanlon, *Joyrider: How Gratitude Can Help You Get the Life You Really Want*. Vermilion, 2023.
Tali Sharot, *The Optimism Bias: Why We're Wired to Look on the Bright Side*. Robinson, 2012.
Lucy Sheridan, *The Comparison Cure: How to Be Less 'Them' and More You*. Orion Spring, 2019.
Farrah Storr, *The Discomfort Zone: How to Get What You Want by Living Fearlessly*. Piatkus, 2021.
Marine Tanguy, *The Visual Detox: How to Consume Media without Letting it Consume You*. Square Peg, 2024.
Bessel van der Kolk, *The Body Keeps the Score: Brain, Mind, and Body in the Healing of Trauma*. Penguin, 2015.

MENTAL HEALTH RESOURCES

If you or someone you know is struggling, please know you are not alone. The following resources offer support, crisis help, therapy directories, and mental health information. **If you or another person are in immediate danger or experiencing a life-threatening emergency, please contact your local emergency services.**

IMMEDIATE CRISIS SUPPORT

- *International (24/7):*
  - International Suicide Prevention (country-specific hotlines): https://findahelpline.com
  - Befrienders Worldwide: https://www.befrienders.org
- *UK:*
  - Samaritans – 116 123 (free 24/7) | https://www.samaritans.org
  - Shout (Crisis Text Line) – Text SHOUT to 85258 | https://giveusashout.org
- *US:*
  - 988 Suicide & Crisis Lifeline – Call or text 988 | https://988lifeline.org
  - Crisis Text Line – Text HELLO to 741741 | https://www.crisistextline.org

RESOURCES

- *Australia:*
  - Lifeline – 13 11 14 | https://www.lifeline.org.au
- *Canada:*
  - Talk Suicide Canada – 1-833-456-4566 | https://talksuicide.ca

THERAPY AND COUNSELLING DIRECTORIES

- *UK:*
  - BACP (British Association for Counselling and Psychotherapy) – https://www.bacp.co.uk
  - Counselling Directory – https://www.counselling-directory.org.uk
  - Self Space – https://theselfspace.com/
- *US:*
  - *Psychology Today* Therapist Finder – https://www.psychologytoday.com/us/therapists
  - Therapy for Black Girls – https://therapyforblackgirls.com
  - Inclusive Therapists – https://www.inclusivetherapists.com
  - Open Path Collective – https://www.openpathcollective.org
- *Australia:*
  - Australian Psychological Society – https://psychology.org.au
- *Global/online therapy:*
  - BetterHelp – https://www.betterhelp.com
  - Talkspace – https://www.talkspace.com

MENTAL HEALTH EDUCATION

- Mind (UK) – https://www.mind.org.uk
- Mental Health Foundation – https://www.mentalhealth.org.uk
- National Alliance on Mental Illness (NAMI) – https://www.nami.org

LGBTQ+ MENTAL HEALTH RESOURCES

- Switchboard (UK) – 0300 330 0630 | https://switchboard.lgbt
- The Trevor Project (US) – https://www.thetrevorproject.org
- LGBT Foundation (UK) – https://lgbt.foundation

SUPPORT FOR SPECIFIC COMMUNITIES

- Black Minds Matter UK – https://www.blackmindsmatteruk.com
- Therapy for Latinx – https://www.therapyforlatinx.com
- Asian Mental Health Collective – https://www.asianmhc.org

List of Practices

While I've chosen to place certain practices in certain chapters, many can be used in different contexts. I've included a full list here, arranged by category, so you can pinpoint any that appeal and see how they might be applied to your situation or state of mind.

BODY-BASED
- The psychological sigh (Stress)
- Body shake (Overwhelm)

COACHING EXERCISES
- What I do in a week (Habits)
- Create a to-don't list (Saying No)
- Brain dump (Overwhelm)
- Should I quit? (Overwhelm)
- Wellbeing cups (Comparison)
- Life coaching audit (Moving Forward)

MEDITATIONS/VISUALISATIONS
- Positive reminiscing (Failure)
- Coping visualisation (Failure)
- Positive change meditation (Moving Forward)

MINDSET-BASED
- The ABCDE model (Stress)
- Playing the tape (Habits)

- Best possible self (Habits)
- Questions to ask yourself before saying yes (Saying No)
- Time tripping (Rejection)
- A compassionate letter (Rejection)
- Three good things (Comparison)
- Do I actually want their life? (Comparison)

PRODUCTIVITY TECHNIQUES
- Tracking energy levels (Procrastination)
- Time logging (Procrastination)
- The ABC Method (Procrastination)
- The priorities matrix (Overwhelm)
- The BUG pyramid (Moving Forward)

References

Introduction

1 Herbert, S. A., *Designing Organizations for an Information-rich World* (Baltimore, MD: Johns Hopkins University Press, 1971), pp. 37–52
2 Hern, A., 'Netflix's biggest competitor? Sleep', *Guardian*, 18 April 2017, https://www.theguardian.com/technology/2017/apr/18/netflix-competitor-sleep-uber-facebook

Chapter 1: Stress

1 Aurelius, M., *Meditations*, trans. by G. Hays (London: Random House, 2003)
2 World Health Organization, 'Stress', 12 February 2023, https://www.who.int/news-room/questions-and-answers/item/stress
3 Keller, A., Litzelman, K., Wisk, L. E., Maddox, T., Cheng, E. R., Creswell, P. D. and Witt, W. P., 'Does the perception that stress affects health matter? The association with health and mortality', *Health Psychology*, 31:5 (2012), pp. 677–8, https://doi.org/10.1037/a0026743
4 McLoughlin, E., Arnold, R. and Moore, L. J., 'The tendency to appraise stressful situations as more of a threat is associated with poorer health and well-being', *Stress and Health*, 40:3 (2023), https://doi.org/10.1002/smi.3358
5 McKay, S., *Brain Health for Dummies* (Hoboken, NJ: For Dummies, 2024)
6 De Nys, L., Anderson, K., Ofosu, E. F., Ryde, G. C., Connelly, J. and Whittaker, A. C., 'The effects of physical activity on cortisol and sleep: A systematic review and meta-analysis', *Psychoneuroendocrinology*, 143 (2022), https://doi.org/10.1016/j.psyneuen.2022.105843
7 Soltani, H., Keim, N. L. and Laugero, K. D., 'Increasing dietary carbohydrate as part of a healthy whole food diet intervention dampens eight week changes in salivary cortisol and cortisol responsiveness', *Nutrients*, 11:11 (2019), https://doi.org/10.3390/nu11112563
8 Institute of Medicine (US) Committee on Sleep Medicine and Research, *Sleep Disorders and Sleep Deprivation: An Unmet Public Health Problem* (Washington, DC: National Academies Press, 2006), https://www.ncbi.nlm.nih.gov/books/NBK19961

9. Nuffield Health, 'Major new survey highlights impact of cost-of-living crisis on mental and physical wellbeing', 2023, https://www.nuffieldhealth.com/article/the-healthier-nation-index-release#sleep. See also US National Heart, Lung and Blood Institute, 'What are sleep deficiency and deprivation?', 2022, https://www.nhlbi.nih.gov/health/sleep-deprivation
10. Dijk, D-J., Duffy, J. F. and Czeisler, C. A., 'Contribution of circadian physiology and sleep homeostasis to age-related changes in human sleep', *Chronobiology International*, 17:3 (2000), pp. 285–311, https://doi.org/10.1081/CBI-100101049; Hua, J., Sun, H. and Shen, Y., 'Improvement in sleep duration was associated with higher cognitive function: A new association', *Aging*, 12:20 (2020), pp. 20,623–44, https://doi.org/10.18632/aging.103948; Ferrie, J. E., Shipley, M. J., Akbaraly, T. N., Marmot, M. G., Kivimäki, M. and Singh-Manoux, A., 'Change in sleep duration and cognitive function: Findings from the Whitehall II study', *Sleep*, 34:5 (2011), pp. 565–73, https://doi.org/10.1093/sleep/34.5.565
11. Benton, D., Bloxham, A., Gaylor, C., Brennan, A. and Young, H. A., 'Carbohydrate and sleep: An evaluation of putative mechanisms', *Frontiers in Nutrition*, 9 (2022), https://doi.org/10.3389/fnut.2022.933898
12. Kriakous, S. A., Elliott, K. A., Lamers, C. and Owen, R., 'The effectiveness of mindfulness-based stress reduction on the psychological functioning of healthcare professionals: A systematic review', *Mindfulness*, 12 (2021), pp. 1–28, https://doi.org/10.1007/s12671-020-01500-9
13. Jungmann, M., Vencatachellum, S., Van Ryckeghem, D. and Vögele, C., 'Effects of cold stimulation on cardiac-vagal activation in healthy participants: Randomized controlled trial', *JMIR Formative Research*, 2:2 (2018), https://doi.org/10.2196/10257
14. Nishida, K., Sawada, D., Kuwano, Y., Tanaka H., Sugawara T., Aoki Y., Fujiwara S. and Rokutan, K., 'Daily administration of paraprobiotic *Lactobacillus gasseri* CP2305 ameliorates chronic stress-associated symptoms in Japanese medical students', *Journal of Functional Foods*, 36 (2017), pp. 112–21, https://doi.org/10.1016/j.jff.2017.06.031
15. Rogge, A.-K., Röder, B., Zech, A., Nagel, V., Hollander, K., Braumann, K.-M. and Hötting, K., 'Balance training improves memory and spatial cognition in healthy adults', *Scientific Reports*, 7 (2017), https://doi.org/10.1038/s41598-017-06071-9
16. Ebrahimi, N., Loripour, M., Sayadi, A., Ardakani, A. M. and Sayadi, A. R., 'Effect of foot reflexology on fatigue, stress and serum cortisol levels in women with multiple sclerosis', *Journal of Evolution of Medical and Dental Sciences*, 9:35 (2020), pp. 2497–501, https://doi.org/10.14260/jemds/2020/543
17. Hopper, S. I., Murray, S. L., Ferrara, L. R. and Singleton, J. K., 'Effectiveness of diaphragmatic breathing for reducing physiological and psychological stress in adults: A quantitative systematic review', *JBI Database of Systematic Reviews and Implementation Reports*, 17:9 (2019), pp. 1855–76, https://doi.org/10.11124/JBISRIR-2017-003848

REFERENCES

18 Koniver, L., 'Practical applications of grounding to support health', *Biomedical Journal*, 46:1 (2023), pp. 41–7, https://doi.org/10.1016/j.bj.2022.12.001

19 Chen, S.-M., Fang, J., Wang, L.-M. and Liu, C.-L., 'Rest a while and run a mile: Relationship between distraction and negative emotions among college students in China', *PLoS One*, 15:9 (2020), https://doi.org/10.1371/journal.pone.0236030

20 Khajuria, A., Kumar, A., Joshi, D. and Kumaran, S. S., 'Reducing stress with yoga: A systematic review based on multimodal biosignals', *International Journal of Yoga*, 16:3 (2023), pp. 156–70, https://doi.org/10.4103/ijoy.ijoy_218_23

21 Fancourt, D., Perkins, R., Ascenso, S., Carvalho, L. A., Steptoe, A. and Williamon, A., 'Effects of group drumming interventions on anxiety, depression, social resilience and inflammatory immune response among mental health service users', *PLoS One*, 11:3 (2016), https://doi.org/10.1371/journal.pone.0151136

22 Palmer, S. and Cooper, C., *How to Deal With Stress* (London: Kogan Page, 2013)

23 Okely, J. A., Weiss, A. and Gale, C. R., 'The interaction between stress and positive affect in predicting mortality', *Journal of Psychosomatic Research*, 100 (2017), pp. 53–60, https://doi.org/10.1016/j.jpsychores.2017.07.005

24 Hou, W. K., Lai, F. T. T., Ben-Ezra, M. and Goodwin, R., 'Regularizing daily routines for mental health during and after the COVID-19 pandemic', *Journal of Global Health*, 10:2 (2020), https://doi.org/10.7189/jogh.10.020315

25 Hoppmann, C. A. and Klumb, P. L., 'Daily goal pursuits predict cortisol secretion and mood states in employed parents with preschool children', *Psychosomatic Medicine*, 68:6 (2006), pp. 887–94, https://doi.org/10.1097/01.psy.0000238232.46870.f1

26 Shen, C., Zhang, R., Yu, J., Sahakian, B. J., Cheng, W. and Feng, J., 'Plasma proteomic signatures of social isolation and loneliness associated with morbidity and mortality', *Nature Human Behaviour*, 9 (2025), pp. 569–83, https://doi.org/10.1038/s41562-024-02078-1

27 Monroy, M., Uğurlu, O., Zerwas, F., Corona, R., Keltner, D., Eagle, J. and Amster, M., 'The influences of daily experiences of awe on stress, somatic health, and well-being: A longitudinal study during COVID-19', *Scientific Reports*, 13 (2023), https://doi.org/10.1038/s41598-023-35200-w

28 Yang, Y. C., Boen, C., Gerken, K., Li, T., Schorpp, K. and Mullan Harris, K., 'Social relationships and physiological determinants of longevity across the human life span', *Proceedings of the National Academy of Sciences*, 113:3 (2016), pp. 578–83, https://doi.org/10.1073/pnas.1511085112

29 Maslach, C. and Leiter, M. P., 'Understanding the burnout experience: Recent research and its implications for psychiatry', *World Psychiatry*, 15:2 (2016), https://doi.org/10.1002/wps.20311

30 Vlemincx, E., Van Diest, I. and Van den Bergh, O., 'A sigh of relief or a sigh to relieve: The psychological and physiological relief effect of deep breaths', *Physiology and Behavior*, 165 (2016), pp. 127–35, https://doi.org/10.1016/j.physbeh.2016.07.004

Chapter 2: Habit

1. 'habit, n.', *Cambridge Dictionary*, https://dictionary.cambridge.org/dictionary/english/habit
2. Mendelsohn, A. I., 'Creatures of habit: The neuroscience of habit and purposeful behavior', *Biological Psychiatry*, 85:11 (2019), https://doi.org/10.1016/j.biopsych.2019.03.978
3. Neal, D. T., Wood, W. and Quinn, J. M., 'Habits – a repeat performance', *Current Directions in Psychological Science*, 15:4 (2006), https://web.archive.org/web/20110526144503/http://dornsife.usc.edu/wendywood/research/documents/Neal.Wood.Quinn.2006.pdf
4. Cleo, G., *The Habit Revolution* (London: Murdoch Books, 2024)
5. Pignatiello, G. A., Martin, R. J. and Hickman Jr, R. L. 'Decision fatigue: A conceptual analysis', *Journal of Health Psychology*, 25:1 (2018), https://doi.org/10.1177/1359105318763510
6. Wood, W. and Rünger, D., 'Psychology of habit', *Annual Review of Psychology*, 67 (2016), pp. 289–314, https://doi.org/10.1146/annurev-psych-122414-033417
7. Lally, P., van Jaarsveld, C. H. M., Potts, H. W. W. and Wardle, J., 'How are habits formed: Modelling habit formation in the real world', *European Journal of Social Psychology*, 40:6 (2010), pp. 998–1009, https://doi.org/10.1002/ejsp.674
8. Schwabe, L. and Wolf, O. T., 'Stress prompts habit behavior in humans', *Journal of Neuroscience*, 29:22 (2009), pp. 7191–8, https://doi.org/10.1523/JNEUROSCI.0979-09.2009
9. Zheng, M., Marsh, J. K., Nickerson, J. V. and Kleinberg, S., 'How causal information affects decisions', *Cognitive Research: Principles and Implications*, 5 (2020), https://doi.org/10.1186/s41235-020-0206-z
10. Hadfield, C., 'What I learned from going blind in space', Ted, March 2014, https://www.ted.com/talks/chris_hadfield_what_i_learned_from_going_blind_in_space
11. Michie, S., van Stralen, M. and West, R., 'The behaviour change wheel: A new method for characterising and designing behaviour change interventions', *Implementation Science*, 6 (2011), https://doi.org/10.1186/1748-5908-6-42
12. Raihan, N. and Cogburn, M., *Stages of Change Theory* (Treasure Island, FL: StatPearls Publishing, 2025)
13. Duhigg, C., *The Power of Habit* (New York: Random House, 2012)
14. Verplanken, B. and Roy, D., 'Empowering interventions to promote sustainable lifestyles: Testing the habit discontinuity hypothesis in a field experiment', *Journal of Environmental Psychology*, 45 (2016), pp. 127–34, https://doi.org/10.1016/j.jenvp.2015.11.008
15. Jackson, S. E., Steptoe, A. and Wardle, J., 'The influence of partner's behavior on health behavior change: The English longitudinal study of ageing', *JAMA Internal Medicine*, 175:3 (2015), pp. 385–92, https://doi.org/10.1001/jamainternmed.2014.7554

REFERENCES

16 Stojanovic, M., Fries, S. and Grund, A., 'Self-efficacy in habit building: How general and habit-specific self-efficacy influence behavioral automatization and motivational interference', *Frontiers in Psychology*, 12 (2021), https://doi.org/10.3389/fpsyg.2021.643753

17 Schultz, W., 'Dopamine reward prediction error coding', *Dialogues in Clinical Neuroscience*, 18:1 (2016), https://doi.org/10.31887/DCNS.2016.18.1/wschultz

18 Di Domenico, S. I. and Ryan, R. M., 'The emerging neuroscience of intrinsic motivation: A new frontier in self-determination research', *Frontiers in Human Neuroscience*, 11 (2017), https://doi.org/10.3389/fnhum.2017.00145

19 Fernandez, J. R. and Kruglanski, A. W., 'The psychology of multiple goal pursuit: Choices, configurations, and commitments', *Journal of the Association for Consumer Research*, 4:1 (2019), pp. 5–12, https://doi.org/10.1086/700845

20 Loewentein, G., Price, J. and Volpp, K., 'Habit formation in children: Evidence from incentives for healthy eating', *Journal of Health Economics*, 45 (2016), pp. 47–54, https://doi.org/10.1016/j.jhealeco.2015.11.004

21 Stojanovic, Fries and Grund, 'Self-efficacy in habit building: How general and habit-specific self-efficacy influence behavioral automatization and motivational interference'

22 Wilson, E., Senior, V. and Tapper, K., 'The effect of visualisation and mindfulness-based decentering on chocolate craving', *Appetite*, 164 (2021), https://doi.org/10.1016/j.appet.2021.105278

Chapter 3: Saying No

1 Erard, M., 'The mystery of babies' first words', *Atlantic*, 30 April 2019, https://www.theatlantic.com/family/archive/2019/04/babies-first-words-babbling-or-actual-language/588289/

2 Baumeister, R. F., Bratslavsky, E., Finkenauer, C. and Vohs, K. D., 'Bad is stronger than good', *Review of General Psychology*, 5:4 (2001), pp. 323–70, https://doi.org/10.1037/1089-2680.5.4.323

3 Alia-Klein, N., Goldstein, R. Z., Tomasi, D., Zhang, L., Fagin-Jones, S., Telang, F., Wang, G.-J., Fowler, J. S. and Volkow, N. D., 'What is in a word? *No* versus *Yes* differentially engage the lateral orbitofrontal cortex', *Emotion*, 7:3 (2007), pp. 649–59, https://doi.org/10.1037/1528-3542.7.3.649

4 Tulshyan, R. and Burey, J.-A., 'Stop telling women they have imposter syndrome', *Harvard Business Review*, 11 February 2021, https://hbr.org/2021/02/stop-telling-women-they-have-imposter-syndrome; Jamison, L., 'Why everyone feels like they're faking it', *New Yorker*, 6 February 2023, https://www.newyorker.com/magazine/2023/02/13/the-dubious-rise-of-impostor-syndrome

5 Schultz, W., Dayan, P. and Montague, P. R., 'A neural substrate of prediction and reward', *Science*, 275:5306 (1997), pp. 1,593–9, https://doi.org/10.1126/science.275.5306.1593; Bunzeck, N. and Düzel, E., 'Absolute coding of stimulus novelty in the human substantia nigra/VTA', *Neuron*, 51:3 (2006), pp. 369–79, https://www.doi.org/10.1016/j.neuron.2006.06.021

6 Lembke, A., *Dopamine Nation* (New York: Dutton, 2021)
7 Gao, Z., Wang, H., Lu, C., Lu, T., Froudist-Walsh, S., Chen, M., Wang, X.-J., Hu, J. and Sun, W., 'The neural basis of delayed gratification', *Science Advances*, 7:49 (2021), https://doi.org/10.1126/sciadv.abg6611
8 Givi, J. and Kirk, C. P., 'Saying no: The negative ramifications from invitation declines are less severe than we think', *Journal of Personality and Social Psychology*, 126:6 (2024), pp. 1103–15, https://doi.org/10.1037/pspi0000443
9 Gandhi, A., *The Gift of Anger: And Other Lessons from My Grandfather Mahatma Gandhi* (London: Michael Joseph, 2017)
10 Hinton Jr, A. O., McReynolds M. R., Martinez, D., Shuler, H. D. and Termini, C. M., 'The power of saying no', *EMBO Reports*, 21 (2020), https://doi.org/10.15252/embr.202050918
11 Schlund, R., Sommers, R. and Bohns, V. K., 'Giving people the words to say no leads them to feel freer to say yes', *Scientific Reports*, 14:576 (2024), https://doi.org/10.1038/s41598-023-50532-3

Chapter 4: Overwhelm

1 'overwhelm, v.', *Cambridge Dictionary*, https://dictionary.cambridge.org/dictionary/english/overwhelm
2 Zhang, Y., Dai, Z., Hu, J., Qin, S., Yu, R. and Sun, Y., 'Stress-induced changes in modular organizations of human brain functional networks', *Neurobiology of Stress*, 13 (2020), https://doi.org/10.1016/j.ynstr.2020.100231
3 Sali, A. W., Ma, R., Albal, M. S. and Key, J., 'The location independence of learned attentional flexibility', *Attention, Perception and Psychophysics*, 84 (2022), pp. 682–99, https://doi.org/10.3758/s13414-022-02469-4
4 Madore, K. P. and Wagner, A. D., 'Multicosts of multitasking', *Cerebrum*, 1 (2019) https://pmc.ncbi.nlm.nih.gov/articles/PMC7075496
5 Sorrell, J. M., 'Tidying up: Good for the aging brain', *Journal of Psychosocial Nursing and Mental Health Services*, 58:4 (2020), pp.16–18, https://doi.org/10.3928/02793695-20200316-02
6 Hostinar, C. E., 'Recent developments in the study of social relationships, stress responses, and physical health', *Current Opinion in Psychology*, 5 (2015), pp. 90–5, https://doi.org/10.1016/j.copsyc.2015.05.004; Childs, E. and de Wit, H., 'Regular exercise is associated with emotional resilience to acute stress in healthy adults', *Frontiers in Psychology*, 5 (2014), https://doi.org/10.3389/fphys.2014.00161; Pressman, S. D., Matthews, K. A., Cohen, S., Martire, L. M., Scheier, M., Baum, A. and Schulz, R., 'Association of enjoyable leisure activities with psychological and physical well-being', *Psychosomatic Medicine*, 71:7 (2009), pp. 725–32, https://doi.org/10.1097/PSY.0b013e3181ad7978
7 Kim, J., Kwon, J. H., Kim, J., Kim, E. J., Kim, H. E., Kyeong, S. and Kim, J.-J., 'The effects of positive or negative self-talk on the alteration of brain

functional connectivity by performing cognitive tasks', *Scientific Reports*, 11 (2011), https://doi.org/10.1038/s41598-021-94328-9

Chapter 5: Procrastination

1 Tice, D. M. and Baumeister, R. F., 'Longitudinal study of procrastination, performance, stress, and health: The costs and benefits of dawdling', *Psychological Science*, 8:6 (1997), pp. 454–8, https://doi.org/10.1111/j.1467-9280.1997.tb00460.x
2 Schlüter, C., Arning, L., Fraenz, C., Friedrich, P., Pinnow, M., Güntürkün, O., Beste, C., Ocklenburg, S. and Genc, E., 'Genetic variation in dopamine availability modulates the self-reported level of action control in a sex-dependent manner', *Social Cognitive and Affective Neuroscience*, 14:7 (2019), pp. 759–68, https://doi.org/10.1093/scan/nsz049
3 Rozental, A., Forsström, D., Hussoon, A. and Klingsieck K. B., 'Procrastination among university students: Differentiating severe cases in need of support from less severe cases', *Frontiers in Psychology*, 13 (2022), https://doi.org/10.3389/fpsyg.2022.783570
4 Ferrari, J. R. and Díaz-Morales, J. F., 'Procrastination and mental health coping: A brief report related to students', *Individual Differences Research*, 12:1 (2014), https://doi.org/10.65030/idr.12002
5 Rozental, A., Forsström, D., Lindner, P., Nilsson, S., Mårtensson, L., Rizzo, A., Andersson, G. and Carlbring, P., 'Treating procrastination using cognitive behavior therapy', *Behavior Therapy*, 49:2 (2018), https://doi.org/10.1016/j.beth.2017.08.002
6 Tice and Baumeister, 'Longitudinal study of procrastination, performance, stress, and health: The costs and benefits of dawdling'
7 Tang, R., Friston, K. J. and Tang, Y.-Y., 'Brief mindfulness meditation induces gray matter changes in a brain hub', *Neural Plasticity* (2020), https://doi.org/10.1155/2020/8830005
8 Wohl, M. J. A., Pychyl, T. A and Bennett, S. H., 'I forgive myself, now I can study: How self-forgiveness for procrastinating can reduce future procrastination', *Personality and Individual Differences*, 48:7 (2010), pp. 803–8, https://doi.org/10.1016/j.paid.2010.01.029
9 Lakein, A., *How to Get Control of Your Time and Your Life* (New York: New American Library, 1973)

Chapter 6: Failure

1 Hemingway, E., *A Farewell to Arms* (London: Arrow Books, 1994)
2 Hajcak, G., 'What we've learned from mistakes: Insights from error-related brain activity', *Current Directions in Psychological Science*, 21:2 (2012), pp. 101–6, https://doi.org/10.1177/0963721412436809

3 de Mooij, S. M. M., Dumontheil, I., Kirkham, N. Z., Raijmakers, M. E. J. and van der Maas, H. L. J., 'Post-error slowing: Large scale study in an online learning environment for practising mathematics and language', *Developmental Science*, 25:2 (2021), https://doi.org/10.1111/desc.13174
4 Overbye, K., Walhovd, K. B., Paus, T., Fjell, A. M., Huster, R. J., Tamnes, C. K., 'Error processing in the adolescent brain: Age-related differences in electrophysiology, behavioural adaptation, and brain morphology', *Developmental Cognitive Neuroscience*, 38 (2019), https://doi.org/10.1016/j.dcn.2019.100665
5 Tangney, J. P., 'Perfectionism and the self-conscious emotions: Shame, guilt, embarrassment, and pride', in G. L. Flett and P. L. Hewitt (eds), *Perfectionism: Theory, Research, and Treatment* (Washington, DC: American Psychological Association, 2002), pp. 199–215, https://doi.org/10.1037/10458-008
6 Atkinson, J. W., 'Motivational determinants of risk-taking behavior', *Psychological Review*, 64:6 (1957), pp. 359–72, https://doi.org/10.1037/h0043445
7 Eskreis-Winkler, L. and Fishbach, A., 'You think failure is hard? So is learning from it', *Perspectives on Psychological Science*, 17:6 (2022), https://doi.org/10.1177/17456916211059817
8 Lee, S. and Park, J., 'Giving up learning from failures? An examination of learning from one's own failures in the context of heart surgeons', *Strategic Management Journal*, 45:10 (2024), pp. 2063–94, https://doi.org/10.1002/smj.3609
9 Eskreis-Winkler, L., Fishbach, A. and Duckworth, A. L., 'Dear Abby: Should I give advice or receive it?', *Psychological Science*, 29:11 (2018), https://doi.org/10.1177/0956797618795472
10 Hobson, N. M., Bonk, D. and Inzlicht, M., 'Rituals decrease the neural response to performance failure', *PeerJ*, 5 (2017), https://doi.org/10.7717/peerj.3363
11 Conroy, D. E., Kaye, M. P. and Fifer, A. M., 'Cognitive links between fear of failure and perfectionism', *Journal of Rational-Emotive and Cognitive-Behavior Therapy*, 25:4 (2007), pp. 237–53, https://doi.org/10.1007/s10942-007-0052-7
12 Radua, J., Stoica, T. Scheinost, D., Pittenger, C. and Hampson, M., 'Neural correlates of success and failure signals during neurofeedback learning', 378 (2018), pp. 11–21, https://doi.org/10.1016/j.neuroscience.2016.04.003

Chapter 7: Rejection

1 Baumeister, R. F. and Leary, M. R., 'The need to belong: Desire for interpersonal attachments as a fundamental human motivation', *Psychological Bulletin*, 117:3 (1995), pp. 497–529, https://doi.org/10.1037/0033-2909.117.3.497
2 Kross, E., Berman, M. G., Mischel, W., Smith, E. E., and Wager, T. D., 'Social rejection shares somatosensory representations with physical pain',

REFERENCES

Proceedings of the National Academy of Sciences, 108:15 (2011), pp. 6270–5, https://doi.org/10.1073/pnas.1102693108; Eisenberger, N. I., Lieberman, M. D. and Williams, K. D., 'Does rejection hurt? An fMRI study of social exclusion', *Science*, 302:5643 (2003), pp. 290–2, https://doi.org/10.1126/science.1089134; Hsu, D. T., Sankar, A., Malik, M. A., Langenecker, S. A., Mickey, B. J. and Love, T. L., 'Common neural responses to romantic rejection and acceptance in healthy adults', *Social Neuroscience*, 15:5 (2020), pp. 571–83, https://doi.org/10.1080/17470919.2020.1801502

3 Slavich, G. M., Shields, G. S., Deal, B. D., Gregory, A. and Toussaint, L. L., 'Alleviating social pain: A double-blind, randomized, placebo-controlled trial of forgiveness and acetaminophen', *Annals of Behavioral Medicine*, 53:12 (2019), pp. 1045–54, https://doi.org/10.1093/abm/kaz015

4 Sansone, R. A. and Sansone, L. A., 'Rumination: Relationships with physical health', *Innovations in Clinical Neuroscience*, 9:2 (2012), pp. 29–34, https://pubmed.ncbi.nlm.nih.gov/22468242

5 Clear, S. J., Zimmer-Gembeck, M. J., Hawes, T., Duffy, A. L. and Barber, B. L., 'Mindfulness, rejection, and recovery of positive mood and friendliness: A Cyberball study', *Emotion*, 21:8 (2021), pp. 1731–43, https://doi.org/10.1037/emo0000987

6 Lakey, B. and Orehek, E., 'Relational regulation theory: A new approach to explain the link between perceived social support and mental health', *Psychological Review*, 118:3 (2011), pp. 482–95, https://doi.org/10.1037/a0023477

7 Shapira, L. B. and Mongrain, M., 'The benefits of self-compassion and optimism exercises for individuals vulnerable to depression', *Journal of Positive Psychology*, 5 (2010), pp. 377–89, https://doi.org/10.1080/17439760.2010.516763

8 Ibid.

Chapter 8: Comparison

1 'self-worth, n.', *Merriam-Webster Dictionary*, https://www.merriam-webster.com/dictionary/self-worth

2 Summerville, A. and Roese, N. J., 'Dare to compare: Fact-based versus simulation-based comparison in daily life', *Journal of Experimental Social Psychology*, 44:3 (2008), pp. 664–71, https://doi.org/10.1016/j.jesp.2007.04.002

3 Deri, S., Davidai, S. and Gilovich, T., 'Home alone: Why people believe others' social lives are richer than their own', *Journal of Personality and Social Psychology*, 113:6 (2017), pp. 858–77, https://doi.org/10.1037/pspa0000105; Davidai, S. and Deri, S., 'The second pugilist's plight: Why people believe they are above average but are not especially happy about it', *Journal of Experimental Psychology: General*, 148:3 (2019), pp. 570–87, https://doi.org/10.1037/xge0000580

4 Kedia, G., Mussweiler, T. and Linden, D., 'Brain mechanisms of social comparison and their influence on the reward system', *NeuroReport*, 25:16 (2014), pp. 1255–65, https://www.doi.org/10.1097/WNR.0000000000000255
5 University of Pennsylvania, 'Want to exercise more? Get yourself some competition', *ScienceDaily*, 27 October 2016, https://www.sciencedaily.com/releases/2016/10/161027122554.htm
6 Swencionis, J. K. and Fiske, S. T., 'How social neuroscience can inform theories of social comparison', *Neuropsychologia*, 56 (2014), pp. 140–6, https://doi.org/10.1016/j.neuropsychologia.2014.01.009

Chapter 9: Moving Forward

1 Covey, S. R., *The 7 Habits of Highly Effective People* (New York: Free Press, 1989)
2 Schacter, D. L. and Addis, D. R., 'The cognitive neuroscience of constructive memory: Remembering the past and imagining the future', *Philosophical Transactions of the Royal Society B*, 362 (2007), pp. 773–86, http://doi.org/10.1098/rstb.2007.2087
3 Cochran, W., and Tesser, A., 'The "what the hell" effect: Some effects of goal proximity and goal framing on performance', in L. L. Martin and A. Tesser (eds.), *Striving and Feeling: Interactions Among Goals, Affect, and Self-regulation* (Mahwah, NJ: Lawrence Erlbaum Associates, Inc., 1996), pp. 99–120
4 Irish, M., Addis, D. R., Hodges, J. R. and Piguet, O., 'Considering the role of semantic memory in episodic future thinking: Evidence from semantic dementia', *Brain*, 135:7 (2012), pp. 2178–91, https://doi.org/10.1093/brain/aws119
5 Frankl, V., *Man's Search for Meaning* (London: Penguin, 2004)
6 Kim, E. S., Chen, Y., Nakamura, J. S., Ryff, C. D. and VanderWeele, T. J., 'Sense of purpose in life and subsequent physical, behavioral, and psychosocial health: An outcome-wide approach', *American Journal of Health Promotion*, 36:1 (2021), pp. 137–47, https://doi.org/10.1177/08901171211038545
7 Morin, A., 'Why New Year's resolutions set you up to fail', *Psychology Today*, 29 December 2024, https://www.psychologytoday.com/gb/blog/what-mentally-strong-people-dont-do/202412/why-new-years-resolutions-set-you-up-to-fail

Acknowledgements

Thank you first and foremost to my literary agent Morwenna Loughman at Aevitas for your unwavering faith and commitment to *Prioritise This*, as well as for navigating my moments of self-doubt (and mini-breakdowns) with such care.

To my editor Jonathan Shipley. You believed in this book from day one and I am endlessly grateful for your encouragement and wisdom. It's been a joy to work with you. Jocasta Hamilton and Iain Campbell at John Murray One – your championing of *Prioritise This* has been unrivalled, you are both brilliant and I feel very lucky to have you on my side. Eleanor Gaffney, Caroline Priestley, Charlie Tonks, Alice Graham, David Bamford, Niamh Brennan – thank you all for everything you've done to get this book out into the world.

To my teachers – Swami Paramananda, Sarah Lo, Dr Siobhain O'Riordan, Dr Stephen Palmer, Dr Sarah McKay, Dr Mary Collins, Naomi Annand, Sonia Sumar and Martha Danzig. Thank you for your knowledge, wisdom and willingness to share.

To my family – Mamma, Spike, Daniel and Jenny for your support and love, and for taking the kids on many occasions so I could write. Pat, for being the best mother-in-law in the world. Eliza and Ida, for being the closest thing I have to sisters. Mal, for providing advice and the sobering (*loving*) voice of my father in his absence. Talana, for holding our family together and treating our children as if they're your own.

To my dad, my first editor, for encouraging rigour in my writing through infuriating lessons such as crossing through entire drafts of school essays and giving the sole feedback: *It's good, just re-write the entire thing.* I know the book would've been better if you were here to help, but I also know we may not have been on speaking terms by now . . . I miss you. We all do.

To Dipal Acharya, for reading every iteration of this book (including the one way back in 2019) and for generally being the most incredible cheerleader for *Prioritise This*. A few more special mentions in that category – Melissa Hemsley, Angela Scanlon and Georgina Graham, you are all the kind of women who mention other women's names in a room full of opportunity, thank you so much for mentioning mine over and over again.

Ash Ruddy, for being all of the above, as well as for our writing time together and the rounds of thoughtful feedback you've so kindly offered. Daisy Uribe-Mosquera, Lawrence Boulanger Bellon and Georgia Levison for bringing The Priorities Method brand to life. Sarah Cresswell for my author portrait. Plus, other much appreciated supporters and early readers: Dan Garber, Zoniel Burton, Michelle Napchan, Tali Knipe, Emily Dolan, Laura Burkitt, Natalie Sytner, Lars Atkin, Olive Young, Rebecca Burn-Callander, Ben Sarner, Lucy Fenn, Liam Freeman, Polly Brown, Boo Hodgetts, James Righton, Nikki Osman. (And anyone else I may have forgotten!)

To Dolly and Zevy, for teaching me the true meaning of priorities, for being the biggest sources of joy and for being so understanding when I've had to work late or miss a school something. I love you more than you'll ever know. (Also, in ink, here is the promise you asked for: I will not write another book this year!)

To Dan. For supporting me, for carrying our family, for never stressing the small stuff, for always having your priorities straight, for making life better, for simply being you. I love you.

To my clients – the individuals, organisations and charities that have trusted me to work alongside you. To the guests from my podcast and the experts I've interviewed for magazines and papers over the years. To anyone who's attended a workshop or retreat, read one of my newsletters or followed me on socials. I am forever grateful to you for everything you've taught me about how to use priorities to live a better life.

And finally, to you, reader, for picking up this book – it means more than you can imagine that you've chosen to give some of your precious time, energy and attention to *Prioritise This*. Thank you.